Customer Relationship Management

Customer Relationship Management

R. Ramachandran

SERIALS PUBLICATIONS
NEW DELHI (INDIA)

First Published - 2011

ISBN: 978-81-8387-433-5

Published by

SERIALS PUBLICATIONS
4830/24, 1st Floor, Ansari Road
Darya Ganj, New Delhi-110002 (India)
Phone : 23245225. Fax : 91-11-23272135
E-mail : serials@sify.com
serialspublications.india@gmail.com
Website : www.serialspublications.com

Dedicated

To My Ever Loving Wife

MRS. KALPPANA RAMACHANDRAN

Who Shows all her Kindness and
Concentration in My Development

Contents

Foreword

The economic scenario has witnessed a paradigm shift in India during the nineties. The first of these shifts occurred during the 1991-94 phase in which the emphasis shifted from growth of profits and balance sheet· size to a clean, transparent and healthy balance sheet, from a regulated and administrated regime to a relatively deregulated one. During the next phase (1994-1998) the financial markets started giving interest rate signals, links between forex and money markets became stronger, as a result deregulation of interest rates led to the intensification of competition in the economic system.

The process of economic liberalization and financial sector reforms brought the issue of 'customer focus' to the forefront. Attempts are being made both by public as well as by private sector to re-shape their structure and functioning keeping customer in view. Any business entity that wishes to either grow in the size of its business operations or improve its profitability must consider the challenges affecting its customer relationships. A momentum of truth refers to any incident when a customer is exposed to any aspect of the service offered and based on the contact, forms an opinion about the quality of the service and the quality of product offered.

The perception about a customer has drastically changed. In the words of P.F. Drucker, the purpose of a business was to attract and retain a customer. There has been a phenomenal change and paradigm shift towards customer focus during the past five decades in the Indian situation.

1961-1970 Servicing the customer

1971 - 1980 Satisfying the customer

1981-1990. Pleasing the customer

1991 - 2000 Delighting the customer

2000 and beyond Relating the customer

Today the relationship between the industries and customer has come under sharp focus at the firm as well as at the customer ends. Customer Relationship Management (CRM) is a comprehensive strategy and process of acquiring, retaining and partnering with selective customers. Thus, it is a holistic concept that envisages a long term relationship with a particular cross-section of customers whose contribution to the organization really matters. It extends the relationship beyond the set periphery punctuated by commercial framework and embraces a profound humane approach based on deep-rooted empathy, which makes sure the existence of customer loyalty.

The biggest management challenge in the new millennium of liberalization and globalization for a business is to serve and maintain good relations with the king - the customer. The changing business environment is characterized by economic liberalization, increasing competition, high consumer preference and selection, enlightened and demording customer, more emphasis on quality and value of purchase. Customer Relationship Management (CRM) is a strategy used to learn more about customers' needs and behaviour in order to develop stronger relationships are with them. Good customer relationships are at the heart of business success. There are many technological components to CRM, but thinking about CRM in primarily technological terms is a mistake. The more useful way to think about CRM is as a strategic process that will help to better understand the customers' needs and how you can meet those needs and enhance the bottom line at the same time. This strategy depends on bringing together lots of pieces of information about customers and market trends make the banks can sell and market their products and services more effectively. The ideas of CRM is that it helps bankers to use technology and human resources to gain insight into the behaviour of customers and the value of those customers. CRM is customer value based strategies not for customer volume based strategies. The aim of CRM is to produce high customer equity. "Customer equity is the tool or the discounted lifetime values of the firm's customers clearly the more loyal the customers, the higher the customer equity, -value equity, Brand equity and Relationship Equity". At this point, close relationship with customers will require strong co-ordination between IT and marketing segments of banks to prove a long-term relation of customers.

It seems that the CRM is a hot cake and the companies use it to attract and retain the customers. From this point, it seems that CRM is one of the most profitable customer strategies of the decade. But, if we consider the statistics of CRM, we find that there are chances of CRM's failure. The statistics show that only one out of six companies that have implemented CRM has been successful. Almost 75% of the projects have failed to deliver the expected ROI. It mostly happened to the larger corporate. This happens generally because smaller projects far better, and mid size organizations have a higher success rate.

Till recently, mostly marketers focused on attracting customers from its target segments using the tools and techniques developed for mass marketing in the industrial era. In this information era, this is proving to be highly ineffective in most competitive markets.

Solving growth rates, intensifying competition, and technological developments made business look for ways to reduce and improve their effectiveness. Business process re-engineering, automation and downsizing reduced the manpower costs. Financial restructuring and efficient fund management reduced the financial costs. Production and operation costs have been reduced through total quality management (TQM), just in time (JIT) inventory, flexible manufacturing systems (FMS), and efficient supply chain management. Studies have shown that while manufacturing costs declined from 55% to 30% and management cost declined from 25% to 15 %, the marketing costs have increased from 20% to 55%. The practice of relationship marketing has the potential to improve marketing productivity through improved marketing efficiencies and effusiveness.

Today's customers are becoming harder to please. They are smarter, more price-conscious, more demanding, less forgiving and are approached by many more competitors with equal or better offers. The challenge is not to produce satisfied customers, which several competitors can do, but to produce delighted and loyal customers. If these customers are retained with the organization, it becomes really profitable by way of increase in purchasing reduced operating costs, price premiums and though referrals. Too many companies suffer from customer chum, i.e. high customer defection. It is like adding water into a leaking bucket. Various strategies such as measuring customer life-time value, efficient complaint management system and service recovery can be really helpful in retaining customers.

Customer value is an interesting and emerging concept in the area of marketing. This is holds an important position in Customer Relationship Management, as relationship needs to be designed and sustained when one party offers some value to the other. So, understanding customer's value to the company and then designing the offer to him would be the most appropriate strategy for ranking companies practicing CRM. In this context, it is appropriate and need of time to analyse different issues confronted in service industry with customer. And it is good and excellence in bringing an edited volume book on CRM.

Dr. R. Ramachandran. works on this is remarkable and recognizable to the field of marketing. It is the third outcome in publication of book and also second one in consumer study. The edited book covers many issues in service industry especially banking, insurance, tourism and hotel with hospital. The contributors are from throughout India is the added flavor for distinguishing feature that it contains a good blend of conceptual, empirical and with a case analysis.

Based on these, all the papers are in lucid, simple and pragmatic. Hence, it is great deal not only to industrialists, policy creators consumers, marketing executives, consumer bodies and society but also to the budding research scholars. The work is a Himalayan task and meticulous treatise on customer relationship management.

I wish and congratulate the editor for his endeavours.

June 2010

Dr. S.B. NAGESWARA RAO
Director
Directorate of Distance Education
Annamalai University
Annamalai Nagar - 608 002.
Tamil Nadu, India.

Preface

Customer Relationship Management (CRM) is the bundling of customer strategies and processes, supported by relevant software, for the purpose of improving customers loyalty and eventually corporate profitability. CRM is a strategy and process which helps improve customer loyalty and eventually corporate profitability. It helps the firm know needs and wants of the customer and satisfy them. It helps to retain the customers.

CRM is imperative for acquiring the right customer, crafting the fight value proposition, instituting the best processes, motivating employees and learning to retain customers. CRM is often considered as database marketing primarily linking marketing segment of the organization with the database of the customers. Some theorists have been considering it as an exercise for customers. Retention as many theories and studies have been emphasizing on the rationale for keeping the customers. This required a variety of techniques, especially post sail initiatives, to keep the customers. For life this was believer to be a mechanism to keep the existing customers happy. So that they remains with the organization and may if possible, generate positive referral for the company's products and services. It was believed that application of it can be effective tool to develop one to one relationship that integrates database with company's marketing strategy that may focus on leveraging the existing customer's base. According to Ammy Hubbel and Mike Roddling the last decade declared the birth of customers relationship management (CRM) as a few businesses have found themselves short of customer data or the means to use it. Increasingly, banks and other financial services companies organize and analyze customer data in order to, drive marketing targeted to customers needs and preferences but is understanding what your customers want enough to enable thou to develop and retains profitable relationship. And if not, where is financial services organization heading in the race to win and retain a high value customer base.

CRM is not a new approach. We can find its roots during the time when the trade began. The history states the Customer Relationship Management originated years before the start of the first millennium in Mesopotamia. At that time, Barter system existed. Farmers who wanted to sell their surplus produces became the pioneers of the customer-oriented process.

With the passage of time, merchants started keeping the records of what was sold and to whom it was sold. This record provided the merchants' comprehensive customer oriented data and it was the beginning of customer orientation. During 1990's companies used more refined customer oriented strategies which formed the ground for the CRM which it now come across with. In this millennium, CRM has become a necessary tool for almost all industries aspiring to make their customers their focal point of success.

In olden days, people did not change their bank unless serious problems occurred. There was a committed relationship between the banker and customer. The banks did not need to develop any customer specific facility. The customers were loyal and there was no need of any extra care. But now a days, banks have to work keeping in view the position of financial market and have to anticipate change in the financial market and prepare themselves accordingly. The customers have become more knowledge and demanding. In such scenario, the banks cannot rely on committed relationships and traditional techniques to attract and retain customers. The banks have to become highly 'Customer Centric' and offer highly personalized services to the 'High Net Worth Customers'. The wealthier the customer are, the more demanding they are. They expect more and more facilities from the bank. It becomes necessary for the banks to understand what the need and wants of their customers are. So that the services industries can meet the expectations of their customers. The only strategic weapon to meet the customers' expectations is CRM. CRM helps all to discover new customers, getting deep knowledge of the need and wants of the customers and retain old customers and turn them into loyal and relative customers.

With great respects, I uphold my hands to thank Professor ***Dr. M. Ramanathan,*** Vice – Chancellor, Annamalai University, Annamalai Nagar, Tamil Nadu for his greatness in granting permission to publish the edited book. I am grateful to my beloved ***Dr. M. Rathinasabapathi,*** Registrar, Annamalai University, Annamalai Nagar, Tamil Nadu for his encouragement and kind help.

I sincerely thank Professor ***Dr. S.B. Nageswara Rao,*** Director, Directorate of Distance Education, Annamalai University, Annamalai Nagar, Tamil Nadu for his support, kindness, encouragement and also for writing "Foreword" to the edited book.

I take this opportunity to thank the ***Reviewers*** and paper, articles and case studies ***Contributors*** for their kind concern and co-operation to bring out the edited book in grand success.

I extend my gratitude to my loving kids, daughter ***Ms. Pranamika Ramachandran*** and my son ***Mr. Tanuj Nagentra Ramachandran*** for their sacrifices and affection shown to me in completion of the work.

I profusely thank ***Shri. S.K. Jha,*** Managing Director, Serials Publications, New Delhi for taking up the strenuous task and meticulous work in neat execution of publishing the edited book.

Above all, I bow my head to ***Lord Nataraja*** for being with me throughout and for blesses in all my walks of life.

R. Ramachandran

List of Contributors

Dr. Narender Kumar, Professor & Head, Department of Commerce, M D University, Rohtak, **Mrs. Kavita,** (Lecturer in Management in U.I.E.T), M.D. University Rohtak.

Dr. N.Y. Rajeshirke, Professor & Head, Commerce Wing, Vivekanand College, Tarabaipark, Kolhapur-416 003.

Mr. Samip Baruah, Regional Manager-East (Modern Trade) ITC Limited, Eastern District Office, 2, Lee Road, 1st Floor, Kolkota- 20, West Bengal, **Prof. P. Bezborah,** Department of Commerce, Dibrugarh University, Dibrugarh-786004, Assam.

Dr. B. Revathy, Associate Professor, Department of Commerce, Manonmaniam Sundaranar University, Tirunelveli.

Dr. Geetha Sankar, Reader, Department of Commerce, Ethiraj College for Women, Chennai-600 008, **Dr. A.S. Saranya,** Reader, Department of Commerce, Ethiraj College for Women, Chennai-600 008

Ms. M. Neela, Lecturer in Business Administration, Cauvery College for Women, Annamalai Nagar, Trichy-620 018, Tamil Nadu.

Dr. Sandeep Tandon, (Associate Professor in Commerce, DDE, University of Jammu), **Ms Jyoti Bahl,** (Lecturer in Commerce, Udhampur Campus, University of Jammu).

Dr. Uma Sankar Prasad Patra, Senior Faculty in Commerce, Semiliguda College, Semiliguda P.O. Dist. Koraput, Orissa-764036.

Dr. (Mrs) Puja Walia Mann, Asst. Professor (Head-Department of Management), Panipat Institute of Engineering & Technology, 70th km milestone Vill- Pattikalyana, Samalkha-Panipat, Haryana-132102, **Mr. Manish Jha,** Sr.Lecturer-Department of Management, Panipat Institute of Engineering & Technology, 70th km milestone Vill- Pattikalyana, Samalkha-Panipat, Haryana-132102.

Dr. Arun Kumar, Reader, Faculty of Commerce, Feroze Gandhi College, Rae Bareli, C.S.J.M. University, Kanpur, **Emmanuel Joseph,** Research Scholar, HNB university, Srinagar, Garhwal.

Ranjit Singh, Research Scholar, Faculty of Commerce, Feroze Gandhi College, Rae Bareli, C.S.J.M. University, Kanpur.

Ms. Sayeda Meharunisa, Senior Lecturer in Commerce, Bangalore.

Dr. S. Jeyalakshmi, AP–III, Department of Commerce, SASTRA University, SRC, Kumbakonam, **Mrs. G. R. Gayathiri,** AP-I, Department of Commerce, SASTRA University, SRC, Kumbakonam.

Dr. Byram Anand, Assistant Professor in Management Studies, School of Management, Department of Management Studies, Pondicherry University, Karaikal Centre, Nehru Nagar, Pondicherry-609605, **Dr. P.Varalaxmi,** Assistant Professor in Commerce & Management, Department of Commerce & Business Mgt., University P.G College, Kakatiya University, Yellandu "X" Roads, Khammam, Andhra Pradesh-507002.

Dr. G. Karunanithi, Lecturer in Commerce, Directorate of Distance Education, Annamalai University, Annamalai Nagar – 608 002., **Dr. (Mrs.) S. Banumathy,** Reader and Head, Dept. of Commerce, V.V.V College for Women, Virudhunagar–626 001.

Dr. A.S. Saranya, Reader, Department of Commerce, Ethiraj College for Women, Chennai–600 008, **Dr. Geetha Sankar,** Reader, Department of Commerce, Ethiraj College for Women, Chennai–600 008.

Dr. T.J. Arun, Lecturer in Commerce, Commerce Wing, Directorate of Distance Education,Annamalai University, Annamalainagar, Chidambaram-608 002, Tamilnadu, **Dr. J. Ashok,** Associate Professor, School of Management Studies, Bannari Amman Institute of Technology, Sathyamangalam-638 401, Erode (dt), Tamil Nadu.

Chirag V. Raval, Lecturer, Aims College of Management & Technology, Vidyanagar-Vadtal Road, Bakrol-388315, Dist. Anand, Gujarat.

Prof. Abirami.P., Faculty, Dept. of Corporate Secretaryship, Guru Nanak College,Velachery,Chennai-42, India.

Mrs. R. Sivakami, Assistant Professor-I, Department of Commerce, Sastra University, Srinivasa Ramanujan Centre, Kumbakonam, **Mrs. B. Maragatham,** Assistant Professor-I, Department of Commerce, Sastra University, Srinivasa Ramanujan Centre, Kumbakonam.

Mrs. Shoby Das, Research Scholar in Management, IMK, University of Kerala, **Dr. G. Raju,** Professor in Commerce, University of Kerala.

Dr. S. Mythili, Head, Department of Commerce, A.D.M College for Women, Nagapattinam, **Mrs. R. Renuka,** Assistant Professor in Commerce, SASTRA University, SRC, Kumbakonam.

P.Nithya Preetha, Ph.D., Research Scholar,GTN Arts College, Dindigul., **Dr. N. Markkandeyan.,** Ph.D., Principal, GTN Arts College, Dindigul.

J. Arunachalam, Lecturer in Commerce, Department of Commerce, Annamalai University, Annamalai Nagar - 608 002, Tamil Nadu.

Dr. R. Rathiha, Associate Professor, Commerce Research Centre, Women's Christian College, Nagercoil, **G. Sweetlin Subi,** Research Scholar, Commerce Research Centre, Women's Christian College, Nagercoil, **S.Priya,** Research Scholar, Commerce Research Centre, Women's Christian College, Nagercoil.

1

Impact of E-CRM in Banking Services

Narender Kumar, Kavita

The present is an era of company loyalty to the customer in order to obtain customer loyalty to the company. Customer is more knowledgeable; companies must be faster, more agile and more creative than a few years ago.

The last several years witnessed the rise of customer relationship management (abbreviated CRM) as an important business approach. Its objective is to return to the world of personal marketing.

CRM consists of three components:

- Customer
- Relationship and
- Management

Customer: The customer is the only source of the company's present profit and future growth. However, a good customer who provides more profit with less resource is always scarce because customers are knowledgeable and the competition is fierce. Sometimes it is difficult to distinguish who is the real customer because the buying decision is frequently a collaborative activity among participants of the decision making process. Information technologies can provide the abilities to distinguish and mange customers.

Relationship: The relationship between a company and its customers involve continuous bi-directional communication and interaction. The relationship can be short-term or long-term, continuous or discrete and repeating or one time. Relationship can be attitudinal or behavioral. Even though customers have a positive attitude towards the company and its products, their buying behavior is highly situational.

Management: CRM is not an activity only within a marketing department. Rather it involves continuous corporate charge in culture and processes. The customer information collected is transformed into corporate knowledge that leads to activities that take advantage of the information and of market opportunities. CRM required a comprehensive change in the organization and its people.

Thus *"CRM implies building long term relationship with customers and understanding their needs and responding through multiple products and services through multiple channels. It enables a targeted, mutually beneficial, profitable relationship with individual and groups".*

Traditional (Mass) marketing doesn't need to use information technology extensively because there is no need to distinguish, differentiate, interact with and customizes for individual customer needs. It is widely acceptable the information technology has a major role in CRM. Because of this, the approach of personal marketing base is transforming from *CRM to electronic customer relationship management* (abbreviated as e-CRM) from the last few years.

Thus *"E-CRM is the phenomenon of building relationship with customers via the internet or the relationship that is web-based is known as electronic CRM (e-CRM)". E-CRM focuses on electronic channels mainly on the Internet and on technologies that enable automated and electronic management of customer relations.*

E-CRM concentrates on the retention of customers by collecting all the data from every interaction, every customer makes with a company from 'all' access point whether they are:

Online : E-mail, website, call centers, online chat.

Offline : Phone, mobile phones, fax, face to face through sales agent.

The term *"touch points"* is used in e-CRM refers to many ways in which customers and firms interact. The companies then use this data for specific business purposes, marketing, service, support or sales whilst concentrating on a customer service centric approach rather than a product centric.

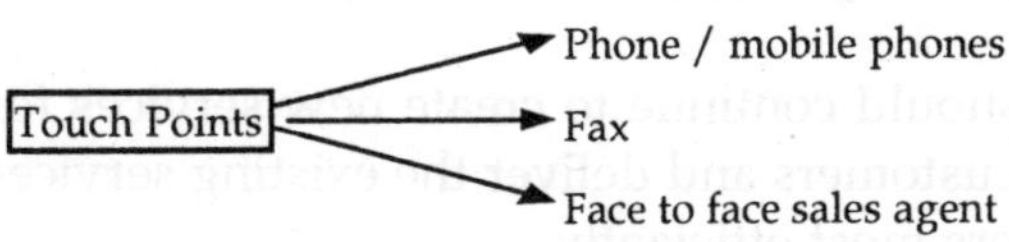

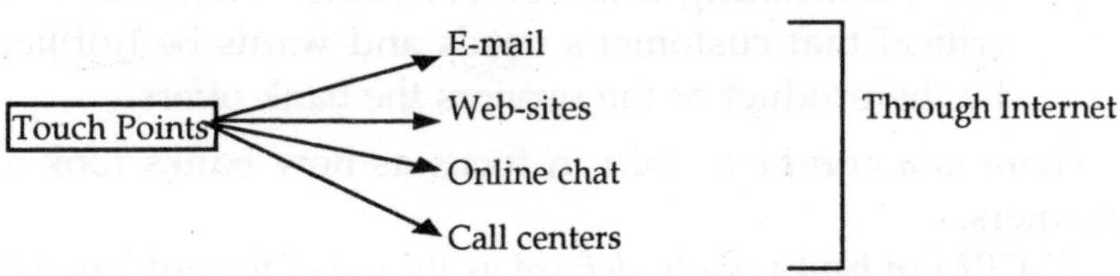

E-CRM in BANKS

Gone are the days when bankers could afford to sit back and wait for businesses to come to their door steps. Today the banker is required to go and knock at the door of customers for getting good business. All the activities of a bank should be focused on its existing or current and prospective customers. Therefore in order to retain existing customers and acquire new customers it is better for the bank to maintain good long term relationship with its customers. This can be done if the bank understands the needs and wants of its customer and then provide the better services/customer services. Therefore, whether a bank is going to succeed or fail in its trade area is determined to a large extent by how well the needs of its customers have been understood and satisfied. Therefore, it is rightly said by Peter F. Drucker that

"The customer defines the business. To satisfy the customer is the mission and purpose of every business".

E-CRM is the marketing concept. Marketing in terms of banking can be defined as the creation and delivery of consumers satisfying products. (goods and services) at a profit to a bank. Every business wants to grow day by day. It wants to attain a growth which knows no end. It must continue to try to attract customers at all times du ring its lifetime without a single day's pause.

If the marketing concept is applied to a bank, it would mean that:

- The bank should continue to create new services for the use of customers and deliver the existing services to consumers most efficiently.
- Bank marketing must be consumer oriented. It is critical that customer's needs and wants be fulfilled by the product or the services the bank offers.

There is a complete shift in focus as how banks look at customers.

"E-CRM in banks can be defined as the use of the web/internet and various other electronic channels, technologies that enable automated and electronic management of customer relations". E-CRM, on the other hand refers to other factors like personalization, customization, one to many and many to many transaction. It permits business speed and real time response to customer or markets through the new tools such as e-mail, internet, telephone, chat facility etc. which reduces the cost of customer contact.

To serve more and retain customers banks in India have changed the old concept of accepting deposits and lending money. Use of technology by banks has increased the productivity very fast through automation of banking operations. The electronic technology instruments adopted by Indian banks are:

- Automated Teller Machines (ATMs)
- Telex
- Fax

- Internet
- Tele Banking / Phone Banking
- E-Banking
- Electronic Clearing Services
- Online Banking
- Infinet
- Swift
- Mobile Banking
- Wireless Banking Services
- Electronic Fund Transfer (EFT)
- Total Branch Mechanization (TBM)

With the introduction, implementation and adoption of above techniques/instruments by the bank have totally revolutionized the functions, operations, administration, decision making and management information system. All these techniques/instruments helped the banks in retaining the existing customers, attracting new customers, and provide lot of services with the help of these instruments to give them satisfaction.

Research Methodology

The present study is empirical in nature which draws its data through both primary and secondary resources. The data was collected with the help of questionnaire from the 10 bank employees of the *Punjab National Bank.* The area selected for the field work was *Rohtak* town. The collected data was analyzed by employing the technique of percentages.

Scope

The concept of e-CRM is very wide, the present paper is includes only some portion of it which is as follows:

- The different touch points used by the bank to interact with their customers.
- There are three areas of e-CRM that is marketing, sales and customer service. Out of these three the customer

service is taken for the study. It covers the different electronic services, the bank is providing to their customers. And what is the impact of these in banking sector.

Objective

The main objective of this paper is to know the impact of e-CRM on different aspects from employee point of view like:

1. Customer loyalty/retention
2. Increase in bank profitability
3. Reduction in frauds and errors
4. Increase in efficiency

Impact of E-CRM

Customer Loyalty/Retention

The main objective of e-CRM is to retain the existing customers and make them loyal. And this can be done only when the bank provides new new services to their customers. With the usage of phones, computers, fax, internet banking, ATM services etcetera. The bank found 26 to 50 percent increase in customer loyalty as showed in table below.

Table Showing %age Increase in Customer Loyalty /Retention after Providing Various Electronic Services

%age of Customer Loyalty/Retention	*No. of Employees*
0%-25%	-
26%-50%	9
51%-75%	1
76%-100%	-
Total	10

Increase in Bank Profitability

The table below shows that 9 employees are of the view that with the usage of computers and providing the new-2 services to customers the bank profits are also increasing. They think that this has increased the profit about 26% to 50% and 1 employee answered that this has increased the bank profitability in the class interval of 0% to 25%. Thus the analysis shows that bank is greatly benefited with the introduction of new-2 services for their customers.

Table Showing %age Increase in Profitability of Bank after Providing Electronic Services

%age of Profitability	*No. of Employees*
0%-25%	1
26%-50%	9
51%-75%	-
76%-100%	-
Total	10

Reduction in Frauds and Errors

Another impact of the use of electronic devices is reduction in the bank frauds and errors. The table below shows the %age reduction of frauds and errors. 9 employees said that with the mechanization of bank branch the frauds and errors are reduced from 0% to 25% whereas 1 employee was of the view that this has reduced the frauds, errors from 51% to 75%. The mechanization of banks thus brings accuracy in transactions.

Table Showing %age Reduction of Fraud, Error by Using the Various Electronic Channels

%age Reduction in Frauds, Errors	*No. of Employees*
0%-25%	9
26%-50%	-
51%-75%	1
76%-100%	-
Total	10

Increase in Efficiency

Although, the fact that electronic tools have resulted into increased efficiency has been established from various parameters like increased profitability, reduced cost, reduction in errors etcetera. Yet it was felt necessary to know specifically from the employees about its impact on overall efficiency of the bank. The results are tabulated in table below.

Table Showing %age Increase in Efficiency with the Usage of Electronic Tools

%age of Efficiency	*No. of Employees*
0%-25%	1
26%-50%	8
51%-75%	-
76%-100%	1
Total	10

The above table shows that most of employees were of the view that their efficiency has greatly been increased through the utilization of phones, internet banking, fax machines etc. 8 employees said that this has increased the efficiency from 26% to 50%. It is so because earlier they used to do only a few transactions in a day but now they are able to handle much more transactions in a day. The study found that the bank now do thousand of transactions through their employees who are sitting in front of the computers. Now they do inter branch transactions, inter-bank transactions because of the usage of the computers. 1 employee was of the view this has increased the efficiency only 0% to 25% and still another employee said that this has increased the efficiency from 76% to 100%.

Conclusion

Customers are the wheel behind which business revolve. All businesses need customers in order that they may exist. Banks are major operators in the service industry and like all other businesses are depicting their desire to woo new customers and try to retain the older ones in the dynamic hard pressured changes that are prevalent all around. With respect to the impact of e-CRM the study concluded that dealing the customers through phones, internet, face to face has greatly benefited the bank business. The cost has greatly reduced customers loyalty has increased by providing them new-2 services. Bank profitability has increased about 26 to 50 percent. Frauds and errors have also reduced about 0 to 25 percent. As now most of the transactions has done on computers. Overall efficiency of the bank has increased with the mechanization of the banking environment. Thus it leads to the conclusion that future of e-CRM in banks is very bright.

References

Cliff Findlay (2000), *CRM what's it all about?* Latitude Solutions Ltd.

Computing (2000), 'IT Playing only a Minor Role in CRM' accessed on *http://www.ununet.com/news/1105945,10.4.2005.*

Dyche Jill (2000), *A Business Guide to customer relationship management,* Addison Welsey, www.crmcommunity.com.

Dyche Jill (2002), *The CRM Handbook,* Pearson Education Asia.

Gray Paul and Byun Jongbok (2001), *Customer Relationship Management, Centre for research on information on technology and organizations,* University of California, Irvine.

Greenberg Paul (2003), *CRM at the speed of light: capturing and keeping customers in internet real time,* 2nd ed, New Delhi, Tata McGraw Hill Publishing.

Upadhaya, Rajiv (1985), "*Management of Commercial Banks in India – Public Relations and Customer Services*", New Delhi, Deep and Deep Publishers.

2

Significant Applicability Trends and Challenges of CRM in Insurance Sector–An Analysis

N.Y. Rajeshirke

Life Insurance Market

The Life Insurance Market in India is an underdeveloped market that was only tapped by the state owned LIC till the entry of private insurers. The penetration of life insurance products was 19 per cent of the total 400 million of the insurable population. The state owned LIC sold insurance as a tax instrument, not as a product giving protection. Most customers were under-insured with no flexibility or transparency in the products. With the coming-up of the private insurers the rules of the work have modified. The private insurers in the life insurance market have already grabbed nearly 9 per cent of the market and the market share is steadily growing. In terms of premium income, the 12 private players have tripled to Rs. 1000 crore in 2002-03 over last year. Meanwhile, state owned LIC's new premium business has fallen.

Innovative products, smart marketing and aggressive distribution–this triple whammy combination has enabled fledgling private insurance companies to sign up Indian customers farter than anyone ever expected. Indians are also slowly moving to the private sector for fulfill their needs and products on offer. However, the state owned companies still dominate segments like endowments and money back policies. But in the annuity or pension products business, the private insurers have already wrested over 33 per cent of the market. And in the popular unit-linked insurance schemes they have a virtual monopoly, with over 90 per cent of customers.

The private insurers are scoring big in persuading people to take out bigger policies. For example, the average size of a life insurance policy before privatization was around Rs. 50,000 that has risen to about Rs.80000. But the private insurers are ahead in this work and the average size of their policies is around Rs. 1.1 lac to Rs. 1.2 lac way bigger than the industry average.

Non-Life Insurance Market

At present, there are 12 general insurance companies with 4 public sector companies and 8 private insurers. Although the public sector companies still dominate the general insurance business, the private players are slowly gaining a foothold. According to estimates, private insurance companies have a 10 per cent share of the market, up from 4 per cent in 2001. In the first half of 2002, the private companies booked premiums worth R. 6.34 billion. Most of the new entrants reported losses in the first year of their functioning in 2001.

Insurance, like project finance, is extended by a consortium. Normally one insurer takes the lead, shouldering about 40-50 per cent of the risk and receiving a proportionate percentage of the premium. The other companies share the remaining risk and premium. The policies are renewed usually on an annual basis through the invitation of bids. And the insurance companies are turning once again to old hands such as NTPC, NHPC and BSES for business.

Re-Insurance Business

Insurance companies retain only a part of the risk assumed by them, which can be safely borne from their own funds. The balance risk is re-insured with other insurers. Re-insurance forms the backbone of the insurance business. Currently all insurance companies have to give 20 per cent of their re-insurance business to GIC. The aim is to ensure that GIC's role, as the national re-insurer remains unhindered. However, GIC re-insurers the amount further with international companies such as Swiss Re in Switzerland, Royale in UK and Munich Re in Germany. Re-Insurance premiums have seen an exorbitant increase in recent period, following the rise in threat perceptions globally.

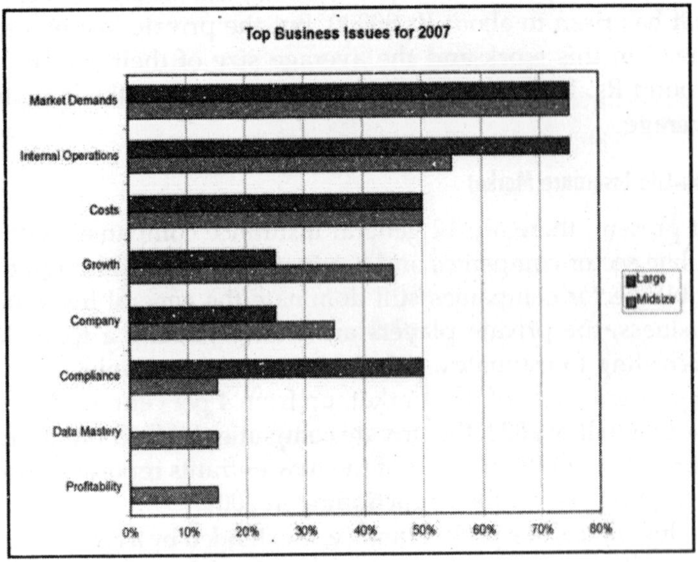

Facets of Challenges for Indian Insurance Market

Industry Challenges

After the liberalization in 1991, the task before the policy makers was to create an entirely new system of incentives for risk-and-profit sharing. Opening up the insurance business was seen as a logical and inevitable way of doing so. The insurance industry has been growing at 20 per cent, but it lags for behind its global counterparts.

A cursory examination of the key issues, which have emerged over the last decade shows the fundamental issue of risk is yet to be addressed satisfactorily in India. Such risks can arise from a host of directions, including, most importantly, demand projections, the contract structure, legal and financial covenants and management. All need to be analyzed and mechanisms have to be found to tackle the problems, which inevitably arise.

Another big problem is the complacency in the insurance industry which is reflected among other things, insufficient responsiveness to customer needs and instability of marketing net works, serious lags in technology. With the entry of private players the service levels are slowly going up.

Penetration is very low. Only about 100 million people have life insurance policies and 30 million are members of group insurance schemes. This is just around 10 per cent of the population. There is no blending between insurance and prudential savings.

Even in the non-life segment, there is no urge amongst the players to tailor their policies to specific customer needs. House protection and accident insurance have been neglected because it is easier to market high value general insurance policies like fire or marine insurance to large firms. As a result, the traditional general insurance products are fire, marine and automobile insurance.

The natural instinct of an insurance firm is to look for ways to not pay. This should not be confused with dishonesty. To ensure that there are no large scale breaches of contract, an enforcement mechanism is needed which cannot be taken for granted. Such a mechanism exists in India but that it doesn't function, as it should. There is an absence of meaningful statistical information of analysis for the future growth of the market. Even the internal costs measurements are flawed as they tend to be systematically biased upwards or downwards. The major thing is computerization is woefully inadequate. This is where the IT industry can make big in roads and boost the insurance business.

Business Challenges

As seen above factors including globalization, product commoditization, industry consolidation, regulatory changes, distribution channels, and shrinking margins have presented the insurance industry with a new reality-securing a new competitive advantage is more difficult than ever. Though there is a considerable increase in technology based investments and the proliferation of internet over the past few years these still remains as major challenges because of existing applications are tightly coupled monolithic and lack of standards.

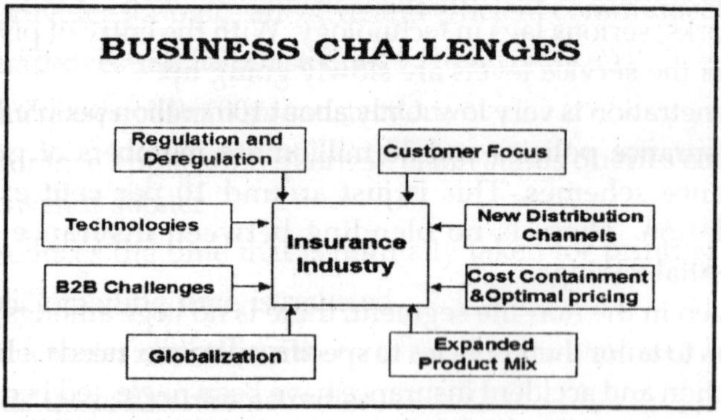

The insurance industry needs better ways to integrate applications and business logic across the value chain:

- Create opportunities for expanded sales channels and added customer value, by exposing services over the internet.
- Convert back-end environments, such as rating, claims and billing, into web based systems, delivering more powerful and integrated business solutions.
- Increase developer productivity, by radically simplifying the task of distributed systems development.
- Provide an inexpensive, standards-based solution for B2B integration issues.
- Provide incremental extension of investments already made in applications and e-Business platforms.

- Expose financial products over the web (e.g. escrow, credit check, loan applications, calculators etc.).
- Provide unified view of customer to customer reps.
- Large amount of automation and cost savings in Claims processing.

CRM Overview

It presents the CRM overview and the distinct areas of CRM initiatives. Following diagram gives high-level representation of the popular CRM structures – Operational CRM, Analytical CRM and Collaborative CRM.

CRM encompasses different organizational groups that are directly or indirectly linked to the end customers. There are a number of models that maps the CRM components with the organization. Each of the above three CRM components are linked to certain organization operations.

Operational CRM

Operational CRM targets at transforming the organization operations towards customer centric view. It impacts functions such as:

- Sales force automation,
- Customer service support,
- Marketing automation.

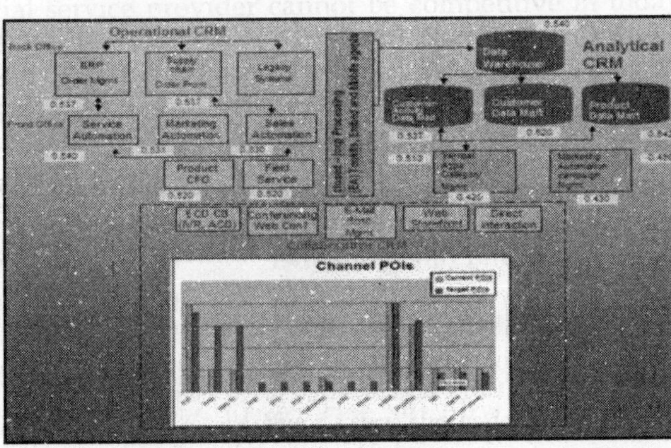

Operational CRM also deals with various channels of customer interaction and provides basic infrastructure for these channels to be efficient in the customer services.

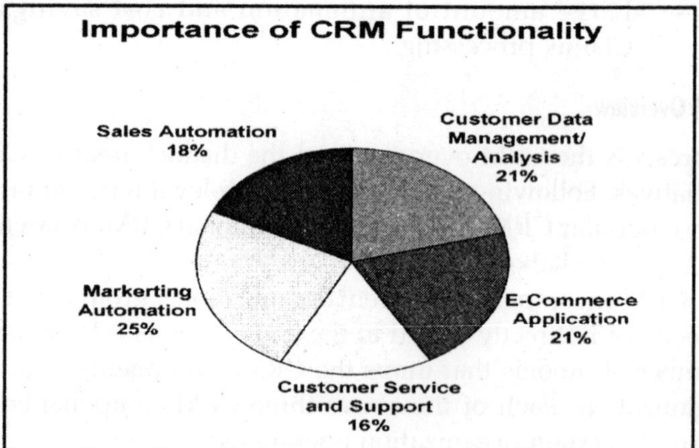

Source: Gartnet Group. Based on a Survey of 132 insurers Worldwide

Sales Force Automation

- Sales force automation functions are the ones carried by most CRM solutions. Within this, providing sales force with customer information, and assigning leads/prospects to sales personnel are the most popular CRM functions.
- Centralizing customer contacts information is the core of automating sales forces.
- For Insurance industry sales force management is critical since the majority of the sales staff are external agents and they must have updated knowledge base of the products, offers, processes and company literature.
- IFA and Broker Management – CRM also helps to collate the call reports and management reports from the agents on a regular and timely manner.

Customer Service–Multi Channel Approach

At a present age, customers use different channels as means of communication with the services provider. While using different channels, customer expects easy interaction, well-defined transactional flow and similar quality of service. Even customer support personnel access to customer interaction data across multiple touch points.

Major channels used by customers and CRM support for these channels as given in the following table

Customer Contact Channel	*CRM Support for Channel*
Email	Many CRM solutions have email-automation feature where customer emails can be linked to business processes that map with appropriate employees in the organization. Many of these processes are also handled by BPO units.
Voice Mail	Call center support solutions. Includes the "switch-board" application that integrates with the back-end processing engines.
Web-based Automation	Customers are increasing transacting using this channel. There are numerous e-Business and internet solutions available to support online transactions.
Insurance Portal	Customers use this portal to access product details, get quotations, receive recent updates etc. There are online content management tools that can assist for such channels.

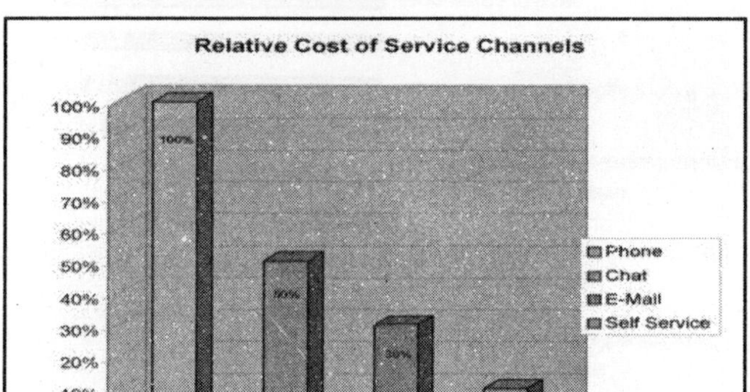

As a competitive factor for both life and non-life companies are using these newer services channels for their competitive advantage.

For example: lower communication cost using channels other than phone

- Average e-mail cost is 30% of a phone call cost
- Average chat cost is 50% of a phone call cost
- Average self-help cost is 10% of a phone call cost

When it comes to channel support, it is important to know the customer behaviour and expectations. CRM implementations must attempt match the expectations and leverage the buyer behaviour in a meaningful way.

Trends in CRM

Customer Relationship Management (CRM) has become a top priority for companies in many industries from insurance and financial services, to manufacturing the healthcare. CRM is the process companies utilize to understand and react to customers' evolving desires, utilizing detailed customer-behaviour and transaction information, to drive customer acquisition, loyalty, satisfaction and profitability.

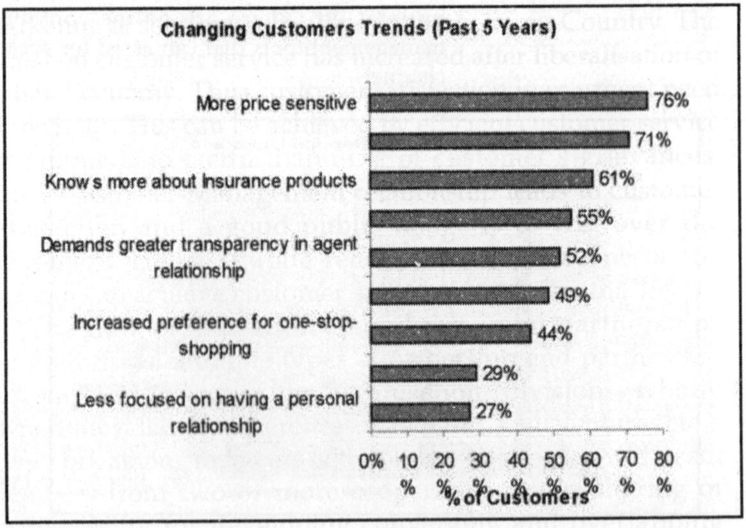

In 2007, spending on packaged CRM application technologies will increase beyond the 2006 levels to exceed the spending boom of 1999/2000. Gartner's 2005 and 2006 surveys of CRM consultants and systems integrators (SIs) show that spending is still being driven primarily by the three main types of CRM applications, which continue to represent more than 70 per cent of all packaged application spending:

- Sales force automation (SFA)
- Campaign management
- Call management

Enterprises are becoming interested in applications that add value by helping sales people sell more effectively, improve sales adoption, target customers more accurately, increase customer insight and advocacy, increase collaboration and support knowledge sharing with customers.

Collaborated and Analytical CRM

The functions of collaborative CRM deal with processes in the interaction between the organization and the customer.

Analytical CRM deals with the capture, storage, extraction, processing and interpretation of customer data to use within the organization. Analytical CRM is also the back-bone of Business intelligence. There are plenty of possibilities with the analytical CRM.

- *Customization:* The primary focus at present seems to be on customizing communication to customers, and generating customized offers.
- *Customer Patterns:* Integrating data across multiple touch points is a feature of the CRM solutions. This is the data warehouse that can be used to identify patterns of customer demands, behaviour. It can also be used extensively for market research functions.
- *Marketing Campaigns:* Using customer data to analyze responses to marketing campaigns is the most frequently used function of analytical CRM solutions.

- *Customer Loyalty:* There are other usages of tools for forecasting customer preferences, tracking customer loyalty, and calculating customer retention rates.
- *Lifetime Value:* This data can be valuable to calculate customer lifetime values.
- *Cross-selling:* Data analysis is important for defining cross-selling strategies across a group of products.

With this brief overview of CRM functions with applications for Insurance industry as such how CRM help to achieve strategic advantage for Insurers.

Applicability

Competitive Factors in Life insurance companies	*CRM Applicability*
Premiums are high compared to non-life	CRM can be used to effectively counter the extra premium points that bother the customer and make the policy more customer friendly.
Market is huge	CRM has a role to segment the market into various customer profiles and target the right customer segment with the right kind of policies. This would be in mutual benefit of customer as well as the company.
Claims are few but of large value	Claims management is one of key areas where customer dissatisfaction is high. Customers are changing the companies just because of the long process involved in it claim settlement. CRM has a big role to play in terms of minimizing delays and making effective use of acquired information for quick settlement. In turn maintaining the customer retention easy.
Product Innovation	Customers have become more market savvy and already looking for newer products. So whenever they find a product suiting their need they shift. Life insurance companies have to be vigilant in this regards have to effective address the concerns of the customer proactively. They need to constantly innovate and provide value added service to the customers. CRM would be providing the framework make it more effective.
Retention of Sales force	This is primarily important in case of Life insurance as the personalized touch and the

Contd.

	customer contact is through the sales agents. These hold the key in acquiring the large customer base on the basis of word-of-mouth. Life insurance companies have to effectively implement CRM to address the internal customer's problems which in turn satisfy them to give more business.

Competitive factors in Non-Life insurance companies	*CRM Applicability*
Premium not too large	CRM needs to address these problems of having single product for single need. The products needs of people should be captured effectively and the customization needs to be done in order to satisfy the populace. The premium collections in turn would automatically rise and also cater to larger goal of customer retention.
Market is huge but the depth is missing	CRM has to address the problem of customer awareness and make the mutual benefit known to them. Very few people get general insurance solutions as per their need and this area of concern leads to loss of business for the companies. CRM has to effectively counter this mentality and make the policies more customer friendly.
Claims are too many and frauds are high	Fraud management is another area of concern for the general insurance companies. These can be countered if there is enough and proper information about the customer. Proper database storage and also history of claims can provide good analysis for major market players. They have to integrate their systems in order to counter claims that are repetitive and also fraudulent at times. CRM has a role in making this into reality.
Complaints management	Customer contact centers providing off the hand information abut the problems can bring customers closer to company. Companies have already employed personnel to bring in the contact centers and complaints management would soon become a need of the hour for all the general insurance companies. CRM implementations and spending have increased in these areas.
Sales automation	Sales automation in this area is very poor frankly due to lack of proper infrastructure and data. The sales are primarily at the point of sale and very few cases of repeat sales once the product is sold. CRM has to bring is the customer back into action with various offerings which can make companies more customer savvy and also product conscious.

Differentiating Factors for Indian Insurers

The implementation model can be used for CRM implementation plan. Depending on the competitive position of the insurer, the roadmap can be defined. We consider three cases here - Non-life insurer, Incumbent Life Insurer, New Life Insurer. Each of the three players has uncommon strategic drivers and hence the roadmap for them would be different. Following factors are considered for each of the above three groups.

The common issue for all and perhaps the greatest challenge is to successfully integrate all customer information acquired through different channels to build a complete and accurate profile of customers, allowing the delivery of tailored advice, increased customer revenue through effective cross-selling and optimized distribution costs from pushing the right customer to the right channel. The key will be to implement CRM correctly-not as an IT project but as a business tool able to, not only retain customers, but cross-sell and acquire new customers. It also has an element of changing the mindset.

CRM Effectiveness in Insurance Processes

Integration of Policy administration system and CRM implementation would be useful for understanding the front office process management.

Customer-Centric Approach

The element of focus is the end-customer, not policies. The CRM implementations need to associate all the relevant information, including owned policies to the customer. With access to complete customer information, including customer demographics, annotations and a complete product portfolio, one can have the additional ability to identify and advance cross-selling opportunities, customer life stage events and expiration date tracking. As a result of its customer-centric design, insurers can either use the solutions inherent to customer management capabilities, or connect with another CRM solutions of their choice.

Strategy Enabling

The CRM architecture should help in perpetually evolving the business functionality and implementing digital innovation to support key strategies. Business and CRM should work in unison to continually and incrementally provide added value without undertaking lengthy and costly projects for every change. This capability is essential to enabling rapid time to market for new policies, for adapting to new business rules and for the spontaneous capture of additional customer and risk data.

Customer Relationship Management

Customer-centric would allow a comprehensive and complete data view of all customer information allowing for complete portfolio selling and management. For example, when viewing a customer, agents or representatives can see at a glance if an auto customer does not have homeowner insurance, if a homeowner's insurance customer also has life insurance policies, or whether a small commercial customer might be a good prospect for your new medical policy. You can also relate customers to specific associations or other groups to manage special marketing campaigns, as well as document relevant contacts of an account for communication purposes.

Operationally Efficient Policy Processing

With streamlined policy processing achieved through reduced paper, workflow management and shorter processing times for new business and changes, CRM solutions would offer a cost efficient means for managing an insurer's business. The system follows user configurable business process definitions in automatically performing the right activities for each type of policy at each stage of its lifecycle. And real-time processing of all transactions means no more waiting for overnight batch cycles and time-consuming follow-ups.

Security and Authority Controls

CRM integration would implement certain security measure as well. One can have different profiles and privileges to administrators so each works within their authority limits for binding and transaction processing, and automatic task management efficiently handles escalation for approvals when required. Producer, and internal user, access to specific customers and policies can also be controlled.

Advantages of this Integration are Many

- New business based on the existing customer information.
- Allowing exploring rate differences for coverage, limit and deductible options one can get the scenario analysis in making the rates/quotes more effective for conversion into a policy.
- Mid-term changes can be put in place.
- Provision for multi-view reports
- Renewals are made easy.
- Underwriting is effective and more streamlir ed.

Technical Hurdles

Some of technical hurdles one has to address are mainly in the areas of product configuration and understanding the implicit needs of the customer.

- The policies govern only the explicit portion in their documentation.
- The customer centric though possible may not each considering the legacy systems in place.
- Data availability is scarce and the sales team is concentrating on business first and data later approach.
- Even the multi-channel multi-tiered systems may be tedious to handle at the beginning of life cycle.

Conclusion

- Bring in training and customer focus within the organization.
- Implementation challenges need to be brainstormed at various forums and need of the hour is to arrive at an effective strategy and not a complex system.

- Policy foundation needs to questioned and the underwriting process problems need to be addressed with due care.
- Explore options for customer contacts and also bring in the customer closer to the organization rather then keep away.

References

Jessica Keyes (2006), Insurance Technology Handbook: The New Partnership, March, CRM Press

Jill Dyche (2007), The CRM Handbook: A Business Guide to Customer Relationship Management, Addison Wesley Information Technology Series.

Len Bass, Rick Kazman, Paul Clements (2005), Software Architecture in Practice, Addison-Wesley Pub.

Martin Fowler (2007), Patterns of Enterprise Application Architecture, Addison-Wesley Publications.

Rasesh Trivedi (2008), Web-services Architecture Models, RCG Information Technology.

http://www.clarabridge.com/resources/downloads/Clarabridge_CRM.pdf

http://www.globalbusinessinsights.com/content/rbtc0092m.pdf http://thinkstrategies.icentera.com/exLink.asp?51683860S36Q26125410385

3

Customer Relationship Management as Driver of Business Success

Samip Baruah, P. Bezborah

Introduction

In today's hyper competitive scenario, more than three quarters of the money and time spent by companies go towards acquiring and retaining customers. Customer-centricity has become the buzzword and the ones with clear and relentless focus on customers, enjoy a better competitive position. This is proved time and again. Yet, companies go through meticulous processes to gradually and consistently mature into an "organization for the customers". But, how would it mature into a customer-focused or customer-centric organization? The answer is: By reading and understanding the customers.

Reading the customer demographics and understanding their needs (both explicit and implicit) is what customer insight is all about. Customer insight is the basic point or the foundation for building a customer centric organization. Everything in the value chain revolves around this. This is the raw material. This is more a conversion process rather, since the end product is Customer Loyalty!

Customer Insight goes through a set of processes to get converted into Customer Loyalty- the finished product. The set of processes include use of machine, process and people to obtain the final outcome - just like a manufacturing process in a factory. The machine here is technology- information technology to be precise, process - the custom made steps based on set objectives; and people - those who are trained to efficiently carry out the conversion process. This whole scheme of activities that begin from customer information and end in processes and interactions that result in customer loyalty - in entirety, is what CRM is all about. CRM relies on customer data to create customer loyalty.

The concept of CRM was again the result of an evolution born out of necessity. When companies understood the need to obtain and maintain customer data, which was exhaustive and scattered in nature and were desperately looking for a tool that could compile, preserve use the data in a way they want, technology came to the rescue with exclusive methods called data mining, data warehousing and thus data base management techniques were born. Technology is mechanistic and didn't know what is required and what is not. A managerial tool was needed to perform the director's role in order to decide the path and processes.

Thus CRM was engineered as a tool to manage customer data using IT enabled techniques.CRM gives a framework for the activities. It decides on what to do - the objectives, what is required to do it - the resources, who should do it - the people, how to do it - the processes, how long to do it - the time frame. CRM could be ready made, tailor-made or handmade depending on the specific objectives it is set to achieve. CRM is unique in the respect that it follows a set of pre-determined processes to accumulate and manage customer data, which was hitherto unpractised. Hence, CRM is defined as:

"Customer relationship management (CRM) is a business strategy to acquire and manage the most valuable customer relationships. CRM requires a customer-centric business philosophy and culture to support effective marketing, sales and service processes. CRM applications can enable effective customer relationship

management, provided that an enterprise has the right leadership, strategy and culture."[1]

As is implicit in the above definition, the purpose of CRM is to improve marketing productivity. Marketing productivity is achieved by increasing marketing efficiency and by enhancing marketing effectiveness. In CRM, marketing efficiency is achieved because cooperative and collaborative processes help in reducing transaction costs and overall development costs for the company. Two important processes for CRM include proactive customer business development and building partnering relationship with most important customers. These lead to superior value creation. The basic concept is that the customer is not someone outside the organisation; he is a part of the organisation.

CRM is "the development and maintenance of mutually beneficial long-term relationships with strategically significant_customers"[2]

The generally accepted purpose of Customer Relationship Management (CRM) is to enable organizations to better serve its customers through the introduction of reliable processes and procedures for interacting with those customers.

In today's competitive business environment, a successful CRM strategy cannot be implemented by only installing and integrating a software package designed to support CRM processes.

A holistic approach to CRM is vital for an effective and efficient CRM policy. This approach includes training of employees, a modification of business processes based on customers' needs and an adoption of relevant IT systems (including soft- and maybe hardware) and/or usage of IT-Services that enable the organization or company to follow its CRM strategy. CRM-Services can even redundantize the acquisition of additional hardware or CRM software-licences.

CRM is "an IT enhanced value process, which identifies, develops, integrates and focuses the various competencies of the firm to the voice' of the customer in order to deliver long-term superior customer value, at a profit to well identified existing and potential customers".[3]

The term CRM is used to describe either the software or the whole business strategy oriented on customer needs. The second one is the description which is correct. The main misconception of CRM is that it is only software, instead of whole business strategy.

Major areas of CRM focus on service automated processes, personal information gathering and processing, and self-service. It attempts to integrate and automate the various *customer serving* processes within a company.

Shani and Chalasani define relationship marketing as "an integrated effort to identify, maintain, and build up a network with individuals' consumers and to continuously strengthen the network for mutual benefit of both sides, through interactive, individualized and value-added contacts over a period of time".

Purpose of Customer Relationship Management

CRM, in its broadest sense, means managing all interactions and business with customers. This includes, but is not limited to, improving customer service. A good CRM program will allow a business to acquire customers, service the customer, increase the value of the customer to the company, retain good customers, and determine which customers can be retained or given a higher level of service. A good CRM program can improve customer service by facilitating communication in several ways: [4]

- Provide product *information,* product use information, and technical assistance on web sites that are accessible *24 hours a day, 7 days a week*
- Identify how each individual customer defines quality, and then *design a service strategy for each customer* based on these individual requirements and expectations.
- Provide a *fast mechanism* for managing and scheduling follow-up sales calls to assess post-purchase cognitive dissonance, repurchase probabilities, repurchase times, and repurchase frequencies.
- Provide a *mechanism to track all points of contact* between a customer and the company, and do it in an integrated

way so that all sources and types of contact are included, and all users of the system see the same view of the customer (reduces confusion).

- Help to *identify potential problems* quickly, before they occur.
- Provide a *user-friendly mechanism* for *registering customer complaints* (complaints that are not registered with the company cannot be resolved, and are a major source of customer dissatisfaction).
- Provide a *fast mechanism for correcting service deficiencies* (correct the problem before other customers experience the same dissatisfaction).
- Use *internet* cookies to *track customer interests* and personalize product offerings accordingly and to engage in collaborative *customization* or real-time customization.
- Provide a fast mechanism for managing and scheduling maintenance, repair, and ongoing support (improve efficiency and effectiveness).
- The CRM program can be integrated into other cross-functional systems and thereby provide accounting and production information to customers when they want it.

Some of the Key CRM principles which needs to be taken care are

Key CRM Principles

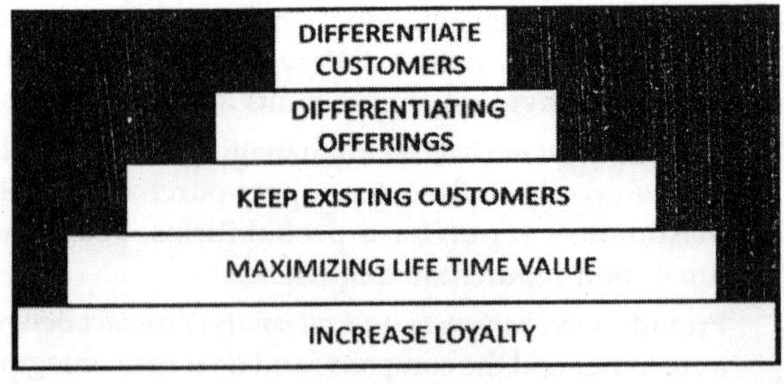

Differentiate Customers

All customers are not equal; recognize and reward best customers disproportionately.

Understanding each customer becomes particularly important. And the same customers' reaction to a cellular company operator may be quite different as compared to a car dealer.

Besides for the same product or the service not all customers can be treated alike and CRM needs to differentiate between a high value customer and a low value customer.

What CRM needs to understand while differentiating customers is:

- Sensitivities, Tastes, Preferences and Personalities
- Lifestyle and age
- Culture Background and education
- Physical and psychological characteristics

Differentiating Offerings

- Low value customer requiring high value customer offerings.
- Low value customer with potential to become high value in near future.
- High value customer requiring high value service.
- High value customer requiring low value service.

Keeping Existing Customers

Grading customers from very satisfied to very disappointed should help the organisation in improving its customer satisfaction levels and scores. As the satisfaction level for each customer improves, so shall the customer retention with the organisation.

Maximizing Life Time Value

Exploit up-selling and cross-selling potential. By identifying life stage and life event trigger points by customer, marketers can maximize share of purchase potential. Thus the single adults shall require a new car stereo and as he grows into a married couple his needs grow into appliances.

Increase Loyalty

Loyal customers are more profitable. Any company will like its mindshare status to improve from being a suspect to being an advocate. Company has to invest in terms of its product and service offerings to its customers. It has to innovate and meet the very needs of its clients/customers so that they remain as advocates on the loyalty curve. Referral sales invariably are low cost high margin sales.[5]

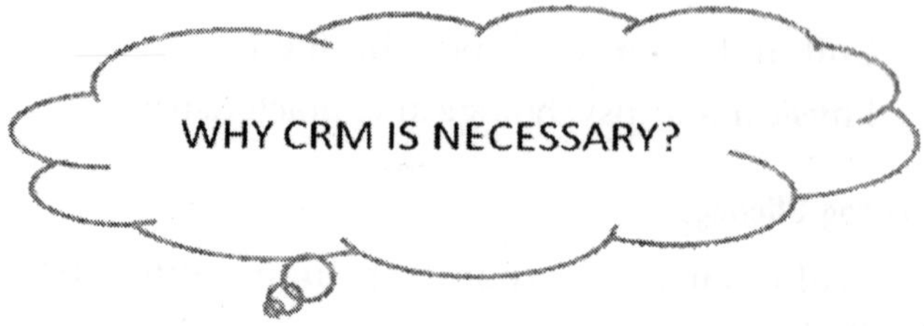

Several companies are turning to customer-relationship management systems and strategies to gain a better understanding of their customer's wants and needs. Used in association with data warehousing, data mining, call centres and other intelligence-based applications, CRM "allows companies to gather and access information about customers' buying histories, preferences, complaints, and other data so they can better anticipate what customers will want. *The goal is to instil greater customer loyalty.*" Other benefits include:

- Faster response to customer inquiries.
- Increased efficiency through automation.
- Deeper understanding of customers.
- Increased marketing and selling opportunities.
- Identifying the most profitable customers.
- Receiving customer feedback that leads to new and improved products or services

Benefits of CRM

Implementing a customer relationship management (CRM) solution might involve considerable time and expense. However, there are many potential benefits. A major benefit can be the development of *better relations with the existing customers,* which can lead to[6]:

- Increased sales through better timing due to anticipating needs based on historic trends.
- Identifying needs more effectively by understanding specific customer requirements.
- Cross-selling of other products by highlighting and suggesting alternatives or enhancements.
- Effective targeted marketing communications aimed specifically at customer needs
- A more personal approach and the development of new or improved products and services in order to win more business in the future.
- Enhanced customer satisfaction and retention, ensuring that your good reputation in the marketplace continues to grow.
- Increased value from your existing customers and reduced cost associated with supporting and servicing them, increasing your overall efficiency and reducing total cost of sales.

Once the business starts to look after its existing customers effectively, efforts can be concentrated on finding new customers and expanding your market. The more it's known about the customers, the easier it is to identify new prospects --improvement. Customer needs change over time, and technology can make it easier to find out more about customers and ensure that everyone in an organisation can exploit this information.

Architecture of CRM

There are three parts of application architecture of CRM:

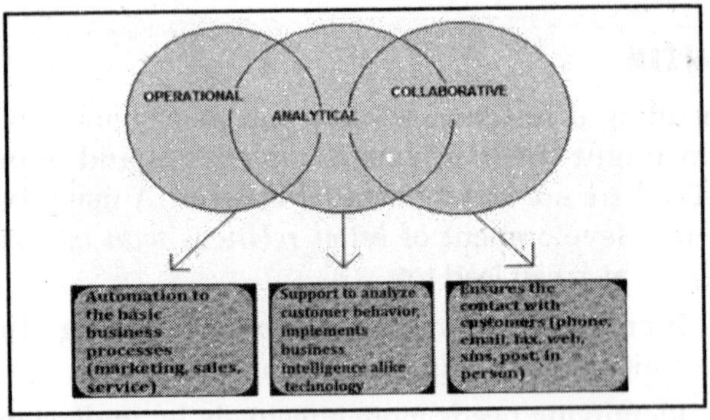

Operational CRM

Operational CRM means supporting the "front office" business processes, which include customer contact (sales, marketing and service). Tasks resulting from these processes are forwarded to resources responsible for them, as well as the information necessary for carrying out the tasks and interfaces to back-end applications are being provided and activities with customers are being documented for further reference.

Operational CRM provides the following benefits:

- Delivers personalized and efficient marketing, sales, and service through multi-channel collaboration.
- Enables a 360-degree view of your customer while the company is interacting with the customers.
- Sales people and service engineers can access complete history of all customer interaction with the company, regardless of the touch point. The operational part of CRM typically involves three general areas of business:

Sales Force Automation (SFA): SFA automates some of the company's critical sales and sales force management functions, for example, lead/account management, contact management, quote management, forecasting, sales administration, keeping track of customer preferences, buying habits, and demographics, as well as performance management. SFA tools are designed to improve field sales productivity. Key infrastructure requirements of SFA are mobile synchronization and integrated product configuration.

Customer Service and Support (CSS): CSS automates some service requests, complaints, product returns, and information requests. Traditional internal help desk and traditional inbound call-centre support for customer inquiries are now evolved into the "customer interaction centre" (CIC), using multiple channels (Web, phone/fax, face-to-face, kiosk, etc). Key infrastructure requirements of CSS include computer telephony integration (CTI) which provides high volume processing capability, and reliability.

Enterprise Marketing Automation (EMA): EMA provides information about the business environment, including competitors, industry trends, and macro-environmental variables. It is the execution side of campaign and lead management. The intent of EMA applications is to improve marketing campaign efficiencies. Functions include demographic analysis, variable segmentation, and predictive modelling occurs on the analytical (Business Intelligence) side. Integrated CRM software is often also known as "front office solutions." This is because they deal directly with the customer. Many call centres use CRM software to store all of their customer's details. When a customer calls, the system can be used to retrieve and store information relevant to the customer. By serving the customer quickly and efficiently, and also keeping all information of a customer in one place, a company aims to make cost savings, and also encourage new customers. CRM solutions can also be used to allow customers to perform their own service via a variety of communication channels. For example, you might be able to check your bank balance via your WAP phone without ever having to talk to a person, saving money for the company, and saving your time.

Analytical CRM

In analytical CRM, data gathered within operational CRM and/ or other sources are analyzed to segment customers or to identify potential to enhance client relationship. Customer analysis typically can lead to targeted campaigns to increase share of customer's wallet.

Examples of Campaigns directed towards customers are:

- Acquisition: Cross-sell, up-sell
- Retention: Retaining customers who leave due to maturity or attrition.
- Information: Providing timely and regular information to customers.
- Modification: Altering details of the transactional nature of the customers' relationship.

Analysis typically covers but is not limited to:

- Decision support: Dashboards, reporting, metrics, performance etc.
- Predictive modelling of customer attributes
- Strategy and research.

Analysis of Customer data may relate to one or more of the following analyses:

- Contact channel optimization
- Contact Optimization
- Customer Acquisition / Reactivation / Retention
- Customer Segmentation
- Customer Satisfaction Measurement / Increase
- Sales Coverage Optimization
- Fraud Detection and analysis
- Financial Forecasts
- Pricing Optimization
- Product Development
- Program Evaluation
- Risk Assessment and Management

Data collection and analysis is viewed as a continuing and iterative process. Ideally, business decisions are refined over time, based on feedback from earlier analysis and decisions. Therefore, most successful analytical CRM projects take advantage of a data warehouse to provide suitable data.

Business Intelligence is a related discipline offering some more functionality as separate application software.

Collaborative CRM

Collaborative CRM facilitates interactions with customers through all channels (personal, letter, fax, phone, web, e-mail) and supports co-ordination of employee teams and channels. It is a solution that brings people, processes and data together so companies can better serve and retain their customers. The data/activities can be structured, unstructured, conversational and/or transactional in nature.

Collaborative CRM provides the following benefits:

- Enables efficient productive customer interactions across all communications channels.
- Enables web collaboration to reduce customer service costs.
- Integrates call centers enabling multi-channel personal customer interaction.
- Integrates view of the customer while interaction at the transaction level.[7]

Now let us look at the functions of Customer Relationship Management:

Functions of Customer Relationship Management[8]

Direct functions (are the basic requirements of a company that are necessary to survive in the competitive marketplace)

- Profit;
- Volume; and
- Safeguard/Maintain

Indirect functions (are the actions necessary to convince the customer to participate in various marketing activities).

- Innovation:
- Market;
- Scout: and
- Access

Functions of Customer Relationship Management[9]

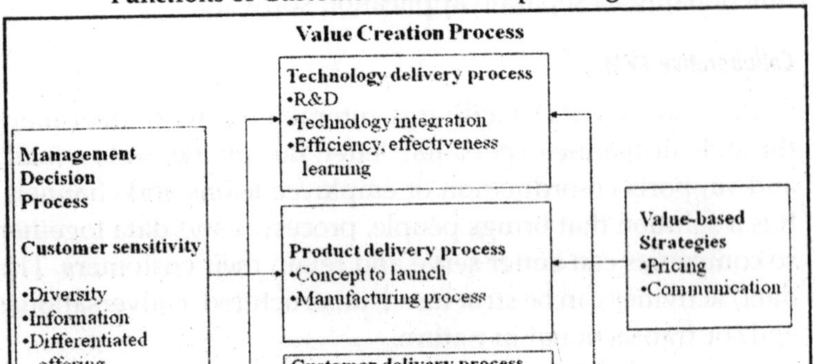

Tools for CRM

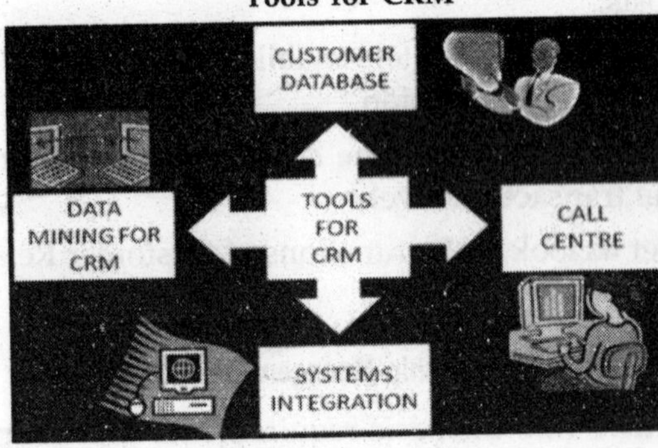

Some of the tools of CRM which are described in details are-

Customer Database

A good customer information system should consist of a regular flow of information, systematic collection of information that is properly evaluated and compared against different points in time, and it has sufficient depth to understand the customer and accurately anticipate their behavioural patterns in future. The customer database helps the company to plan, implement, and monitor customer contact. Customer relationships are increasingly sustained by information systems. Companies are increasingly adding data from a variety of sources to their databases. Customer data strategy should focus on processes to manage customer acquisition, retention, and development.

Call Centre

A *call centre* is a centralized office used for the purpose of receiving and transmitting a large volume of requests by telephone. A call centre is operated by a company to administer incoming product support or information, inquiries from consumers. Outgoing calls for telemarketing, clientele, and debt collection are also made. In addition to a call centre, collective handling of letters, faxes, and e-mails at one location is known as a *contact centre.* A call centre is often operated through an extensive open workspace, with work stations that include a computer, a telephone set/headset connected to a telecom switch, and one or more supervisor stations. It can be independently operated or networked with additional centres, often linked to a corporate computer network, including mainframes, microcomputers and LANs. Increasingly, the voice and data pathways into the centre are linked through a set of new technologies called computer telephony integration (CTI). Most major businesses use call centres to interact with their customers. Examples include utility companies, mail order catalogue firms, and customer support for computer hardware and software. Some businesses even service internal functions through call centres. Examples of this include help desks and sales support.

Systems Integration

While CRM solutions are front office automation solutions, ERP is back office automation solution. An ERP helps in automating business functions of production, finance, inventory, order fulfilment and human resource giving an integrated view of business, where as CRM automates the relationship with customer covering contact and opportunity management , marketing and product knowledge, sales force management, sales forecasting, customer order processing and fulfilment, delivery, installation, pre-sale and post-sale services and complaint handling by providing an integrated view of the customer. It is necessary that the two systems integrate with each other and complement information as well as business workflow.

Therefore, CRM and ERP are complementary to one another. This integration of CRM with ERP helps companies to provide faster customer service through an enabled network, which can direct all customer queries and issues through appropriate channels to the right place for speedy resolution. This will help the company in tracking and correcting the product problems reported by customers by feeding this information into the R&D operations via ERP.

Data Mining for CRM: Some Relevant Issues

Data mining is an important enabler for CRM. Advances in data storage and processing technologies have made it possible today to store very large amounts of data in what are called data warehouses and then use data mining tools to extract relevant information. Data mining helps in the process of understanding a customer by providing the necessary information and facilitates informed decision-making.

CRM technology has been, and still is, offered as on-premises software that companies purchase and run on their own IT infrastructure. Vendors include: Oracle Corporation, SAP AG, and Amdocs. In 2009, SaaS represented approximately 20% of all customer relationship management spending, and continued its trajectory of outselling on-premises software by a ratio of 3-to-1.[10]

Some CRM Service providers are SAP, Siebel, Sales Force.com, Chordiant & Oracle

Implementation of CRM

How to Implement CRM

The implementation of a customer relationship management (CRM) solution is best treated as a six-stage process, moving from collecting information about your customers and processing it to using that information to improve your marketing and the customer experience.[11]

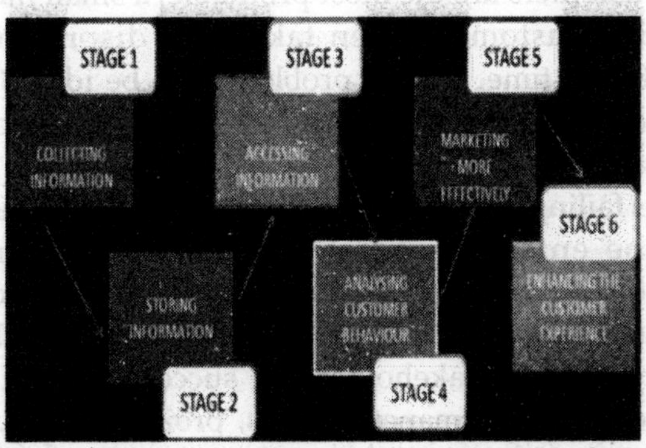

Diagram: Implementation of CRM (Six Stage Process)

Stage one- Collecting information: The priority should be to capture the information you need to identify your customers and categorise their behaviour. Those businesses with a website and online customer service have an advantage as customers can enter and maintain their own details when they buy.

Stage two- Storing information: The most effective way to store and manage your customer information is in a relational database- a centralised customer database that will allow you to run all your systems from the same source, ensuring that everyone uses up-to-date information.

Stage three- Accessing information: With information collected and stored centrally, the next stage is to make this information available to staff in the most useful format.

Stage four- Analysing customer behaviour: Using data mining tools in spreadsheet programs, which analyse data to identify patterns or relationships, one can begin to profile customers and develop sales strategies.

Stage five - Marketing more effectively: Many businesses find that a small percentage of their customers generate a high percentage of their profits. Using CRM to gain a better understanding of one's customers' needs, desires and self-perception, and can reward and target the most valuable customers.

Stage six - Enhancing the customer experience: Just as a small group of customers are the most profitable, a small number of complaining customers often take up a disproportionate amount of staff time. If their problems can be identified and resolved quickly, the staff will have more time for other customers.

CRM is failing because the correct capabilities are not being built at the enterprise level. The requisite changes in organizational culture, behaviour and attitude are not being implemented. Overall, in failed projects, there is little or no alignment between stakeholders on success criteria, critical success factors, performance metrics, project drivers, nor on the dynamics of how these parameters may change over the project life cycle. The requirements of the customer are either misunderstood, or not taken into account. The result is an inconsistency in focus, with less than optimum system design and implementation.

Hence CRM is failing due to two primary reasons: a) technical; due to the size, complexity, and lack of knowledge of technology, and b) human behaviour; due to general change management issues in the organization. What is required is a coherent, all encompassing strategy that focuses on key stakeholder requirements. Companies underestimate the complexities of CRM projects, lack clearly defined business objectives, and tend to invest inadequately in the provision of CRM software.

Let us look at some models of CRM based on Review of Literature

Some Models of Customer Relationship Management

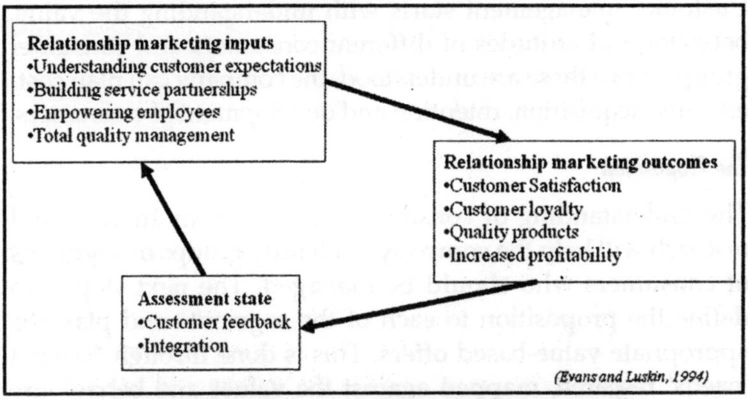

Model of Customer Relationship Management[12]
(The Evans and Luskin (1994) model)

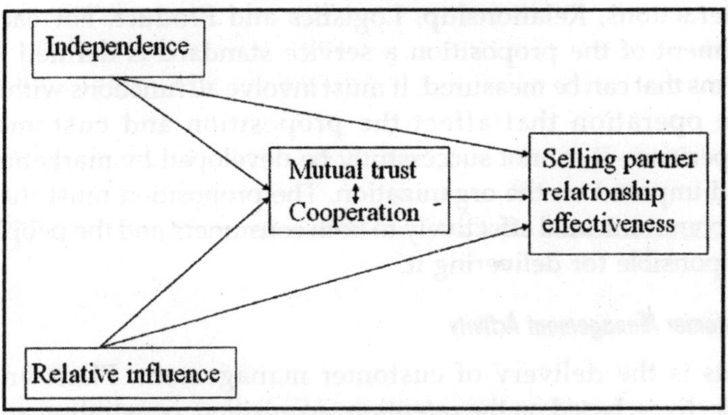

Model of Customer Relationship Management[13]
(The Brock and Barcklay (1999) model)

A Model of CRM[14] (Consumer Insight)

QCi, a specialist CRM consulting company, has developed a straightforward way of representing what doing CRM involves. Rather than describe CRM as a high-level concept, it describes it simply as a list of management activities, which when put together result in consumers being managed better. We describe it below.

Analysis and Planning

Customer management starts with understanding the value, behavior and attitudes of different consumers and consumer groups. Once these are understood, the company can plan cost-effective acquisition, retention and development of consumers.

The Proposition

The understanding of consumers derived from analysis and research will help the company to identify groups or segments of consumers who should be managed. The next step is to define the proposition to each of the segments and plan the appropriate value-based offers. This is done through focused 'needs' research, mapped against the values and behaviours discovered during analysis. The proposition is normally defined in terms of Brand, Price, Service, Transactional interactions, Relationship, Logistics and Product. For each element of the proposition a service standard is defined in terms that can be measured. It must involve all functions within the operation that affect the proposition and customer experience–it cannot successfully be developed by marketing and imposed on the organization. The proposition must then be communicated effectively to both consumers and the people responsible for delivering it.

Customer Management Activity

This is the delivery of customer management. Plans and objectives, based on the retention, acquisition, penetration and efficiency findings of the analysis, and the needs of consumers, lead to activity throughout the consumer lifecycle from prospect, through new consumers and on into mature consumers. This involves day-to-day working practices of marketing, sales and service support functions' in: Targeting, acquisition and retention activity like

- Handling enquiries;
- Support for new and upgrading consumers;
- Getting to know consumers and how they want to be managed;

- Account management (service, billing, technical support, field, third-party telephone);
- Identifying and managing dissatisfaction;
- Winning back lost consumers.

People and Organization

People deliver activity. Companies should identify and develop required competencies. Leaders must create and support customer management objectives, in an organizational structure that facilitates good customer management. Clear, understandable customer management objectives should be linked to business goals and employee satisfaction. Suppliers should support the organization with skills not available internally.

Measuring the Effect

Companies should measure how people, processes, profitability, proposition delivery, channel performance and consumer activity (such as campaigns) support achievement of the vision and objectives. Identifying performance relative to plan allows a company to refine and redefine plans and activity.

Understanding Consumers Experience

CRM is about managing consumers. So companies need to ask consumers:

- How well are we doing?
- What can we improve?
- What do competitors do better than us?

They should do this for each experience customers have with them, especially the ones that they consider most important.

Information and Technology

Information and technology underpin the whole model. Information needs to be collected, stored and used in a way that supports the strategy, the way people work and the way consumers want to access the organization. Technology needs to be used to enhance the way consumers are managed (from analysis to data at point of contact) and enabled.

Now let us look at some industry implementation of CRMs

Canon and CRM

- Canon needed a comprehensive customer database that could be made available to front office personnel.
- It purchased and implemented a Siebel CRM package, which implemented a Call Centre CRM strategy in the sales department, among other things.
- Information that was stored for a period of 15 years was used in an attempt to achieve customer satisfaction. Canon had 2200 users involved in its implementation.
- Overall improvement was seen in three main areas – Call Centre, Sales and Service.

DHL and CRM

- DHL Global Mail needed a CRM solution that could cater to a global network and ultimately provide a holistic view of the customer right across the globe.
- DHL used *Salesforce.com* as its CRM platform in the dispatch and delivery of parcels, and business post etc.
- The CRM suite was installed simultaneously around the globe within six months and integrated with the existing systems to ensure data centralization.
- It achieved an integrated approach to the customer worldwide and a *single view of the customer as well.*

Tata Motors and CRM

- Tata Motors was looking for real-time availability of customer and product data from its entire dealer network, faster response to customer requests, increased productivity and revenue generation, and a system that would give it a 360- degree view of customers across all possible touch points
- The solution jointly deployed by Oracle, SAP and IBM had been implemented in phases since 2003.
- The on-line CRM initiative now supports over 15,000 users, within the company and among its channel partners in India and abroad, to conduct all customer-facing transactions
- Besides achieving the above objectives, the CRM package also helped in leveraging data to improve customer interactions and streamline product development and planning, which has helped Tata motors provide additional value added service to customers.

TCS and CRM

CRM has evolved from customer data management to building and managing long-term relationships. TCS works with enterprises to devise and implement CRM solutions that become the backbone of their customer acquisition and retention strategies. With a framework that ensures alignment to the organization's strategic objectives, TCS' approach addresses the key dimensions of people, process, and technology, helping enterprises succeed in their CRM initiative with the best technology.[15]

Aviva and CRM

AVIVA

- Aviva decided to implement a CRM suite even before it commenced its Indian operations. The idea was to have a better interface with customers. It also wanted to integrate its customer-facing departments.
- It picked Talisman from among four vendors after a stringent evaluation exercise.
- Aviva took six months to implement the e-CRM suite. It implemented all the e-CRM modules except for the chat module. Today there are 450 users of the e-CRM suite at the company.
- The e-CRM implementation enabled Aviva to tap the potential of the Indian insurance market by tailoring its products and services, and quickly analyzing and adjusting its marketing initiatives

Summary & Conclusions

The purpose of Customer Relationship Management (CRM) is to enable various organizations serve customers better through introducing them to a series of processes and procedures that better the buying experience for customers. This is done through implementing a successful CRM strategy through a software package that has been specifically designed to support these business processes and procedures.

The work of CRM involves focusing on service automated processes, information gathering and processing, integrating and automating various customer serving processes in a company. It also manages to keep track of customer preferences, buying habits, deals with service requests, information requests, complaints etc. It deals directly with the customer. For ex call centres use Customer Relationship Management to store customer information. It enables them to retrieve and store information and serve the customer efficiently. It also helps them to encourage new customers, cater to the needs of the older ones and basically achieve customer retention. Finding a CRM software vendor is easy work but what's important is getting one that works for the company.

CRM can be implemented having even one customer. That is the barest minimum required. As such small industries too benefit from CRM implementation. In CRM terms a small business would generally constitute an organization having around 10 employees. Medium enterprises are enterprises having 11-100 employees. CRM works for a small entrepreneur, a 100 employee firm and a million dollar corporation as well. Fundamentally its application transcends to almost all industries.

Hence the saying that the CRM Software if chosen right can be the key to scalability and efficiency[16]

The overall extract of this information leads us to the conclusion that CRM is a boon to the industries, and has bought immense innovation in the field of industrialization. In this innovation by CRM, Business Communication plays a huge role. It is evident hat effective and proper communication leads to a better customer relation, whereas on the contrary ineffective communication has a negative effect on the relationship development. Today organizations have left no stones unturned regarding communication, to gain customers and are constantly moving towards it. CRM Software provides added strength to your existing plan.

CRM software is not a "cure-all" for the CRM program in your business. Successful launch of a CRM software campaign requires a strong CRM plan for your business, with complete objectives and clear priorities. CRM software can offer incredible accuracy, track-ability and detailed follow-up capabilities.

CRM is a new business philosophy based on trust and value. The core function of CRM is the value creation process. The basic premise of CRM is to offer superior value to customers in an effort to turn prospects into customers, customers into loyal customers, and loyal customers into partners.

Some of the growing trends which need to be noted are

The growing *de-intermediation process* in many industries due to the advent of sophisticated computer and telecommunication technologies that allow producers to directly interact with end-customers needs to be taken on board. For example, in many industries such as airlines, banks insurance, software or household appliances and even consumables, the de-intermediation process is fast changing the nature of marketing and consequently making relationship marketing more popular. Databases and direct marketing tools give them the means to individualize their marketing efforts.

Advances in information technology, networking and manufacturing technology have helped companies to quickly match competition. As a result product quality and cost are no longer significant competitive advantages.

Another force driving the adoption of CRM has been *the total quality movement.* In companies it became necessary to involve customers and suppliers in implementing the program at all levels of the value chain. This needed close working relationships with the customers. Thus several companies such as Motorola, IBM, General Motors, Xerox, Ford, Toyota, etc formed partnering relations with suppliers and customers.

Customer expectations are changing almost on a daily basis. Hence we need to address the needs of the newly empowered customers who choose how to communicate with the companies across various available channels. Also nowadays consumers expect a high degree of personalization.

Emerging real time, interactive channels including e-mail, ATMs and call centre that must be synchronized with customer's non-electronic activities. The speed of business change requiring flexibility and rapid adoption to technologies.

In the current era of *hyper competition,* marketers are forced to be more concerned with customer retention and customer loyalty.

As several researchers have found out *retaining customers is less expensive* and more sustainable competitive advantage than acquiring new ones hence CRM tools to be enabled.

On the supply side it pays more to develop closer relationships with a *few suppliers* than to develop more vendors.

The *globalization* of world marketplace makes it necessary to have global account management for the customers.

The basics of CRM include a business strategy that focuses on developing and retaining the relationships existing between customer and organization. The general perception is that CRM is nothing but a hype and the chance of CRM failure is high. Despite this, experts have speculated that billions of dollars are going to be poured into the CRM industry making it one of the fastest growing sectors in the market. It can be software or a customer loyalty card or a program enabler for retaining customers like the Super Value Stores and Vijeta stores of HUL but the need to retain customers' needs and working with the customers' needs to be taken care of, is addressed by CRM.

Hence CRM can be a reality, once a company wants to build on its existing customers as well as win new customers, which is the only way to grow market share in value and volume.

References

Buttle (2000), www.wikipedia.org/com

Plakoyiannaki and Tzokas, 2001

Grant, A.W.H. & Sclisinger, L.A (1995), Realize your Customer's Full Potential.

Gary Robbins (1999), The Marriage of Category Management & Customer Management published in RIS, July.

Hull, M. (2002,Feb), CRM Analytics, The Integration Channel. DM review (online) www.dmreview.com

Humburger, T. (2000, Sep), DM Review(online) www.dmreview.com

Merlin Stone, Alison Bond & Bryan Foss- Consumer Insight , First South Asian Edition 2005(Market Research in Practice) Chp-4 pg. (88-110)

Nair Suja-Retail Management Fourth Edition(2009) Himalaya Publishing House, Chp-12 CRM , pg.(332-373)

Saunders J. (1999), Manufacturers Build on CRM, Chp-25, pg.(17-18)

Simon Knox, Stan Maklan, Adrian Payne, Joe Peppard, Lynette Ryals- Customer Relationship Management: Perspectives from the

Marketplace Reprinted 2009-Butterworth-Heinemann- An imprint of Elsevier, Chp- 3, 7

Shanmugasundaram S. (2008), Customer Relationship Management: Modern Trends and Perspectives by Prentice- Hall of India Private Limited, New Delhi Part I- pg (3-31)

www.harvardbusinessreview.com

www.wikipedia.com

www.crmassist.com

www.crmcommunity.com

www.crmxchange.com

www.crm.guru.com

www.crm2day.com

www.destinationcrm.com

www.intelligentcrm.com

www.insightexec.com

www.searchcrm.com

www.spencersretail.com

www.customerservicemanager.com

www.google.co.in

http://www.crmasiasolutions.com/crm-solutions/benefits-of-crm.aspx

http://www.chinabi.net/blog/user1/141/archives/2005/92.html

Gartner, Inc. (6 June 2009) What's 'Hot' in CRM Applications in 2009 (http://en.wikipedia.org/wiki/Customer_relationship_ management#cite_note-hot-0)

http://crm.dynamics.com/customers/allcasestudies.aspx

Gartner, Inc (2009-06-15). "Gartner Says Worldwide CRM Market Grew 12.5 Percent in 2008". (http://en.wikipedia.org/wiki/Customer_relationship_management)

http://siebel.ittoolbox.com/documents/strategic-issues-in-customer-relation

http://en.wikipedia.org/wiki/Siebel_Systems

http://www.mycustomer.com/item/134150

http://www.oracle.com/us/corporate/press/017718_EN?rssid=rss_ocom_pr

http://www.avidian.com/contact-management-software/compare-siebel-crm-to-prophet-crm-software.aspx

4

Customer Relationship Management in Health Care Sector

B. Revathy

Introduction

Hospitals are the most important element in any health care delivery system. Hospitals play a major role in maintaining and restoring the health of the people. Care of the sick and injured, preventive health care, health related research and training of medical and paramedical staff are the broad functions of a hospital. An important resource in a hospital is human resource.

Hospitals should maintain high degree of transparency and accountability in their services, so as to ensure durable relationship with their patients. In fact, an effective CRM practice is one of the key strategies for efficient hospital services. In health care, CRM practices are essentially patient-focused strategies that involve effective management of hospital interface and interaction with patients. One of the major impacts of current interest in CRM is the change in focus from customer acquisition to customer retention. A repeat customer may be some one who has received extra value from an organisation in the form of services. The CRM could be viewed as hospital wide growth strategy aimed at knowing and serving patients, using the latest technology, to create a personal caring and service oriented interface.

A state of complete physical, mental and social well being and not merely an absence of disease is 'Health'. The basic expectation of all the individuals is to have good health. The health is being influenced by too many factors. When there is some ailment, or sickness, the person expect the service of doctors and in some cases the services of the hospital. The patients are the customers of the hospital. Their wants and needs are different according to their ailment. So it is essential that the institution should understand the needs and requirements of the patients.

A management process of acquiring customers by understanding their requirements more than their expectations and attraction of new customers through specific strategic marketing approaches with total commitment on the part of the entire organisation in evolving and implementing relationship strategies that would be rewarding to all concerned is customer relationship management. CRM is the application of one to one marketing.

Health Care Marketing

Marketing ideas were first developed half centuries ago, in business and industry. Several non-profit sectors also adopted these ideas. There is an inbuilt tendency to think that, if the hospital is good, the wards will be full. If the doctor is with specialisation, crowds will flow. If adequate equipments are organized, more will be the cash flow. All these factors read to better profitability of any hospital. Health care marketing is a new style of thinking and direction which a hospital can adopt in its exchange system to target patients who are in constant search for better health care services. A new thinking and direction has emerged among the health professionals in the recent times which are contributed by the following factors such as-

- Patients' attitude towards professional services
- Financial implications of hospital care
- Increasing number of patients leaving against medical advice
- Patients with Chronic diseases
- Utilization of health services by the community
- The Consumer Protection Act, 1986

Many hospitals are able to succeed because of well developed marketing programmes supported by budget allocation. Every hospital in addition to the existing customers aims at attracting new potentials, without losing the present ones. The advertisement and sales promotion of the hospital aims at securing future customers. It keeps a track of changing factors in the macro environment, especially the media, which has a definite influence on the public.

Hospitals would be wise to keep themselves updated with the changing trend, modify their policies and programmes. Hospitals should plan, implement and control their programmes so as to bring about a desired exchange with the target customers for the purpose of mutual gain. It includes the adaptation and co-ordination of services, pricing, promoting and placing for achieving an effective response. The most important task is to know the market trend, the market segment, the target group and in particular, to position themselves in the market.

Customer Relationship Management in Hospitals

CRM is a strategic device in health care marketing services. Health care awareness with technological application is an emerging term. This trend attracted the planners and policy makers, government and non-government organisations to provide fair health care facilities. The concept of hospital which was confined to taking treatment for ailments has undergone a sea-change for health education, awareness to treatment for critical, high risk diseases and for confidence building.

CRM practices for hospital services can be described as organized endeavors to establish and improve relationship between the hospital and the patients and their relatives. CRM practices also have major implications on the vision, mission, values, culture, processes and services structure of a hospital. CRM strategies help hospitals to enhance many of their relationships with patients and their relatives. Delivering value is building block of relationships. Value is not just the price of the services delivered or discounts offered. In fact, patient's perceptions of value are based on number of factors that include quality of service, ease of delivery without hassles, speed, responsiveness, flexibility and service excellence. It is always possible to improve hospital productivity and reduce cost while improving or maintaining service quality at the same level.

Outpatient Service and CRM

Outpatient services are one of the most important areas of a hospital which provide diagnostic, curative, preventive and rehabilitative services. It is not uncommon that hospitals are overcrowded and patients have to spend considerable part of their time waiting at different places. Hospitals and clinics generally function for about 5-6 hours a day (3-4 hours in the morning and 1-2 hours in the afternoon). In some hospitals, a doctor is charged of a clinic examination for about 21-40 patients per hour. This is considered to be excessive, as a doctor should not be expected to attend to more than about 10 patients (new and old) per hour. However, in practice a doctor is constrained to attend to more patients. Normally, a doctor should not be expected to attend more than 20 patients per hour in any case.

Inpatient Service and CRM

Inpatient services are an important element in health care delivery. Inpatient service may be provided in hospital wards which can be of general type like male, female wards or special wards which include maternity ward, isolation wards or wards for patients who need hospitalization in particular specialties such as orthopedics, pediatrics, psychiatry etc. Intensive care units are essentially the wards for critically ill patients. During patient's hospitalization, medical and nursing staff extends utmost personalized care to the patients undergoing treatment.

Medical staff should provide all relevant and possible information to patients for their adequate understanding of treatment options, risks involved in various procedures, duration and likely expenditure for treatnent. Patient's fear need to be allayed by the attending doctors. Non-verbal communication such as facial expressions, eye contact, pleasing gestures and a comforting touch helps in building up this relationship which may help in providing anxiety free stay for the patient in hospital. In inpatient services, nurses play major role in building strong relationships with patients.

The housekeeping staff helps in keeping the hospital clean and tidy. Many of them come in direct contact with patients. Their services are important aspect of CRM practices as their activities contribute directly to the patients comfort and peace of mind. During the patients stay in the hospital, their physical comfort contributes greatly to their recovery. Hence, maintenance services assume significance in CRM practices in the health care sector. The maintenance crew is expected to attend to the complaints as early as possible, diagnose the faults and rectify them.

Emergency Medical Services and CRM

Medical emergency is a situation in which a patient needs urgent and high quality medical care. It works 365 days and 24 hours a day. The foremost requirement of emergency services is that it should be done without any delay. Patients of cardiac problems, strokes, fire in high rise buildings, accidents, suicides, building collapse, natural calamities or critical health conditions are dealt with in emergency medical services. An ambulance brings a patient to the hospital. The emergency department provides round the clock service. Ambulance alarm and communication system is an important CRM feature of ambulance service which helps to minimize the delay. The post-discharge customer care management has two important roles to play -

- Maintenance of the record for each patient
- The regular interaction with the patients

Traditionally hospitals expected the patients to maintain medical records. But in this competitive market, the hospitals should maintain computerised database of each and every patient in detail. This database will help in the CRM activities of the post discharge period, i.e. maintaining relationship with the patients even after the discharge of the patient.

Review of Literature

[1]Peer Mohammad. H and Sagadevan in their study have stated that a hospital is an indispensable service centre which offers diagnostic and treatment facilities providing boarding and lodging, medical care and continuous nursing care for alleviation or cure of disease, illness or injury to inpatients, outpatients and for emergency patients. The hospital provides the facilities and services to meet the countries true health needs and serves as a beneficent to the society.

[2]Russell S. Winter has established what managers need to know about their customers and how that information is used to develop a complete CRM perspective. The basic model contains a set of seven components:

- A database of customer activity
- Analyses of the database
- Given the analyses, decisions about which customers to target
- Tools for targeting the customers
- Devices to build relationship with the targeted customers
- Privacy issues
- Metrics for measuring the success of CRM program

[3]CRM is very useful in the sense that, the company in control, makes business better, and tracks customers by transaction needs, treats customers as segments, customers feel stalked, organized around products and services. CRM helps in-

- Understanding customer's buying behavior for better targeting of offers
- Spreading customer information across the enterprise to allow customer-facing personnel to be more efficient
- Creating greater operational efficiency to reduce expense

[4]Ramachandran. P states that effective segmentation and positioning is the key to the success in health care marketing. Although many hospitals emphasize sophisticated specialty care, it is seen that maternity patients are most profitable. Some other health care providers target their services to the older individuals. This segment consists of individuals aged above 50 years. In India, this segment is growing faster and it offers an opportunity to the health care providers, as this group is responsible for more patient days than other segments.

[5]Health services are highly intangible, which cannot be tested or examined before consumption. The patients may not have the requisite knowledge to verify and evaluate the quality of services provided by a doctor. Due to limited educational background and low awareness of the health care issues, a majority of the patients are not able to evaluate service quality.

[6] The behavior of the doctors, nurses and public relation officers is found more sensitive, particularly with reference to raising the standard of services. Like other services, the medical services also need improved research and training facilities especially to the staff directly concerned with the patients. The channel for the distribution of services also occupies a significant place.

[7]Every patient should be given a feed back form to measure the level of satisfaction. All complaints should be sorted out as soon as possible and the management should make regular review to take immediate action in various areas. The facilitation desk which should work for 24 hours a day should provide an additional channel for patients who seek information, direction and redressal. The 24 hours reception should be ready to help the patients.

Statement of the Problem

Due to the recent technological changes, shrinking product life cycle, mass production and services, many hospitals are struggling to maintain competitive advantages. The present heath care system (and its escalating costs) is not sustainable due to its inefficiency and a lack of aligned incentives for improving performance. But behind all this glitter there are some ominous signs of the ills that pervade the health care system. A coherent and sustainable plan that addresses the healthcare needs of the masses is strikingly absent. There are no national standards by which physicians, nurses, pharmacists and hospitals are trained. Quality management remains an elusive dream; it is not sufficient to know the mortality rate of a surgical operation; one must know if the care was timely and appropriate. Judging from the incredible advances that have been made in information technology in India, it is noteworthy that these advances have not been applied on a large scale to healthcare. The lack of an Electronic Health Record (EHR) prevents the development of transparency throughout the healthcare system. And compounding all this is the widespread use of spurious drugs that interfere with proper treatment.

India has made rapid strides in the health sector since Independence: life expectancy has gone up markedly, the infant mortality rate has been halved, 42 percent of children receive the essential immunisations. We have a huge private healthcare infrastructure. And yet, critical health issues remain: infectious diseases continue to claim a large number of lives, babies continue to die needless deaths from diarrhea and respiratory infections, and millions still do not have access to the most basic healthcare. A country that has leapfrogged from rotary phones to a ubiquitous presence of mobile phones must make a similar change in healthcare. It will not be easy and it will not be inexpensive. But it has been done in other parts of the world before and it can be done here too. The potential to create the best healthcare system in the world exists. It is time to commence the debate, develop a plan and execute it.

Significance of the Study

Health has always been a high priority area in any country. It has been recognised as an important component in the process of economic and social development. Sanitation and hygiene, nutrition as well as safe drinking water are the basic determinants of good health. The indicators like infant mortality and maternal mortality rates, life expectancy and nutrition levels, birth rate and death rate, along with the incidence of communicable and non-communicable diseases reflect the health status in an economy. The existence of proper and well-defined health care facilities are vital not only for having a healthy productive workforce and promoting general welfare, but also for attaining the goal of population stabilisation as well as enhancing the overall quality of life of people.

Over the years, India has built up a vast health infrastructure and manpower, with a wide variety of hospitals and dispensaries being set up at different levels and run both by public and private sectors. They are being managed by qualified doctors and trained nurses. Expansion in access to healthcare services combined with technological advancements in this field has resulted in substantial improvement in health indices of the population and a steep decline in mortality rates.

Effective CRM practices should become one of the key strategies for efficient hospital services. In health care, CRM practices are essentially patient - focused strategies that involve effective management of hospital interface and interaction with patients. Effective CRM practices in a hospital mean providing services related information to a patient very quickly, responding to the patient appointment and admission requests promptly, dealing with patient queries and complaints expeditiously, and exercising all kind of flexibilities in serving patients and extending best of care and courtesies to the patients. The CRM in hospitals is a strategy to serve, satisfy, retain and attract patients. CRM could be viewed as hospital-wide growth strategy aimed at knowing and serving patients using the latest technology to create a personal, caring and service oriented interface.

Objective of the Study

- To identify the awareness among the respondents on health care.
- To measure the influence of personal variables on health care.
- To ascertain the periodical of medical check up by the respondents.
- To identify the level of satisfaction of the respondents regarding service guidance in the hospitals.
- To rank the factors of CRM in the health care sector on the basis of respondents' perception.

Scope of the Study

Five leading hospitals in Ambasamudram namely-Seetha Lakshmi Hospital, Loganathan Hospital, Sankaranarayanan Hospital, Sakthi Hospital and Tamil Selvi Hospital are chosen for the survey.

Methodology of the Study

- *Sampling*- The desired sample size is obtained by collecting a sample of 40 each from five hospitals. 40 samples from each hospital is through convenience sampling method.
- *Sources of Data* - The study is based on both primary and secondary data. Primary data are collected from the sample respondents with help of a specially designed questionnaire, which consists of the key factors determining CRM in the health care sector. Ten factors of CRM in health care sector are identified and Likert's 5 point scaling technique is used to rank the factors of CRM in the health care sector on the basis of respondents' perception. Secondary data are collected from the records of the hospitals, articles from journals and magazines.
- *Statistical Tools Used*- Data are analysed with the help of classification table, percentage analysis, chi square test and simple and weighted averages.

Analysis and Interpretation

To analyse the influence of personal variables on the opinion of respondents regarding health care, *four* variables namely – sex, age, marital status and monthly income are considered. Further the CRM in health care sector is analysed with the help of the following *ten* dimensions of CRM: Reception, Medical check up, Diagnosis, Availability of equipments, Conducive environment, Patient education, Personalised care, Loyalty, Hospital charges and Follow up.

Table 1
Distribution of Sample Respondents Based on Personal Variables

Personal Variables	*Category*	*Sample Respondents*	
		Number of Respondents(200)	*Percentage of Respondents*
Sex	Male	112	56
	Female	88	44
Age	Below 20 years	28	14
	21-40 years	56	28
	41-60 years	70	35
	Above 60 years	46	23
Marital Status	Married	142	71
	Unmarried	58	29
Monthly Income	Below Rs.5000	20	10
	Rs.5001-Rs.10000	48	24
	Rs.10001-Rs.15000	62	31
	Above Rs.15000	70	35

Source: Primary Data

Out of the total 200 respondents, 56% constitutes male and the balance 44% female. 35% of respondents are of the age group between 41- 60 years, a higher proportion of respondents are of the age group 41-60 years. It is evident from the table that with the increase in the age of the respondents there is a proportionate need for the health care. The exception here is with regard to the respondents above 60 years of age which may be interpreted due to high mortality rate. As to marital status, 71% of the respondents are married and the balance 29% of the respondents are unmarried. Thus higher is the health ailment for the married respondents. The table depicts that there is proportionate increase in the number of respondents with a corresponding hike in their monthly income.

Respondents with Family Doctor

The table highlights the number and percentage of respondents with family doctors. Out of the total respondents, it is found that majority of the respondents prefer to have family doctors with regard to their health matters. Out of 200 respondents, 41% male respondents have family doctors and 38% female have their family doctors. With regard to age, 23% of the respondents between 21 to 40 years of age have family doctors and 10% of the respondents of age below 20 years also have family doctors. It is found that more respondents between 41 to 60 years of age prefer to have family doctors. As far as marital status is concerned, 59% of the respondents of married category have family doctors and 20% of the respondents of unmarried category have family doctors. Thus it is found that married respondents normally have preferred to have family doctors. With regard to the income of the respondents, 28% of the respondents who earn above Rs15000 as monthly income have family doctors for their consultation. The ratio of respondents with family doctors proportionately increases with corresponding hike in monthly earnings. Thus the respondents with better income prefer to have family doctors.

Regular Checkup

Prevention is better than cure. Regular check-up helps to detect the diseases and disorders at an early stage. It prevents unwanted anxiety and tensions. After certain years of age regular medical check up is advisable. With regard to sex, out of the total 200 respondents 30% male and 21% female respondents have undergone regular medical check-ups and 26% and 23% male and female respondents respectively have not undergone regular medical check-ups. With regard to the age factor and preference to undergo medical check-up, it is found that, 21% of the respondents of the age group between 41-60 years of age have undergone regular medical check-ups

Table 2
Respondents with Family Doctor

Variables	Yes		*No*		*Total*	
	Number of Respondents	*Percentage of Respondents*	*Number of Respondents*	*Percentage of Respondents*	*Total Number of Respondents*	*Percentage of Respondents*
Sex						
Male	82	41	30	15	112	56
Female	76	38	12	6	88	44
Total	158	79	42	21	200	100
Age						
Below 20 years	20	10	8	4	28	14
21-40 years	46	23	10	5	56	28
41-60 years	56	28	14	7	70	35
Above 60 years	36	18	10	5	46	23
Total	158	79	42	21	200	100
Marital status						
Married	118	59	24	12	142	71
Unmarried	40	20	18	9	58	29
Total	158	79	42	21	200	100
Monthly income						
Below Rs.5000	16	8	4	2	20	10
Rs.5001- Rs.10000	40	20	8	4	48	24
Rs.10001-Rs.15000	46	23	16	8	62	31
Above Rs.15000	56	28	14	7	70	35
Total	158	79	42	21	200	100

Source: Primary Data

Table 3
Regular Check-up

Variables	Yes		No		Total	
	Number of Respondents	Percentage of Respondents	Number of Respondents	Percentage of Respondents	Total Number of Respondents	Percentage of Respondents
Sex						
Male	60	30	52	26	112	56
Female	42	21	46	23	88	44
Total	102	51	98	49	200	100
Age						
Below 20 years	8	4	20	10	28	14
21-40 years	36	18	20	10	56	28
41-60 years	42	21	28	14	70	35
Above 60 years	16	8	30	15	46	23
Total	102	51	98	49	200	100
Marital status						
Married	74	37	68	34	142	71
Unmarried	28	14	30	15	58	29
Total	102	51	98	49	200	100
Monthly income						
Below Rs.5000	8	4	12	6	20	10
Rs.5001-Rs.10000	26	13	22	11	48	24
Rs.10001-Rs.15000	32	16	30	15	62	31
Above Rs.15000	36	18	34	17	70	35
Total	102	51	98	49	200	100

Source: Primary Data

and only 4% of the respondents below 20 years of age have undergone medical check-ups. Thus it is evident that middle aged people prefer to undergo regular medical check-ups. As far as the regular check-ups and the marital status are concerned, it is found that, only 37% of the respondents of married category have undergone regular medical check-ups. While analyzing the monthly income, more respondents with higher income have undergone regular medical check-ups.

Variables	*Degrees of Freedom*	*χ2 Value*	*Table Value at 5% Level of Significance*	*Statistical Inference*
Sex	1	0.67	3.841	Not significant
Age	3	16.8	7.815	Significant
Marital status	1	0.39	3.841	Not Significant
Monthly income	3	1.20	7.815	Not Significant

Source: Primary Data

Hypothesis

Ho: Personal variables of the respondents do not influence the regularity of medical check up

With regard to the personal variables sex, marital status and monthly income of the respondents, as the calculated value of ÷2 is less than the table value at 5% level of significance, the null hypothesis, Ho: Personal variables sex, marital status and monthly income of the respondents do not influence the regularity of medical check up is accepted. Thus it is statistically proved that personal variables sex, marital status and monthly income of the respondents have not influenced the regularity of medical check up. But there is significant relationship between respondents' personal variable age and the regularity of medical check up. Age of the respondents has significantly influenced the regularity of medical check up.

Frequency of Medical Check-Up

Most of the respondents prefer to undergo medical check-up once in 3 months as they are well aware of the fact that early

Table 4
Frequency of Medical Check-Up

Variables	Once in 3 months		Once in 6 months		Once in a year		Total	
	Number of Respondents	Percentage of Respondents	Number of Respondents	Percentage of Respondents	Number of Respondents	Percentage of Respondents	Total No. of Respondents	Percentage of Respondents
Sex								
Male	28	28	18	17	14	14	60	59
Female	32	31	10	10	-	-	42	41
Total	60	59	28	27	14	14	102	100
Age								
Below 20 years	8	8	-	-	-	-	8	7
21-40 years	14	14	16	15	6	6	36	35
41-60 years	30	29	6	6	6	6	42	41
Above 60 years	8	8	6	6	2	2	16	17
Total	60	59	28	27	14	14	102	100
Marital status								
Married	50	49	24	23	-	-	74	73
Unmarried	10	10	4	4	14	14	28	27
Total	60	59	28	27	14	14	102	100
Monthly income								
Below Rs.5000	8	8	-	-	-	-	8	8
Rs.5001-Rs10000	20	19	6	6	-	-	26	26
Rs.10001-Rs.15000	14	14	18	18	-	-	32	31
Above Rs.15000	18	18	4	4	14	14	102	100
Total	60	59	28	27	14	14	102	100

Source: Primary Data

detection and diagnosis is preferable. Undergoing medical check-up is not a one time affair. It should be periodical and regular as attack of diseases and disorders cannot be predicted. Causes of diseases and health hazards are due to the changes in environment, climate, and are due to addiction to evil habits or due to irregular food habits. Out of 102 respondents, who underwent frequent medical checkups, 28% male respondents have undergone medical check up once in 3 months and 31% female respondents have undergone medical check up once in 3 months and rest of them once in 6 months with the exception of 14 male respondents who have undergone medical checkup once in a year. It is evident that a higher proportion of female respondents have undergone medical check-up once in 3 months. Regarding marital status, 49% of the respondents of married category have undergone medical check-up once in 3 months and 10% of the respondents of unmarried category have undergone check-up once in 3 months. With regard to income, 18% of respondents whose monthly income is above Rs 15000 have undergone medical check-up once in 3 months.

Hypothesis

Ho : Personal variables of the respondents do not influence the Frequency of Medical Check-Up

Variables	*Degrees of Freedom*	*χ2 Value*	*Table Value at 5% Level of Significance*	*Statistical Inference*
Sex	2	99.74	5.991	Significant
Age	6	19.62	12.592	Significant
Marital status	2	33.47	5.991	Significant
Monthly income	6	3.48	5.991	Not significant

Source: Primary Data

With regard to the personal variables sex, age and marital status of the respondents, as the calculated value of ÷2 is more than the table value at 5% level of significance, the null hypothesis, Ho: Personal variables sex, age and marital status of the respondents do not influence the frequency of medical check- up is rejected. Thus it is statistically proved that personal variables sex, age and marital status of the respondents have significantly influenced the frequency of medical check up. But there is no significant relationship between respondents' personal variable monthly income and the frequency of medical check up.

Choice of Hospitals

There are so many hospitals in the study area with better infrastructure, special features and add on service facilities. However, while selecting the hospital, patients may consult others and collect information regarding the quality of service, efficiency in diagnosis and regarding post operative care. As far as sex is concerned, out of the total 200 respondents, 29% and 21% male and female respondents respectively have selected the hospital of their own choice and rest of them have not decided the hospital on their own. Regarding the age factor, around 50% of respondents of different age group selected the hospital of their own choice and rest of them have consulted others to select the hospital for treatment. Regarding marital status, 41% of the respondents of married category have consulted others for the choice of the hospital and 20% of the respondents of unmarried category have decided on their own. 20% of the respondents who earn above Rs.15000 as monthly income have opted for consulting others to select the hospital for their treatment.

Source of Knowledge Regarding the Choice of Hospitals

From the table, it is observed that, 40 respondents have consulted their family doctors to select the hospital and 24 have consulted their friends and 36 respondents their relatives for the purpose. While analyzing the age factor, the respondents below 20 years of age have not consulted their family doctors and 20 respondents between 41 - 60 years of age have availed the help of their family doctors for selecting the hospital to undergo treatment. With regard to the marital status, more respondents of married category have consulted their family

Table 5
Choice of Hospitals

Variables	Self		Others		Total	
	Number of Respondents	Percentage of Respondents	Number of Respondents	Percentage of Respondents	Total Number of Respondents	Percentage of Respondents
Sex						
Male	58	29	54	27	112	56
Female	42	21	46	23	88	44
Total	100	50	100	50	200	100
Age						
Below 20 years	18	9	10	5	28	14
21-40 years	28	14	28	14	56	28
41-60 years	32	16	38	19	70	35
Above 60 years	22	11	24	12	46	23
Total	100	50	100	50	200	100
Marital status						
Married	60	30	82	41	142	71
Unmarried	40	20	18	9	58	29
Total	100	50	100	50	200	100
Monthly income						
Below Rs.5000	10	5	10	5	20	10
Rs.5001-Rs10000	20	10	28	14	48	24
Rs.10001-Rs15000	40	20	22	11	62	31
Above Rs15000	30	15	40	20	70	35
Total	100	50	100	50	200	100

Source: Primary Data

doctors for selecting the hospital to undergo treatment. As far as monthly income is concerned, 10 respondents earning monthly income of above Rs.15000 have consulted their family doctor for selecting the hospital to undergo treatment. The number of respondents who have consulted their friends and relatives has increased gradually with proportionate increase in their monthly income.

Table 6
Source of Knowledge Regarding the Choice of Hospitals

	Friends	*Relatives*	*Family doctor*	*Total*
Variables	*Number of Respondents*	*Number of Respondents*	*Number of Respondents*	*Number of Respondents*
Sex				
Male	12	21	21	54
Female	12	15	19	46
Total	24	36	40	100
Age				
Below 20 years	4	6	-	10
21-40 years	6	6	16	28
41-60 years	6	12	20	38
Above 60 years	8	12	4	24
Total	24	36	40	100
Marital status				
Married	18	31	33	82
Unmarried	6	5	7	18
Total	24	36	40	100
Monthly income				
Below Rs.5000	3	3	4	10
Rs.5001-Rs10000	5	5	18	28
Rs.10001-Rs15000	6	8	8	22
Above Rs.15000	10	20	10	40
Total	24	36	40	100

Source: Primary Data

Satisfactory Guidance in the Hospital

Most of the hospitals in the study area provide timely response to the patients and give them proper guidance as to which

Table 7

Satisfactory Guidance in the Hospital

Variables	Yes		No		*Total*	
	Number of Respondents	*Percentage of Respondents*	*Number of Respondents*	*Percentage of Respondents*	*Total Number of Respondents*	*Percentage of Respondents*
Sex						
Male	76	38	36	18	112	56
Female	44	22	44	22	88	44
Total	120	60	80	40	200	100
Age						
Below 20 years	18	9	10	5	28	14
21-40 years	34	17	22	11	56	28
41-60 years	42	21	28	14	70	35
Above 60 years	26	13	20	10	46	23
Total	120	60	80	40	200	100
Marital status						
Married	96	48	46	23	142	71
Unmarried	24	12	34	17	58	29
Total	120	60	80	40	200	100
Monthly income						
Below Rs.5000	10	5	10	5	20	10
Rs.5001-Rs.10000	20	10	28	14	48	24
Rs.10001-Rs.15000	60	30	2	1	62	31
Above Rs.15000	30	15	40	20	70	35
Total	120	60	80	40	200	100

Source: Primary Data

place in the hospital they should move for their treatment. The person who is entering as a patient in a hospital basically expects that he will be given proper guidance in the reception. Sometimes illiterates who intend to undergo treatment find it difficult to ascertain as to where he has to proceed for next course of action. Out of the total 200 respondents, 60% of the respondents felt the guidance in the hospital to be satisfactory and the rest did not. 21% of the respondents of the age group 41–60 years of age are satisfactory regarding the guidance in the hospital. 40% of the respondents are dissatisfied regarding the guidance in the hospital. This alarming percentage has to be brought down to ensure satisfactory quality service in hospitals.

Hypothesis

Ho : There is no relationship between respondents' personal variables and their perception on guidance in the hospital.

Variables	*Degrees of Freedom*	*χ2 Value*	*Table Value at 5% Level of Significance*	*Statistical Inference*
Sex	1	68.8	3.841	Significant
Age	3	12.27	7.815	Significant
Marital status	1	11.93	13.841	Not significant
Monthly income	3	50.87	7.815	Significant

Source: Primary Data

With regard to the personal variables sex, age and monthly income of the respondents, as the calculated value of ÷2 is more than the table value at 5% level of significance, the null hypothesis, Ho: There is no relationship between respondents' personal variables sex, age and monthly income and their perception on guidance in the hospital is rejected. Thus it is statistically proved that there is significant relationship between respondents' personal variables sex, age and monthly income and their perception on guidance in the hospital. But for the personal variable marital status of the respondents, the calculated value of ÷2 is less than the table value at 5% level of significance. So the null hypothesis, Ho: There is no relationship between respondents' marital status and their perception on guidance in the hospital is accepted. Marital status of the respondents has not significantly influenced respondents' perception regarding guidance in the hospital.

Appointment Confirmation Before Treatment

All the patients, both the residents of rural and urban, have the awareness to get the prior appointment in the hospital so as to avoid undue delay and waiting time. The hospital authorities, due to the heavy crowd in most of the hospitals normally insist on getting prior appointment in the hospital. This will reduce unwanted delay, and the waiting time in the hospital for the patients who are already suffering from ailment. Especially in multispecialty and corporate hospitals prior appointment is essential. While analyzing this factor with the sex category, out of the total 200 respondents, it is observed that 29% and 25% male and female respondents respectively got the prior appointment and the rest of them did not. With regard to age, 54% respondents composed of different age groups have got the prior appointment and the rest of them did not. With regard to the marital status of the respondents, 78 respondents of married category have confirmed their appointment before treatment. Thus majority of the married respondents have confirmed their appointment prior to treatment. With regard to the income level of the respondents, it is observed that 24% of the respondents earning above Rs15000 per month preferred to confirm the appointment prior to the treatment.

Types of Treatment

The patients may approach the hospital for different types of treatment. In the study area, it is found that there are some hospitals which permit the doctors to perform surgery only in their hospitals on rental basis for the operation theatre. The reason is, establishing an operation theater is a costly affair. While we analyse the nature of treatment with the variable

Table 8
Appointment Confirmation before Treatment

Variables	Yes		No		Total	
	Number of Respondents	*Percentage of Respondents*	*Number of Respondents*	*Percentage of Respondents*	*Total Number of Respondents*	*Percentage of Respondents*
Sex						
Male	58	29	54	27	112	56
Female	50	25	38	19	88	44
Total	108	54	92	46	200	100
Age						
Below 20 years	8	4	20	10	28	14
21-40 years	34	17	22	11	56	28
41-60 years	40	20	30	15	70	35
Above 60 years	26	13	20	10	46	23
Total	108	54	92	46	200	100
Marital status						
Married	78	39	64	32	142	71
Unmarried	30	15	28	14	58	29
Total	108	54	92	46	200	100
Monthly income						
Below Rs.5000	8	4	12	6	20	10
Rs.5001- Rs.10000	22	11	26	13	48	24
Rs.10001-Rs.15000	30	15	32	16	62	31
Above Rs.15000	48	24	22	11	70	35
Total	108	54	92	46	200	100

Source: Primary Data

Table 9
Types of Treatment

Variables	*Outpatient*		*Consultation*		*Inpatient & Admission*		*Surgery*	
	Number of Respondents	*Percentage of Respondents*	*Number of Respondents*	*Percentage of Respondents*	*Number of Respondents*	*Percentage of Respondents*	*No. of Respondents*	*Percentage of Respondents*
Sex								
Male	10	5	42	21	56	28	4	2
Female	6	3	30	15	38	19	14	7
Total	16	8	72	36	94	47	18	9
Age								
Below 20 years	-	-	12	6	17	8.5	-	-
21-40 years	3	1.5	22	11	31	15.5	-	-
41-60 years	13	6.5	20	10	26	13	11	5.5
Above 60 years	-	-	18	9	20	10	9	4.5
Total	16	8	72	36	94	47	18	9
Marital status								
Married	16	8	46	23	62	31	18	9
Unmarried	-	-	26	13	32	16	-	-
Total	16	8	72	36	94	47	18	9
Monthly income								
Below Rs.5000	6	3	6	3	8	4	-	-
Rs.5001- Rs.10000	-	-	19	9.5	20	10	9	4.5
Rs.10001- Rs.15000	-	-	25	12.5	32	16	5	2.5
Above Rs.15000	10	5	22	11	34	17	4	2
Total	16	8	72	36	94	47	18	9

Source: Primary Data

sex, out of 200 respondents it is observed that only 16 respondents composed of 10 male and 6 female have approached the hospital as out patients and 94 respondents are admitted in the hospitals for treatment. More respondents of the age group 21-40 years are under the admission category. 34 respondents who earn above Rs.15000 per month are given treatment in hospitals as inpatients.

Respondents' Perception on CRM

'Conducive Environment' is the factor of CRM which has secured the highest score. Thus the public is much aware and conscious of conducive environment in the hospitals, a major determinant of good health. Hygiene environment is the primary determinant of the reputation and fame of the hospital. Next to Environment the respondents' perception is towards the 'Diagnosis' in the hospital. Wrong diagnosis damages the goodwill of the hospital and endangers its survival. Followed by it are Reception, Medical checkup and Availability of medicines & equipments in the hospitals which are also crucial factors of CRM in health care sector. The CRM factor "Loyalty" has scored the sixth rank and 'Personalised Care' in health care sectors the seventh rank. The CRM factor, 'Follow up' in the hospitals was ranked eighth. Nineth rank is for the CRM factor 'Hospital charges' as respondents do not want to sacrifice service quality for the sake of economy in cost. 'Patient Education' has scored the final rank as respondents have not recognized the value of it.

Findings

1. Out of the total 200 respondents, 56% constitutes male and the balance 44% female. 35% of respondents are of the age group between 41-60 years, a higher proportion of respondents are of the age group 41-60 years. With the increase in the age of the respondents there is a proportionate need for the health care. As to marital status, 71% of the respondents are married and the balance 29% are unmarried. Thus higher is the health ailment for the married respondents. There is proportionate increase in

Table 10
Ranking the Factors of CRM

Factors	*Highly Dissatisfied*	*Dissatisfied*	*Neutral*	*Satisfied*	*Highly Satisfied*	*Total*	*Weighted Average*	*Rank*
Reception	10	60	150	160	350	730	3.65	III
Medical checkup	16	48	135	188	340	727	3.64	IV
Diagnosis	18	42	126	120	445	751	3.76	II
Availability of medicines and equipments	10	70	156	96	395	727	3.64	IV
Conducive Environment	11	36	120	156	460	783	3.92	I
Patient education	92	78	120	72	55	417	2.09	X
Personalised care	20	50	144	128	375	717	3.59	VII
Loyalty	16	56	129	172	350	723	3.62	VI
Hospital charges	70	80	150	120	50	470	2.35	IX
Follow up	15	80	171	120	290	676	3.38	VIII

Source: Primary Data

the number of respondents with a corresponding hike in their monthly income.

2. Out of the total respondents, it is found that majority of the respondents prefer to have family doctors with regard to their health matters. Out of 200 respondents, 41% male respondents have family doctors and 38% female have their family doctors. With regard to age, 23% of the respondents between 21 to 40 years of age have family doctors and 10% of the respondents of age below 20 years also have family doctors. It is found that more respondents between 41 to 60 years of age prefer to have family doctors. As far as marital status is concerned, 59% of the respondents of married category have family doctors and 20% of the respondents of unmarried category have family doctors. Thus it is found that married respondents normally have preferred to have family doctors. With regard to the income of the respondents, 28% of the respondents who earn above Rs15000 as monthly income have family doctors for their consultation. The ratio of respondents with family doctors proportionately increases with corresponding hike in monthly earnings. Thus the respondents with better income prefer to have family doctors.

3. Out of the total 200 respondents 30% male and 21% female respondents have undergone regular medical check-ups and 26% and 23% male and female respondents respectively have not undergone regular medical check-ups. With regard to the age factor and preference to undergo medical check-up, it is found that, 21% of the respondents of the age group between 41-60 years of age have undergone regular medical check-ups and only 4% of the respondents below 20 years of age have undergone medical check-ups. Thus it is evident that middle aged people prefer to undergo regular medical check-ups. As far as the regular check-ups and the marital status are concerned, it is found that, only 37% of the respondents of married category have undergone regular medical check-ups. While analyzing the monthly income, more

respondents with higher income have undergone regular medical check-ups.

4. It is statistically proved that personal variables sex, marital status and monthly income of the respondents have not influenced the regularity of medical check up. But there is significant relationship between respondents' personal variable age and the regularity of medical check up. Age of the respondents has significantly influenced the regularity of medical check up.
5. Most of the respondents prefer to undergo medical check-up once in 3 months as they are well aware of the fact that early detection and diagnosis is preferable. Undergoing medical check-up is not a one time affair. It should be periodical and regular as attack of diseases and disorders cannot be predicted. Causes of diseases and health hazards are due to the changes in environment, climate, and are due to addiction to evil habits or due to irregular food habits. Out of 102 respondents, who underwent frequent medical checkups, 28% male respondents have undergone medical check up once in 3 months and 31% female respondents have undergone medical check up once in 3 months and rest of them once in 6 months with the exception of 14 male respondents who have undergone medical checkup once in a year. It is evident that a higher proportion of female respondents have undergone medical check-up once in 3 months. Regarding marital status, 49% of the respondents of married category have undergone medical check-up once in 3 months and 10% of the respondents of unmarried category have undergone check-up once in 3 months. With regard to income, 18% of respondents whose monthly income is above Rs 15000 have undergone medical check-up once in 3 months.
6. Personal variables sex, age and marital status of the respondents have significantly influenced the frequency of medical check up. But there is no significant relationship between respondents' personal variable monthly income and the frequency of medical check up.

7. Out of the total 200 respondents, 29% and 21% male and female respondents respectively have selected the hospital of their own choice and rest of them have not decided the hospital on their own. Regarding the age factor, around 50% of respondents of different age group selected the hospital of their own choice and rest of them have consulted others to select the hospital for treatment. Regarding marital status, 41% of the respondents of married category have consulted others for the choice of the hospital and 20% of the respondents of unmarried category have decided on their own. 20% of the respondents who earn above Rs.15000 as monthly income have opted for consulting others to select the hospital for their treatment.
8. 40 respondents have consulted their family doctors to select the hospital and 24 have consulted their friends and 36 respondents their relatives for the purpose. While analyzing the age factor, the respondents below 20 years of age have not consulted their family doctors and 20 respondents between 41 - 60 years of age have availed the help of their family doctors for selecting the hospital to undergo treatment. With regard to the marital status, more respondents of married category have consulted their family doctors for selecting the hospital to undergo treatment. As far as monthly income is concerned, 10 respondents earning monthly income of above Rs.15000 have consulted their family doctor for selecting the hospital to undergo treatment. The number of respondents who have consulted their friends and relatives has increased gradually with proportionate increase in their monthly income.
9. Out of the total 200 respondents, 60% of the respondents felt the guidance in the hospital to be satisfactory and the rest did not. 21% of the respondents of the age group 41 – 60 years of age are satisfactory regarding the guidance in the hospital. 40% of the respondents are dissatisfied regarding the guidance in the hospital. This alarming percentage has to be brought down to ensure satisfactory quality service in hospitals.

10. There is significant relationship between respondents' personal variables sex, age and monthly income and their perception on guidance in the hospital. Marital status of the respondents has not significantly influenced respondents' perception regarding guidance in the hospital.
11. Out of the total 200 respondents, it is observed that 29% and 25% male and female respondents respectively got the prior appointment and the rest of them did not. With regard to age, 54% respondents composed of different age groups have got the prior appointment and the rest of them did not. With regard to the marital status of the respondents, 78 respondents of married category have confirmed their appointment before treatment. Thus majority of the married respondents have confirmed their appointment prior to treatment. With regard to the income level of the respondents, it is observed that 24% of the respondents earning above Rs15000 per month preferred to confirm the appointment prior to the treatment.
12. Out of 200 respondents it is observed that only 16 respondents composed of 10 male and 6 female have approached the hospital as out patients and 94 respondents are admitted in the hospitals for treatment. More respondents of the age group 21-40 years are under the admission category. 34 respondents who earn above Rs.15000 per month are given treatment in hospitals as inpatients.
13. 'Conducive Environment' is the factor of CRM which has secured the highest score. Thus the public is much aware and conscious of conducive environment in the hospitals, a major determinant of good health. Hygiene environment is the primary determinant of the reputation and fame of the hospital. Next to Environment the respondents' perception is towards the 'Diagnosis' in the hospital. Wrong diagnosis damages the goodwill of the hospital and endangers its survival. Followed by it are Reception, Medical checkup and Availability of medicines &

equipments in the hospitals which are also crucial factors of CRM in health care sector. The CRM factor "Loyalty" has scored the sixth rank and 'Personalised Care' in health care sectors the seventh rank. The CRM factor, 'Follow up' in the hospitals was ranked eighth. Nineth rank is for the CRM factor 'Hospital charges' as respondents do not want to sacrifice service quality for the sake of economy in cost. 'Patient Education' has scored the final rank as respondents have not recognized the value of it.

Suggestions

Based on the above findings, the following suggestions are made with a view to ensure cordial Customers Relationship in the Health Care Sector.

- In order to avoid health complications, it is suggested to have a family doctor so that early detection of diseases is made feasible, which in turn is also advisable.
- The strengths and weaknesses of the health care service shall be ascertained only when feed back information is collected from the patients. So it is suggested to get the feed back forms filled up by the patients at the time of discharge from the hospital. This may help the hospitals to improve their competitive advantage.
- It is found that undergoing regular medical check-up is not so common among unmarried respondents. It is suggested that every individual should undergo regular medical check up because in the current scenario health ailments are increasing at an abundant rate.
- A separate help desk may be arranged so that the patients will be free from any confusion. This arrangement may be made in addition to the regular reception counter.
- Most of the respondents do not prefer to get the prior appointment from the hospitals. This state should be

avoided, by confirming the prior appointment unnecessary waiting time shall be avoided.

- From the views of the respondents, it is suggested that better and sophisticated equipments should be purchased and installed in the hospitals.
- If the patients are assured of proper and courteous treatment in the hospital, their loyalty towards the hospital would also increase. When they share their experiences with others, it becomes a good advertisement for the hospital. The study reveals that the quality of services in the hospital is not so encouraging. To eradicate this criticism, sophisticated medical equipments shall be bought by the hospital authorities and few add-on services may also be provided.
- Adequate advertisement may be flashed in the local dailies to educate the people to undergo periodical check ups for the sake of early detection of diseases.
- Doctors and other health care service providers should interact with the patients to create better relationship with them.
- Many hospitals do not entertain follow up actions. It is suggested that reminder card mentioning the date of next check-up shall be sent to the patients so that their level of satisfaction and their loyalty regarding the hospital gets enhanced.
- As the question of public relation is very important, there should be a medical staff committee in each hospital consisting of the superintendent and all honoraries or full time Head of the departments.
- In the future, hospitals should move from patient centric to service-centric strategies. The future of the hospital rests in the ability to provide quality health care services which exceed beyond the patients' expectations.

- Globally, consumerism has become the new watchword. As more and more patients get into the self-pay category they demand more accountability in pricing, safety and quality. Transparency will be the key to success. Preventive care and disease management is the way forward to reduce cost and manage demand.
- Hospitals should develop multi-specialty group practices. It is much easier to teach the techniques of sophisticated medical care to a group of employed physicians than to physicians as a whole. It is also important that doctors are paid adequately for what they do.
- Hospitals should benchmark their services level vis-à-vis other hospitals by undertaking benchmarking exercises or comparing with service level databases maintained by several hospitals.
- The government should appoint a commission which makes recommendations for the healthcare system and monitors its performance.

Conclusion

Health care sectors play a key role in maintaining good health for the citizens of India. As varieties of diseases are becoming common in the present time, modernization, research and development of new medicines and equipments are much expected in the field. Communication plays a very effective role in health care marketing. Television with its wide net work and coverage now is reaching 85% of the Indian population but this health care field has become very competitive. Around three fourth of the doctors have engaged themselves in urban area. The patients of upper income group have a wide choice to make from a number of clinics and hospitals. Therefore, many hospitals have abandoned traditions and adopted marketing strategies to bring more patients to their clinic. Indian doctors who have experience of highly sophisticated hospitals in abroad are coming back and setting up hospitals with good equipments and sophisticated updated investigative machineries. Thus India has emerged as a global hub for healthcare and this has led to more and more doctors and clinicians looking back towards India to continue and take forward their practices. The reversal of the brain drain is not restricted to the IT field alone. We are witnessing an increased number of specialists showing interest to shift their work base back to India from countries like the U.K. and the U.S. This indicates the growth of India as a leader in the healthcare industry. In fact, the head of critical care at Wockhardt's new facility in Bangalore has returned from the U.S. Deregulation, globalisation and fundamental breakthroughs in science with strategic influence of information technology are blurring geographic boundaries. New age professionals from various service sector industries are seriously looking at different opportunities that are available in the healthcare sector where they can play a vital role.

References

Books

Direct/yankelovitch Survey (2008) presented at the National Center for Database marketing conference, Philadelphia.

Lovelock C.H. (2001) "Services marketing" Prentice Hall International, USA.

Murugaiyan.S (2007) paper presented in the international seminar: "CRM in hospitals".

Peer Mohammad.H and Sagadevan.A. (2009)"Customers Relationship Management - A step by step approach", Vikas Publishing House Pvt Ltd, New Delhi.

Ramachandran. P, (2009) "Innovation in Health Care Marketing", paper published in services marketing, Sinha P.K, Himalaya Publishing House, New Delhi.

Russell .S. winter, (2007) "Customer Relationship Management, A framework, research directions, and the future", published by Haas school of business, University of California at Berkeley.

Shantha Meena.V(2009) paper presented in international seminar "CRM in hospitals".

Journals

Indian Journals of Marketing - volume XVI, No.1, September 2003

Indian Journals of Marketing - volume XVI, No.1, December 2003

Website

www.wikipedia.com

www.customer satisfaction.com

5

Effective CRM through Complaint Management

Geetha Sankar, A.S. Saranya

An organization's future health and vitality depends to a sizable extent on the importance it attaches to complaint management. It should view complaints as opportunities to target improvement efforts in the different areas. The key concept in complaint management is *defensive marketing,* which involves retaining existing customers. Its counterpart offensive marketing refers to attracting new customers.

Tools such as advertising, pricing, sales promotion, and personal selling are the traditional way of thinking about marketing, and the "four P's" paradigm- i.e., viewing marketing as making decisions about promotion, price, place, and product. This is the offensive marketing perspective. Defensive marketing, on the other hand, focuses on retaining existing customers by concentrating on customer satisfaction and complaint management. Since defensive marketing increases customer retention, it has a positive impact on market share reducing the necessity of attracting new customers (replacements) by reducing offensive marketing cost.

There are other benefits in addition to customer retention. Customers come back only if they are sufficiently happy, which means that the side effect of defensive marketing is positive word-of mouth, which tends to attract new customers. Also, long-term customers may tend to do more business with the firm, ask fewer questions and cause fewer problems, reducing the costs of serving them. All of these positive effects of defensive marketing enhance the lifetime value of the customer.

The urgency with which an organization views a complaint is related to the future value of the customer. Research to date indicates that the benefits of turning around a complaining customer are dramatic. In some circumstances, 95% of complainers will return if the complaint is handled satisfactorily and an unhappy customer who is listened to, regardless of the final outcome, is twice as likely to return.

Happy customers may tell others that they are happy and unhappy customers may tell others that the company is no good. According to one industry report, a dissatisfied customer tells an average of 9-10 people about the bad experience.

Service researchers have some startling figures to quote on complaints from dissatisfied customers reported in various newspapers and quoted in books viz,.

- Only one out of 20 dissatisfied customers bother to complain.
- Twelve positive experiences are required to erase one negative experience.
- Each dissatisfied customer shares his experience with 9 to 10 people.
- Around 50 per cent of attempts at service recovery are botched up, leaving customers even more dissatisfied.
- The most startling finding is that 86 per cent of the bad memories quoted by respondents are more than five year old experiences.

These findings do provide insight into the extent of problems, or opportunities that the service companies face. Some more insights into complaining behaviour, pertain to reasons why the customers complain, and why they do not.

Why Customers Complain

Some of the commonly documented reasons for complaining behavior are:

- To appear intelligent or discerning to others
- To get control over the service provider
- To build a consensus or to validate their viewpoint; and
- To let off steam, as an emotional release of stress.

Why Customers Don't Complain

Similarly, there are many documented reasons why many customers do not complain such as:

- They don't know where or how to do it
- They don't think it'll help;
- They doubt their own evaluation as being subjective;
- They are uncomfortable in complaining face to face; and
- They feel they lack the technical expertise (doctor's treatment, car repairs).

Therefore service marketers design a suitable complaint management process to deal with all types of situations

Most relatively enlightened companies realize that nothing is gained by ignoring complaints, not responding to complaints, or making complaining more difficult. They realize that retaining the customer is very important because of the lifetime value of the customer, and they try to think of ways to make the customer happy. Usually this is done by making it up to the customer in someway, that is, "buying the customer off". Unfortunately, this practice also may not have the desired effect on retention, that is, the customer may be satisfied but if he thinks about the quality of the job that the company did, the perception of the company is still likely to be low. Thus it is far better to solve the root problem than it is to compensate for failure in delivering the service.

Complaint Management in the Telecom Industry

Just about a decade ago, India had only 8 million phones for a billion people-teledensity (phones per 100 persons) of 0.8 %. Today, the Indian telecommunications network is the fifth largest in the world and the second largest among the emerging economies of Asia. It is at present the fastest growing service sector in the world. With teledensity approaching 6.9 per hundred the target to achieve 15 per hundred by 2010 looks well within reach. Three things changed the Indian telecom scenario for good- the new telecom policy of 1999, the entry into the mobile sector of MTNL and BSNL and the introduction of CPP(calling party pays) making incoming calls free. Now, India has about 42 million landlines and about 47 million cell phones.

Private operators have made mobile telephony the fastest growing (over 90%) in India. Four main private groups- Bharti, Tata, Reliance and Vodafone are braving the hazards of competing with the public sector incumbents.

The industry is currently in a state of high flux and there is rapid introduction of schemes creating both convenience and stress.

Quality in the Telecom Sector

Quality of service is the main indicator of the performance of a telephone network and of the degree to which the network conforms to the stipulated norms. Building lasting relationships with customers is one of the most vital operational functions, since the present day markets are no longer seller markets, but buyer markets. High cost of customer acquisition is making today's businesses understand the importance of retaining the customers for long-run sustainability in businesses. The cost of acquiring a customer is 6 times more than the cost of retaining them. Losing an existing customer is like losing a fortune especially in service centric industries which are characterized by active switch-over (churn) of customers, high acquisition costs, ceaseless price wars and near-saturation.

Due to intense competition in the telecom industry, prices are cut to such an extent that further cuts would mean only losses beyond recovery. At present, the service providers are resting on undifferentiated pricing strategy, hence price variation is not an issue for switch over. Customers now expect cost-efficient, high-end and user friendly value added services for the same price. It is at this point that churn occurs. According to research firm Gartner, the churn rate in the mobile segment in India is anywhere between 3.5% to 6%, which is the highest in the Asia- pacific region, where the industry standard is 2%. In order to control churn, most companies follow an internally developed monitoring system- complaint management system and to control churn. For this purpose, the subscriber's perception of the Quality of Service (QOS) is determined by around 21 performance factors (source; TRAI). The most important of these with respect to basic services and mobile services are,

Basic Service

Performance Factors

- Provision of a telephone after registration of demand(100% in < 7 days)
- Fault incidence (number of faults / 100 subscribers/ month)
- Mean time to repair (< 8 hrs)
- Percentage of repeat faults
- Dial tone delay
- Call completion rate within a local network (> 65 %)
- Response time to other operator assisted services
- Response time to the customer for assistance, % of calls answered (electronically as
- well as voice to voice)
- Time taken for refund of deposit after closures

Cellular Mobile Service

Performance Factors

- Fault incidence (no. of faults / 100 subscribers / month) and faults cleared within 24 hrs.

- Call success rate (the probability that call attempts made from mobile within the Coverage area, in 90 % of the cases, will be signaled to the called network within the Specified time)
- Call set-up success rate (within licensees own network)
- Blocked call rate (when there is no free channel to serve a call attempt)
- Service coverage.

Customer centric organizations (e.g, Telecom industry) are innovative in their overall approach and grow into learning organizations by concentrating on effective customer care and complaint management systems and also by developing the culture of total employee involvement towards total customer satisfaction. Such organizations have a well planned system for monitoring complaint data to know number of complaints, nature of complaints, number of justified complaints, analysis of complaints as product-centered, process-centered, and person-centered.

Proposed remedial actions including modifications of products/procedures/systems/ and identification of training needs are also standardized.

Such complaint data are used to initiate improvements and to benchmark services in relation to its competitors, customers and industry leaders. 'Root cause analysis' of all complaints and 'Duration wise complaint resolution analysis' are performed to identify where majority of the problems begin. All supervisors, team leaders and customer service representatives are made accountable. They are trained to adopt basic principles of handling customer complaints and thereby achieve total quality.

Some best practices of companies are linking complaint management visions to corporate missions and to clearly understand the link between complaint resolution and customer satisfaction.

Principles of Complaint Management in the Telecom Industry

Several principles followed for successful complaint management in the telecom industry are

- Communication links from the front line to the information system
- Immediate advocacy
- Authority to settle complaints
- Responsiveness
- Not further inconveniencing the customer
- Give customers a chance to complain.
- Give guarantees.
- Develop capacity of learning from complaints.

'Communications links' are invaluable in resolving complaints. This gives the capability of being able to tell the customer exact details about the product or service, so that they feel reassured about using the service. Database access, giving all relevant information about a customer, is fast becoming a requirement rather than a competitive advantage.

'Immediate advocacy' is another important principle. This means that someone from the company is immediately on the customer's side, working to bring about a successful resolution to the complaint. This is not the same as immediate resolution of the problem. Some problems take a long time to solve. However, someone in the company is always there to represent the complaining customer's interests.

Another key principle is the 'authority to settle complaints'. The more service oriented the advanced economies become, the more decentralized complaint resolution becomes. For this reason, authority to settle complaints is usually best handled at the front line because speed of resolution is important. A key to successful delegation of authority is thus "employee empowerment".

Related to this principle is 'responsiveness', which means that the complaint is to be resolved quickly, If the complaint can't be resolved quickly, the company communicates this fact to the customer quickly, and indicates exactly what is being done to address the problem. The principles discussed above go hand in hand with responsiveness. For example, the better the communication links and databases the faster the response in many instances. Likewise, an empowered front line tends to have the authority to resolve problems quickly; In general, two things is done to ensure that the customer considers the company to be responsive, regardless of whether the problem is solved immediately or not, i.e, the company responds immediately to all communication by the customer, preferably by phone, and informs the customer of what is being done to solve the problem and how long it is likely to take.

The next principle of successful complaint management is 'don't further inconvenience the customer'. Whenever the organization has made a mistake, it is the organization's sole responsibility to make things right. A fast acknowledgement, followed up with a fast resolution helps a customer cool down and thereby makes him feel important, which in turn can also make him a loyal customer. If a fast resolution is not possible, telling him when it can be resolved, and following up on it will be greatly appreciated by the customer. He would be delighted if he did not have to call a second time for the same complaint.

Customers are 'encouraged to give feedback regularly' through methods such as surveys, toll-free telephone lines, email addresses etc.

Where possible, 'guarantees' can be given to customers, so that they are encouraged to speak their mind, instead of taking their business elsewhere.

The attitude of developing the capability of 'learning from complaints' results in continuous improvements by implementing suggestions from their employees.

Complaint Resolution Procedure in the Telecom Industry

The entire market is classified into geographical zones. Each zone handles three types of market segments, viz, 'residential', 'commercial' (shops) and 'corporate' (small , medium and large companies). The fourth market segment is 'enterprise' segment (very large companies) which is handled exclusively by a separate department of the organization.

Complaints are first categorized zone-wise and then segment-wise and finally based on the nature of the complaint;

they are handled by the respective department. Complaints from the customers will land at the 'customer care' department which will give a ticket number to the customer and pass on the complaint to the respective zone coordinator. For e.g., billing query of a customeı, will be transferred by the particular zone coordinator to 'the billing and credit control' department. Similarly complaint that the phone is dead will be handled by the 'fault repair' department. A service mechanic will be in charge of rectification of the fault, and feedback will be sought from the customer regarding his satisfaction with the service rendered. Performance ratings of the service engineers are based on the service level agreements (SLA) in hours as stated below.

Categories of Complaints

Complaints	*Sla (hrs)*
Access to call centre	4
Activation related	72
Bill charges	8
Bill delivery	8
Billing request	4
Bri – basic rate interface	4
Call back related	4
Cancellation related	16
Correspondence related	4
Customer care services	16
Customer related	4
Disruption in services	1
Dsl hard ware	4
Dsl installation related	16
Dsl related	4
Dsl soft ware	4
Executive related	4
Hardware related	4
Installation and provisioning	8
Leased line	8
Marketing	8
Marketing related	16 - 56
Mass outage	8

Contd.

Complaints	*Sla (hrs)*
Migration related	24
Miscellaneous category	04 - 56
Non billing related	8
Out going related	4
Payment related	4 - 24
Phone not working	4
Phone working with defects	4 - 16
Primary rate interface	4
Provisioning related	4
Sales related	04 - 56
Selfcare related	16
Service gaurantee claim	4
Tariff_scheme change	8
Threat to cancel	16
Vas related	4 - 16
Waiver related	4

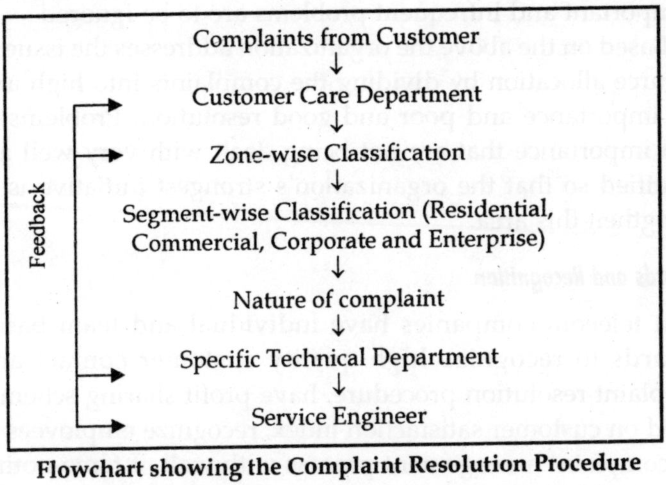

Flowchart showing the Complaint Resolution Procedure

Data Analysis Procedure in Telecom Industry

In large organizations numerous complaints received over a period of time are sorted, counted, and catalogued to suggest the areas in which the greatest improvement is needed. Valuable insights using some very simple 'data analysis' and some simple 'quadrant analysis' can be got.

The first step is to obtain a sorted list of all the complaints, grouping similar complaints together. Each type of complaint will now have a count associated with it, reflecting the number of times that complaint occurred

The second step is to identify which complaints have the biggest impact by rating complaints on a five -point rating scale, for example, from "very low impact" to "very high impact, " or some similar variant.

The third step is to analyze which complaints are most important, and how complaint resolution resources should be allocated. First, the complaints are divided into low and high impact and low and high frequency. Frequent problems of high impact are the most important problems to solve immediately. High frequency and low impact problems and low frequency and high impact problems also may be important. However unimportant and infrequent problems are to be ignored.

Based on the above the organization addresses the issue of resource allocation by dividing the complaints into high and low importance and poor and good resolution. Problems of high importance that are not being dealt with very well are identified so that the organization's strongest initiative is to strengthen this area.

Rewards and Recognition

Most telecom companies have individual and team based rewards to recognize high quality customer contact and complaint resolution procedure, have profit sharing schemes based on customer satisfaction index, recognize employees in the complaint management process with wall of fame-noting exceptional work and give gift certificates to employees who are positive role models in the complaint process. By and large companies do not link reward to compensation because of their apprehension of manipulation of data. The ultimate objective of an effective reward and recognition system is to institutionalize, a systematic and continuous customer driven learning by the employees and the organization.

Indian Telecom Market-Future Scenario

Indian telecom market has been estimated to be around $8.1 billion and is estimated to reach around $ 18 billion by the financial year 2010 with a compounded average growth rate of 12% as per study by research and consulting firm, McKinsey. Telecom sector is one of the most attractive and fastest growing sectors in the country.

As a result of the combination of the state of the art Telecom infrastructure, with raising affordability in the rural markets and growing spending levels in the middle class in the country-Indian Telecom space will be one of the most exciting areas in the emerging global scenario over the next five to seven years.

References

N.M. Shanthi, S.Bhaskaran., Implementation of CRM in Services.

B. Balaji (2002), Services Marketing and Management., S.Chand and Company Limited.

Kenneth E. Clow , David . L. Kurtz., Services Marketing.

Christopher Lovelock, Jochen Wirtz, Jayanta Chatterjee (2004), Services Marketing., Pearson Education Inc.

Shailendra Nigam., Total Quality Management.

John . S. Oakland., Total Quality Management.

Reynolds. J. (2002), Practical Guide to CRM: Building More Profitable Customer Relationships., Gilroy, CA, USA.

6

Customer Relationship Management in Insurance Sector

M. Neela

Introduction

In today's dynamic world, the importance of good customer service is becoming more and more apparent. With the blurring up of differences between banking, broking and insurance, coupled with industry consolidations; demutualization; shrinking margins; profitability pressures; and new distribution channels; the insurance companies are being forced to rethink their business models for survival. Today's customers are more sophisticated and are more willing to explore alternatives to traditional insurance products and how they are delivered. The task of getting and keeping customers requires even greater skill and effort. Getting closer to customers and effectively responding to their needs is a great way to boost their loyalty and encourage deeper business relationships.

Ever increasing competition, low interest rates and declining margins have driven firms to discover the customer as the basic element in their business equation. In search of a magic wand that attract and retain customers, companies have turned to technology to find out what makes their customers tick, and what keeps them both loyal and profitable, and have identified a tool commonly known as customer relationship management(CRM). This new technology in the past few years has emerged as one of the important tools of the business success. This is applicable to Insurance sector also. It is seen a strategic tool, which offers customers an insight into Companies and help transform market practices for betterment of the company. CRM plays a critical role in shaping up corporate strategy and operations. According to Cap Gemini Ernst & Young, 32% of business heads feel that CRM plays a critical role in business success, where as 41% feel that it is gaining ground and it will take some time to emerge as a tool which will help facilitate business success.

Though CRM as an idea is not a new development but the new technological developments have facilitated its implementation and helped companies build long term profitable relationship with customer, get closer to customers, and maximize company's share of customer's wallet.

Customer relationship management is the establishment, development, maintenance and optimization of long-term mutually valuable relationships between consumers and the organizations. Successful customer relationship management focuses on understanding the needs and desires of the customers and is achieved by placing these needs at the heart of the business by integrating them with the organization's strategy, people, technology and business processes.

The Concept of CRM

CRM as a concept focuses on increasing company's abilities to understand the customer's current needs, what they have done in the past and what they plan to do in the future to meet their own objectives. Its primary goal is to optimize revenue through effective customer interaction, which creates more satisfaction and in turn yields more loyalty. No wonder, this new concept proved to be a magic wand for many companies shaping them to march in a new business environment. Customer relationship management defines a business objective to deliver a level of customer satisfaction that ensures that the best customers will return. The new focus is to deploy end-to-end systems that can deliver this satisfaction, while also streamlining the organizations deployment of resources to make the promise of mass customization and rapid fulfillment not only possible, but also profitable.

The three phases of CRM are acquisition, enhancement and retention. Each phase has a different impact on the customer relationship and each can more closely tie the company to its customer's.

The concept of CRM is developed as a way to collect and manage customer service and sales information so the business would have more comprehensive view of their customer contact.

CRM system provides unique oppourtuinity with tremendous capabilities for sales Management, Sales forecasting, customer order processing and complaint handling supported by automated database and user friendly solutions of information technology.

The Requirements of CRM

- A belief in the strategy of being "customer-centric", rather than "product centric".
- Clear understanding of the need for CRM strategy and willingness to invest moderate money, as solutions are expensive.
- Careful evaluation of CRM solution vendor, to ensure that current and potential needs are understood, and business focus is retained rather than getting distracted by IT.
- Right kind of marketing and technical expertise in the company, to handle the complex strategies and tools of CRM. Change in enterprises attitude towards the traditional definitions of quality and productivity.
- Well defined cross-functional processes along with the ability to innovate and improve continuously.
- A scientific assessment of CRM functionalities and synchronizations between front-end and back-end activities through integration with solutions and technologies like ERP, SCM, Data Warehousing, Data mining etc.

Assumptions of CRM

- Shift of focus form "mass production" to "mass customization". Hence by understanding the customers' needs and desires better, companies can retain them longer and sell more to them.
- Sustainable competitive advantage lies more in retaining existing loyal customers than in acquiring new ones.
- Management is concerned about customers and their satisfaction and not about capacity utilization.
- Appropriate mix of technology and people along with necessary set-up is the key to success.
- Harvesting each interaction to improve targeting and personalizing services.
- Customer relationship is a must to ensure repeat business. It is not a new marketing mantra to push products, however IT has rejuvenated it.
- CRM in itself is not meant for,"pricing" of a product. It is the "value" or "satisfaction" of a customer derived during usage of products and services and experience with respect to an organization.

The Role of CRM

- Helps to focus and differentiate the most profitable customers and helps to serve them better than before, as well as better than competitors, to gain loyalty.
- Helps promote, offer and design product/services for target customer groups in a cost-effective manner, since, the entire cycle begins with capturing the customer's requirements.
- Clearly differentiates between customer requirements and product requirements and concentrates on the customer's real needs and likings.
- Collects customer data at one place, making it widely available and leverages customer databases, to find best customers and their needs.

- Increases customer loyalty and hence profitability, by more effective planning, marketing, selling and servicing throughout the customer life cycle.

CRM in Insurance Sector

Today, with an increase in the number of insurance players on the insurance landscape and consumers becoming aware of different products, insurers are urged to do away with the traditional strategy of selling and become customer-centric.

Unlike the other financial companies, insurance companies are faced with an additional challenge of keeping in touch with their customers regularly by way of interacting with them continuously. Moreover, attracting new customers and retaining high value ones have become more challenging with the banks and other financial firms exhibiting novel ways of integrating insurance products into their distribution channels

The benefits of adopting CRM strategies such as acquiring new customers and at the same time retaining the older ones. CRM facilitates capturing, consolidating, integrating and analyzing customer data. Implementing CRM strategies can offset the lack of coordination among the various departments and people in the insurance industry.

Insurance industry is facing several challenges in the form of increased demand for better service and simultaneous reduction in costs.Key stakeholders namely, employers, providers, agents, members and new consumers demand exceptional service. CRM-integrated self-service results in increased efficiency, convenience and stakeholder awareness. CRM implementation brings about a convergence between people and processes thereby increasing the business of the agent and employer group. It also plays a key role in identifying the right mix of tools and information for optimal profitability

The changing attitudes of customers and their efforts to explore alternatives to traditional insurance products has urged insurers to find new products and adopt a better service methodology to deliver these products.

Today, CRM is recognized as a valuable corporate asset. The process of CRM in insurance, which involves three steps, namely identifying the most potential customers, understanding the needs and buying patterns of the customers and interacting with the customers to meet their expectations is elaborated. The culture of the insurance industry that resists changes in technology, communicating the information to the actual point of customer contact and lack of technology to integrate the customer data are identified as the major challenges for implementing CRM.

A majority of insurers are not aware of what their customers really want, and those who are aware are unable to deliver the goods due to several organizational constraints. The structure of the organization and the way it does business can be cited as organizational constraints.

CRM practices of a company contribute to the overall performance of an insurance player. If the customer service of the organization is satisfactory, the customer does not look elsewhere but remain loyal to the organization. He would, in reality, act as a brand ambassador for the insurance company and assist in acquiring new customers.

Significance and the need for insurers to aim at increasing the insurance orientation of the customers. This can be achieved by explaining all possible coverage that can be obtained for their diverse needs. In the Indian insurance industry, which is still at an evolving stage, maintaining a long-term association with the customer becomes all the more challenging. The insurer should be able to do need-based selling, that is, suggesting a product that would best suit the customers' needs.

Insurers can no longer sit back and relax after clinching a deal. Today, they are under pressure to deliver customer satisfaction. Insurers need to enhance their service standards. They have to focus on understanding the customer well and should appropriately respond to the real as also imaginary grievances of the customers. They need to earn customer's trust and be keen on providing after-sales service. CRM implementation promotes stronger relationship and leads to customer delight.

The stiff competition in the industry has left the insurers with no option but to deploy CRM solutions to retain existing customers and simultaneously acquire new ones. Insurance companies are investing a considerable amount on CRM software and services. Through customized solutions insurers are able to provide individual attention to the customers. Leveraging on modern CRM technologies, insurers are able to sell multiple insurance and pension plans to the same customer.

In a highly competitive environment, Business Intelligence (BI) acts as a key driver for understanding the customers. The usage of BI technologies is quite low due to non-automation of core business processes. This aspect needs to be focused upon by the insurance companies. Data mining is a useful tool that can be exploited to build contacts and relationships with customers. The launch of a new product should be made known to the targeted customers. For this, the existing customer database and customer profiles need to be mined. It argues that the cost of acquiring new customers is much more than that incurred in offering better services and acquiring repeat business from the existing ones describes the crucial role Business Intelligence (BI) tools like data warehousing, OLAP, and data mining play in the insurance industry. BI tools provide crucial information to the corporate clients, which can bond the insurer's relations with the clients.

Insurance value chain, CRM process, Channel management are a few of them. It suggests that to effectively interact with customers and design the right products, the CRM strategy adopted by the insurers should utilize the potential of technology to the maximum extent.

Benefits of CRM

CRM helps in maximizing revenue by carefully targeting the customers and offering more products, and services. One can cross-sell and up-sell. Also these targeted customers could be upgraded to newer versions of products or sold additional products and solutions. And also it helps to interact with their customers in amore informal manner. Customer service can also be offered on multiple channels to ensure that customers have easy and convenient access to service representatives within the organization. Effective customer service leads to improved customer satisfaction and increased revenues in the long term from the same customers.

Since most insurance companies are not adequately equipped to help their agents deal with customer centered problems CRM insurance enables insurance organizations to survive in a tough economic climate by using the data the insurance company has on the existing customers and then use it to increase the level of profitability. It manages to enhance your customer relationships based on customer's unique requirements.

A wealth of customer data is available but insurance companies do not have it readily assessable nor is it coherent. CRM insurance software creates a holistic view of the customer which helps eliminate customer irritation experienced due to this, when they need to identify themselves repeatedly. Insurance CRM assists Customer Service Representatives when they are not able to properly access customer data. Having ample customer information on hand enables a CSR to be more confident of dealing with the client. It removes the chance of errors.

CRM enables customers themselves to do research on products, have answers to their questions etc. In addition to this policyholders or beneficiaries can check their claim status, change their account information, submit complaints etc. Insurers find that CRM is assisting them in their marketing efforts as well through a comprehensive understanding of the client base. CRM aids the insurance companies by ensuring that campaigns are more affective.

In Short

- Insurance CRM decreases the time required to make product changes
- A holistic integrated customer view
- Targeted marketing

- Customer retention
- Increased growth
- Increased policy sales
- Increased insurance market share
- CRM Insurance integrates marketing with other operations
- Efficient distribution channels are secured
- CRM provides the chance to reduce operating expenses
- It provides for more affective and efficient communication
- It improves the response time
- It increases customers satisfaction
- Insurance application queries/ claim status queries can be answered sooner
- It reduces the time that is normally taken for printing
- Policy mailing time is reduced
- It decreases overall costs
- Aids the call centre activities
- Insurance CRM guarantees lead management

Guidelines for CRM Success

- To avoid failures implementing CRM, Companies should spend time in strategic planning.
- Identify corporate needs and problems. Find the solution to that problem, discuss it with the management and field force, ensure that they are willing to accept the change, and then decide how to implement it.
- Identify key technology matching company's requirements and invest wisely in key components such as data warehouse and analytical tools and help employees understand its uses and benefits.
- Define Clear, Measurable business Objectives and monitor ROI on business moves.
- Offer the same customer service level via all channels.

Conclusion

Today, CRM is a boon to the insurance industries with a little help form CRM software, insurance firms can sell multiple insurance policies and pension plans to the same customer but, Indian Companies are slow in adopting CRM. In the past, CRM was identified with call centres. At present, CRM is expected to serve as an integrated approach to provide differentiated customer experience while identifying, acquiring and retaining customers to ensure efficiency in the insurance industries. Today's insurance companies certainly face a daunting challenge in maintaining and increasing their competitive edge. But by focusing on three key imperatives—gaining a unified enterprise view of customers, retaining customers with great service and controlling costs while expanding—insurance companies can turn challenges into strategic competitive advantage and enhance their long-term viability and profitability.

Since profits are drying up in the face of increased competition and customers are moving very fast form one firm to another on service and complete solution provision dimension, it becomes important to have an integrated customer relationship management strategy across the whole organization for generating higher customer life-time value. Without this awareness and constant attention to varying customer needs a financial service provider cannot be competitive in today's world. Integration of process, people, technology and information will offer a greater value to the customers.

The available customer information is to be strategically utilized and segmented to target the new customer prospects. Whenever new insurance needs have been discovered and new products have been developed Insurance sector can expand its customer value both horizontally and vertically.

"The customer is the most important visitor to our establishment
He is not dependent on us; we depend on him
He does not disturb us in our work; he is the purpose of it;
He is not alien in our business; he is a part of it;
We do not do him a favour when we serve him, he does us a favour
By making it possible for us"

—*Mahatma Gandhi*

References

BalaSubaamaniyan,Usha Priya S, Hema K. (2007), "*Essence of Customer Relationship Management-Emerging e-business Concepts and Cases*", Learntech Press.

Balu V. (2005),"*Services Marketing*",Sri Venkateswara Publications, Chennai.

Braj Mohan Chaturvedi (2004), "Effective CRM Concepts and Applications", ICFAI University Press.

Drucker.P. (1999), "*Management Challenges for the 21st Century*", Harper Business, New York.

Gosney. John.W. (2000), "*Customer Relationship Management Essentials*", Prentice Hall of India, New Delhi.

Iyer,Gopalakrishnan R., Anthony D,Miyazaki Dhruv Grewal and Maria Giordano (2002), "*Linking Web based Segmentation to Pricing Tactics*" ,Journal of Product and Brand Management, Volume11(5), pg. 288-300.

Jagdish N Sheth (2001), "*Customer Relationship Management*",First Edition, Tata McGraw Hill,Publishing Company Limited.

Mohamed, Peeru.H. & Sagadevan (2005), "*Customer Relationship Management*",Vikas Publishing House,New Delhi.

Murty G.R.K. (2002), "*CRM in Banks-A Tool Edge-out Competition*",IBA Bulletin, July 2002.

Paul Grenberg (2001), "*CRM at the Speed of Light*",Tata McGraw Hill.

Ravichandran.K.(2007), "*Recent Trends in Insurance Sector*",Delhi Abhijeet Publications.

Ron Hasty and James Readon (1997), "*Retail Management*", McGrawHill.

SCN Education B.V. (2001), "*Customer Relationship Management*",First Edition April, Frider Vieweg & Sohn Veralsgesselschaft mbH.

Websites

http://www.irdaindia.org/regulations/TheInsuranceAct1938er126042004.docakhtar@ expresscomputeronline.com

http//www.bharatbook.com/Market-Research-Reports/CRM-Market-2007-2010.html

www.bharatbook.com

"http://www.articlesbase.com/management-articles/importance-of-crm-market-and-its-applications-1468715.html"

http://www.cheathouse.com/essay/essay_view.php?p_ essay_id=33890#ixzz0flT573O

http://www.crminfoline.com/crm-articles/crm-insurance.htm

http://www.customerthink.com/news/attention_retention

http://www.entrepreneur.com/tradejournals/article/179285412.html

http://www.expresscomputeronline.com/20040216/indiatrends02.shtml

http://www.insurancetech.com/resources/fss/showArticle.jhtml?articleID=14705394

http://www.licindia.com/history.htm

7

CRM and Value Chain Management- A Case Study of Commercial Banks in Jammu & Kashmir

Sandeep Tandon, Jyoti Bahl

Background

Customer satisfaction is one of the formidable challenges in marketing of services in Banking Industry in our Country. The thrust on customer service has increased after liberalisation of Indian Economy. Thus customer satisfaction is an urgent need of the hour. This can be achieved by efficient customer service and immediate tactful handling of customer's grievances. Better Customer-Management relationship leads to customer satisfaction and a good public image is to win over the customers. Hence, Public relations should be one of the strategies to achieve customer satisfaction (Ambastha 1999).

The new organisation's emphasis is on partnerships between firms; multiple types of ownership and partnership and partnering within the organisation (divisions, wholly owned subsidiaries, differences, franchises, joint ventures etc.); teamwork among members of the organisation, often with team members from two or more cooperating firms; sharing of responsibility for developing converging and overlapping technologies; and often less emphasis on formal contracting and managerial reporting, evaluation, and control systems. The best visual image of these organizations may be a "wheel" instead of a pyramid, where the spokes are "knowledge links" between (focal) organisation at the hub and strategic partners around the rim (Badaracco 1991). These for as were pioneered in such industries as heavy construction, fashion and computers, where markets often span geographic boundaries, technology is complex, products change quickly and doing everything oneself is impossible. These confederations of specialists are called by many names including "networks" (Miles and Snow 1986; Thorelli 1986), "value-adding partnerships" (Johnston and Lawrence 1988), "alliances" (Ohmae 1989), and "shamrocks" (Handy 1990). All are characterised by flexibility, specialisation, and an emphasis on Relationship Management instead of market transaction. They depend upon administrative processes but they are not hierarchies (Thorelli 1986); they engage in interactions within ongoing relationships and they depend on negotiation rather than market-based process, as a principal basis for conducting business and determining prices.

Managing Customer Loyalty and Development

Managing customer-developing process is one of the critical dimensions of relationship marketing. Basically it involves a twin focus customer catching, and customer keeping 'Customer catching' is the process of attracting new customers (inviting new blood), while the customer keeping aims at the process of retaining the existing customers (encouraging old blood).

Customer catching process will have to effectively deal with the suspects, prospects and disqualified prospects. To start with, suspects include everyone who might possibly buy the organ station's product or service. But the firm is interested in sensing, serving and satisfying the prospects who possess both the ability and willingness to buy the product or service. Accordingly, the marketer must be available to precisely assess and identify the prospects among the suspects in the market and at the same time exclude the disqualified prospects who are unprofitable for the organisation to serve.

The relationship centered organisation should undertake proper and adequate efforts to converse many of its qualified prospects into first-time customers, satisfied first-time customers into repeat customers repeat customers into clients.

Commitment and trust lead directly to cooperative behaviour. This is conducive to relationship marketing success. This is precisely due to the following main reasons:

1. Relationship commitment and trust encourage marketers to work at preserving relationship investments by cooperating with exchange partners;
2. Resist attractive short-term alternatives in favour of the expected long-term benefits of staying with existing partners, and
3. View potentially high-risk actions as being prudent because of the belief that their partners will not act opportunistically (Yodapadithaya, 1999).

Banking system has a significant role to play in the rapid growth of economy. The banks that do well in 1990s and 2000 A.D. will be those rediscover the customer through cutting the edge known as relationship banking (Vaishnar, 2000). Effectiveness of banking system depends upon the customer's satisfaction and infact, customer is the kingpin of the banking industry. Customer satisfaction is dependant on the climate in which contacts between customers and the bank take place. Healthy climate promotes pleasant transactions for both the parties. No industry in the service sector can afford to ignore its customers and as Banks are required to give top priority in providing satisfactory and efficient service to their customers.

Objectives

The main objectives of the paper are:

1. To study the actual level of customer's satisfaction in four commercial banks i.e., State Bank of India, Punjab National Bank, Central Bank, of India and Jammu & Kashmir Bank Ltd. By analysing their attitude towards:

- Bank
- Employees
- Management

2. To make a comparative analysis of level of customer's satisfaction in four banks.

Methodology

For preparing the present paper 111 customers were selected with stratified random sampling method which formed a sample of more than 20% of the employees, taken up for study. Customers have been split up in three categories viz. businessmen, service-class and practitioners, 33 customers from State Bank of India, 26 from Punjab National Bank, 20 from Central Bank of India and 32 from Jammu & Kashmir Bank Ltd. were selected.

Findings

Customers Satisfaction in State Bank of India

Table 1 shows that a total of 33 customers of the bank have reported overall highest satisfaction which is evident from the mean score of 3.20, which is above average, out of these, service class is the highest satisfied lot (3.47) while businessmen have put up the lowest mean score (2.86). It falls in the below average range. Practitioners seems to be moderately satisfied as they are showing mean score of 3.27. Table further shows that mean scores of Service class, customers and practitioners are higher than the overall average for the bank.

Comparative analysis of the three variables for the study shows that customers are showing good response towards management of the bank which is clear from the mean score of 3.22, which is higher than those of other two variables i.e., Attitude towards Bank (3.20) and attitude towards Employees (3.17). Thus table makes it clear that staff of the bank has not been able to make customers happy with their behaviour. That is why table is showing the lowest mean score (3.17) regarding this particular variable.

Table1
Customers Satisfaction in Banks State Bank of India

Number of Customers	*Category-I Attitude Towards Bank*	*Category-II Attitude Towards Employees*	*Category-III Attitude Towards Management*	*Average Mean Score*
*B=11	2.91	2.61	3.04	2.86
*S=11	3.43	3.55	3.42	3.47
*P=11	3.26	3.35	3.19	3.27
Average Mean Score	3.20	3.17	3.22	3.20

*B- Business. S- Service Class. P- Practitioners.

A comparative analysis of overall mean score and actual means of different variables shows that regarding customers attitude towards bank, mean score of service class (3.43) and practitioners 3.26) are higher than overall average. Mean score of 2.19 is lower than the overall mean score.

As regards second variable i.e., attitude towards Employees except businessmen (2.62), other two categories of customers have responded well i.e. 3.55 of service class and 3.35 of practitioners.

Customers have reported highest mean score of 3.22 towards management of the bank. It is also higher than actual average of Businessmen (3.04) and practitioners (3.19). To sum up, it may be stated businessmen, though having the frequent dealings with the bank, still is the least satisfied lot especially with the behaviour of employees.

Customers Satisfaction in Punjab National Bank

An overall mean score of 3.06 has been shown in the Table 2 comparing the actual response with the overall response, it may be stated that it is lower than those of service class customers (3.33) and practitioners (3.14). Conversely, it is higher than that of businessmen (2.17).

A comparative analysis of overall averages with the actual mean score, table under reference shows that overall mean score (3.05) is lower than averages for service class (3.32) and practitioners (3.23) but higher than that of business class (2.60), so far as attitude towards bank is concerned.

Table 2
Customers Satisfaction in Punjab National Bank

Number of Customers	*Category-I Attitude Towards Bank*	*Category-II Attitude Towards Employees*	*Category-III Attitude Towards Management*	*Average Mean Score*
*B=8	2.60	2.52	3.01	2.71
*S=9	3.32	3.45	3.21	3.33
*P=9	3.23	3.04	3.16	3.14
Average Mean Score	3.05	3.00	3.13	3.06

Customers do not seem happy with the staff of the bank which is clear from the mean score of 3.00, which is just average. It is again higher than that of businessmen responses (2.52) while it is lower than those of service class (3.45) and practitioners (3.04).. Highest degree of satisfaction has been shown towards management of the bank (3.13) which is lower than those of service class and practitioners i.e. 3.21 and 3.16 respectively, but higher than of businessmen (3.01).

Customers Satisfaction in Central Bank of India

Table 3 signifies almost similar position as that of two banks discussed above. Though Central Bank is a small bank, still its customers are most satisfied i.e., 3.30. This when compared to actual averages shown by different categories of customers, it becomes clear from the table under reference that it is higher than those of businessmen responses (3.04) and practitioners (3.9) but lower than that of service class (3.67).

Table 3
Customers Satisfaction in Central Bank of India

Number of Customers	*Category-I Attitude Towards Bank*	*Category-II Attitude Towards Employees*	*Category-III Attitude Towards Management*	*Average Mean Score*
*B=8	3.18	3.01	2.92	3.04
*S=6	3.51	3.55	3.96	3.67
*P=6	3.25	3.28	3.04	3.19
Average Mean Score	3.31	3.28	3.31	3.30

Table further shows that comparing the variable wise position of the bank regarding Ist variable i.e. attitude towards Bank, overall average (3.31) is higher than that of businessmen and practitioners (3.25) while lower than service class. It clarifies the fact that businessmen and practitioners are more satisfied with the bank. Same is the position regarding variable attitude towards management i.e. (3.31).

As regards third category i.e. attitude towards management overall mean is lower than that of service class customers (3.96) and higher than in case of practitioners (3.04) very poor response has been shown by businessmen as clear from the below average mean score of 2.92, second variable i.e. attitude towards employees shows lowest mean score of 3.28 which is lower than that of service class customers (3.55) but higher than that of businessmen (3.01). It is equal to that of practitioners (3.28).

Customers Satisfaction in Jammu & Kashmir Bank Ltd.

The position of Jammu and Kashmir Bank Ltd. Is different from other banks so far as mean score of practitioners is concerned. Their mean score has been estimated at 2.90 which is below average range. Lowest overall mean score of 3.01 has been worked out against which mean score of service class customers is the highest (3.41) as compared to businessmen (2.71) and practitioners 2.90) as shown in Table 4.

Table 4
Customers Satisfaction in Jammu & Kashmir Bank Ltd

Number of Customers	*Category-I Attitude Towards Bank*	*Category-II Attitude Towards Employees*	*Category-III Attitude Towards Management*	*Average Mean Score*
*B=12	2.93	2.75	2.44	2.71
*S=10	3.45	3.01	3.78	3.41
*P=10	3.11	2.87	2.71	2.90
Average Mean Score	3.16	2.88	3.03	3.01

Comparative analysis of the actual mean score of customers with the overall mean scores, variable wise, reveals that the highest degree of satisfaction lies in case of their attitude towards Bank (3.16). As against this overall average, mean scores of business class customers (2.93) and practitioners (2.71). Customers responses regarding employees are very poor as is evident from the mean score of 2.88 which is lower than that of majority of service class customers (3.01) employees show dissatisfaction towards bank.

Table 5
Customer's Satisfaction in Four Commercial Banks
A Comparative Analysis Between 3 Categories

Number of Customers	*Category-I Attitude Towards Bank*	*Category-II Attitude Towards Employees*	*Category-III Attitude Towards Management*	*Average Mean Score*
SBI	3.20	3.17	3.22	3.20
PNB	3.05	3.00	3.13	3.06
CBI	3.31	3.28	3.31	3.30
J&K	3.16	2.88	3.03	3.01
Average Mean Score	3.18	3.08	3.17	3.14

Above table shows the customer's satisfaction in all the four commercial banks through judging their attitude towards three categories viz. attitude towards bank, attitude toward employees, attitude towards customers.

Comparative analysis of the level of customers satisfaction in four banks shows that overall average mean score has been estimated at 3.14 which is little above average. This shows that the customers are not fully satisfied with the services offered by the banks. On comparing it with the actual mean scores of four Banks, table shows that customers of Central Bank of India have shown a highest level of satisfaction i.e. 3.20, whereas, State Bank of India has been ranked second in order of satisfaction amongst customers. Customers of Punjab National Bank and Jammu and Kashmir Bank are showing almost same mean score i.e. 3.06 and 3.0 respectively which is lower than the overall average mean score. It shows the dissatisfaction is prevailing in these two banks. Through Central Bank of India, being a bank with few number of branches is having good relations with its customers. Likewise other three banks should also try to raise the level of customers satisfaction by providing maximum facilities to them. Good relation with customers depends upon efficient CRM as CRM is the ability to understand customers across their various interaction with the banks.

Suggestions

To improve the level of customers satisfaction following suggestions are made:

1. Bank personnel should be willing and ready to serve the customers.
2. They should be quick and prompt in offering the services.
3. Personnel should be knowledgeable and skillful and the same should be reflected in their behaviour.
4. Quality Service should be maintained consistently.
5. All the risks and side-effects, if any, should be conveyed to customers.
6. Banks should be conveniently located.
7. All dealings with customers must be kept confidential.
8. Employees should be properly equipped with communication facilities for easy access.
9. Physical facilities should be attractive.
10. Personnel should be polite, respectful, flexible, friendly and accommodating.

References

Ambastha, Manoj Kumar and Kumari Sunita, (1999). "Customer Satisfaction in Banking Industry" Marketing Strategy and challenges. Indian Journal of Commerce Vol.52, P.60, Oct-Dec.

Yedapadithaya, P. (1999). Relationship Marketing, Emerging issues an challenges in the New Millennium. The Indian Journal of Commerce, Vol.52, P.23 Oct-Dec.

Yaishnay, B.L., (2000). Services Marketing: Global Perspectives. The Indian Journal of Commerce, Vol.52, P.23 July-September.

N. Sheth Jagdish, Parvatiyar, Shainesh (2001). "Customer Relationship Management", Page 28.

Dyche Jill, Page 179, "The CRM Handbook. A business Guide to Customer Relationship Management".

8

Emerging Trends in CRM- A Study on Indian Banking Industry

Uma Sankar Prasad Patra

Introduction

The biggest management challenge in the new millennium of liberalization and globalization for a business is to serve and maintain good relations with the king-the customer. The changing business environment is characterized by open economy, increasing competition, high consumer choice, enlightened and demanding customer, more emphasis on quality and value of purchase. Customer Relationship Management (CRM) is a strategy used to learn more about customers' needs and behaviors in order to develop stronger relationships with them. Good customer relationships are at the heart of business success. The idea of CRM is that it helps businesses use technology and human resources to gain insight into the behavior of, products and services for the customer. CRM software is used to support information on customers and prospective customers.

CRM and Technology

Customer relation management analysts say CRM is "a buzzword that's really not so new. What's new is the technology is allowing us to do what we could do at the turn of the century with the neighborhood grocer. He had few enough customers and enough brainpower to keep track of everyone's preferences.

Technology has allowed us to go back to the future to this model." The aim of CRM is optimize the use of technology and human resources for the business to gain insight into the behavior of customer. Technology is now an essential part of CRM but buying technology before defining CRM business goals is a recipe for disaster. It is important to remember that technology used for CRM should be 'tailor made' depending on the type of consumer base of the company and the business goals. Companies need to understand CRM in relevance to customers and customers only. The CRM services consist of the following major segments such as Consulting services, Implementation services, CRM Outsourcing services and Training service.

Indian companies are jumping into the CRM bandwagon to seize a chunk of the global market; both products as well as services, catering primarily to the American and European markets that are coming up in and around the metros. With the easing of infrastructure constraints, India is likely to emerge as a significant player in this segment.. The CRM enabled companies include Tata Telecom, TVS Electronics, HP India, Tata InfoTech, Carrier Refrigeration, Tata Teleservices, Satyam Info way, Planet M, and Epicenter Technologies among many others.

CRM Software Packages

Off shoring which started with near shore ventures has moved on to outsourcing to countries such as India has become essential to survive in today's competitive market. The banks that have opted for off shoring have definitely increased profits and had proved to be a major beneficiary. When companies consider implementing a CRM strategy, they usually talk about either Campaign Management or Sales Force Automation. Although CRM is much more than either of those parts, software packages are usually based around one or the other idea (with SFA being the most popular).

Operational CRM provides support to "front office" business processes, including sales, marketing and service. A sale is a type of Operational CRM that is designed to automate sales-force-related activities, such as lead tracking. Analytical CRM analyzes customer data for a variety of purposes: Design and execution of targeted marketing campaigns to optimize marketing effectiveness

Campaign management software is marketing-oriented CRM software that combines elements of Operational and Analytical CRM and allows campaigns to be run on an existing client base. Campaign Management is used when you need to create personalized offers when it is prohibitively expensive to personally contact each client. The function of the Customer Interaction System or Collaborative Customer Relationship Management is to coordinate the multi-channel service and support given to the customer by providing the infrastructure for responsive and effective support to customer issues, questions, complaints, etc.

Geographic CRM (GCRM) is a customer relation management information system which collaborates geographic information system and traditional CRM. gCRM combines data collected from route of movement, types of residence, ambient trading areas and other customer and marketing information which are matched with relevant road conditions, building formations, and a floating population.

Customer focus on Banking Services

As the intense competition becomes a way of doing business, it is the customer who calls the shot in deciding the nature of products and services offered in the market. The customers are becoming demanding, dominant and selective. In fact the perceptions and the expectations of the customers have undergone a sea change, with the availability of banking services to the customers at their door steps through the help of technology. Marketing of customer services aims at two important goals: prosperity to the bank and satisfied customers. Banks offer tangible services like loan schemes, interest rates and kinds of account and the intangible services like behavior and efficiency of staff, speed of transactions and the ambience. There are four strategies available to customer relations' managers:

- To win back or save customers
- To attract new and potential customers
- To create loyalty among existing customers and
- To up sell or offer cross services.

Customer Relationship Management in Banking Industry

Customer Relationship Management (CRM) is fundamental to building a customer-centric organization. CRM system links together the customer data into single and logical customer repository. The goal of CRM is to manage all aspects of customer interactions in a manner that enables banks to maximize profitability from every customer. By using knowledge of the customer, banks can turn customer relationship into a key competitive advantage. Banks can develop customer relationships across a broad spectrum of touch point's branches, kiosks, ATMs, internet, electronic banking, smart cards, call centres and phone banking.

Highlighted are some of the relevant issues that banks face to-day:

Standardization is the Key

The method a bank adopts literally emanates what school of thought it follows, and can very well be an indicator of their growth strategy for the coming years and organization can cause a lot of confusion in operations. Also, in applications at each level and each segment might result in hindrance in output by the organization. This can be simply avoided by standardizing processes, eliminating redundancies and rationalizing the applications. Standardization of processes and technology used acts as a launch pad for inducting any new product in the organization and it also helps the bank elevate from processing obstacles.

Reduce Operational Discrepancies

Cost reduction is one of the most important concerns for any organization. This cost reduction can take place through standardization of processes. Standardizing processes would help to recognize similarity in various functions and enable in clubbing together similar processes.

Customer Relationships

Customer relationship is of prime importance in any business, but even more so in the service industry. Financial institutions must, therefore, place customer relationship building and maintenance as top priority. Banks need to keep in mind that this cannot be achieved with the implementation of CRM alone. This has to be coupled with data storage systems.

Foundation to Design your Product

Understanding the customer profile is key to choose the right product. Choosing the right product design can help understand and analyze the customer needs and even make forecasts for the same. The right product design will act as a catalyst in assessing important strategies and their effectiveness.

Complying with Regulations

In the recent past one has seen many banking institutions faltering from complying with the set of regulations introduced. For e.g.: AML (anti money laundering), SOX (Sarbanes-Oxley Act) etc.These regulations can pose challenges in compliance because of technological constraints and can impact profits that the bank is making. But from a different perspective, one must comply with these regulations not only because they are mandatory but also because it will help in reputation building and customer and culture orientation.

Buzz Around Basel II

While the first phase of banking, the economic rationale was to focus on implementation of various core banking solutions, the second phase will see deployment of the Basel II. Basel II is a complex new standard for measuring risk in financial services firms that has been published by the Basel committee on banking supervision. It is a committee of the Bank for International Settlements, specifically in areas of risk that include credit, operations and the market.

Therefore, by this guideline, to have an operational system in place becomes integral. The urgent need is to integrate a operational management system (ORM) that will help banks assess and monitor operational risks and calculate the capital required for the same.

Powerful Customer Knowledge Systems for the Future

The pace of implementation of integrated delivery channel architectures will quicken and eventually prevail at top banks. The deployment of powerful customer knowledge systems will also increase as more and more useful information can be distilled from the myriad of resources in the bank IT network. With most of the technology in place, banks must begin to form strategies around the use of information in the day-to-day contact with its customers.

As the capability to build on this flow of information grows, it has the potential to outpace the customer's acceptance of the bank's knowledge. Privacy is an emotional issue and, so, not entirely rational. Technology and policy can only go so far in ensuring that the use of information at the point of contact is not intrusive to the customer's comfortable level of privacy. Ultimately, the management of customer information at the point of interaction is about service, about keeping the customer happy, and, simply put, about keeping the customer. It's about strengthening the relationship and showing the customer that the bank's knowledge can lead to real benefit. It's about increasing the bank's benefit as well, and doing it in a way that does not sacrifice the customer's long-term well-being.

Conclusion

The recent trend of globalization and liberalization has posed serious problems to domestic banks. The entry of new foreign banks and private sector banks with their advanced knowledge base of automation in the banking operations and aggressive marketing strategies has pushed public sector banks to a tight corner. Potential customers have started moving towards foreign banks and private sector banks.

To survive and succeed, banks must identify their marketing areas, develop adequate resources, convert these resources into healthy and efficient services and distribute them effectively satisfying the manifold tastes of customers. The success of any business depends on how well it treats its customers. Try the following 10 tips to improve the level of customer service in your company and boost its image. They are:

- Stay in contact with customers.
- Create a customer focus group.
- Resolve customer complaints quickly.
- Be available to your customer easily.
- Treat your client well.
- Be polite to your client.
- Listen to your customer.
- Build strong relationship with your customer.
- Always keep your promises.
- Treat your customer as you would like to be treated.

By following these simple customer service tips that we have put together for you, you will be creating a loyal customer base which will return to you again and again. One satisfied customer is equivalent to many marketing dollars in terms of favorable word-of-mouth!

Some of the recommendations are suggested to have strong customer relationship base.

- Banks needs to do away with the strategy of going in for such IT enabled strategies mostly during times of recession. They should plan for such strategies and not react on immediate stimulus. This was evident in India when banks went on to embrace CRM during recession of early 2000 but moderated the initiative once good times are back again.

- Neglect of the business process issues surrounding CRM implementations has impacted efficiency gains achieved post implementation. And hence, though technical aspects needs to be given due importance, other strategic aspects should not be compromised upon.
- The basic pre-requisite of CRM is "enterprise wide consistent and uniform customer knowledge".
- The time has come to make the shift from customer volume based strategies to customer value based strategies. Banks need to understand the actual value of each relationship and should base their actions on this information to provide mutually beneficial customer relationship.

References

R.K. Suganthi (2005) Customer Relationship Management, New Age International (P) Ltd, New Delhi.

John W. Gosney and Thomos P. Boethm (2006) Customer Relationship Management Essentials, Prentice Hall of India.

Monika Chowdhary (2004) Text Book of Marketing of Services, The Indian Experience NIMIT Chowdhary.

www.networkmagazine.com

www.kmworld.com

www. crm2day.com

Sheela Rani (2008), Customer Relationship Management, Margham Publications, Chennai.

Bligh, Philip; Douglas Turk (2004) CRM unplugged Releasing CRM's Strategic Value, Hoboken; John Wiley & Sons.

Gartner, Inc (2007) Commonly Deployed CRM Application Vendors in 2006.

9

Comparative Study of IVRS- A Case Study of Cellular Service Providers

Puja Walia Mann, Manish Jha

Customer Relationship Management(CRM)

Customer relationship management is achieved by creating a team relationship among sales, marketing, and customer support activities within an organization. Many perceive CRM only as customer retention in which a variety of after marketing tactics are used for customer bonding or staying in touch with the customers after the sale is made to ensure post purchase satisfaction.

CRM maybe defined as " the strategic use of information, processes, technology and people to manage the customers relationship with your company (Marketing, Sales, Services and support) across the whole customer life cycle" (*Kincaid W. Judith, 2003*)

CRM, in its broadest sense, means managing all interactions and business with customers. This includes, but is not limited to, improving customer service. A good CRM program will allow a business to acquire customers, service the customer, increase the value of the customer to the company, retain good customers, and determine which customers can be retained or given a higher level of service. Relationship expectations from customers point of view could also be used as a segmentation variable to identify customer relationship profiles and address them with specific means (*Dimitriadis and Stevens, 2008*).

The CRM systems are increasingly using technology as a means to be in touch with the customers due to the following benefits:

- Faster response to customer inquiries.
- Increased efficiency through automation.
- Deeper understanding of customers buying patterns and preferences.
- Increased marketing and selling opportunities by being available online.
- Identifying the most profitable customers by studying buying habits of regular customers.
- Development of better relations with existing customers.
- Increased value from existing customers.
- Reduced cost associated with supporting & servicing customers.
- Increasing overall efficiency by reducing total cost of sales

Relationship Marketing (RM) has been widely accepted as an important determinant of long-term business success and is believed to be especially well suited for services because of the personal contact between customers and service providers *(Liljander & Roos, 2002)*. A major benefit can be the development of better relations with existing customers, increased value from existing customers and the development of new and improved products and services in order to win more business in the future. It is also envisaged that there is a positive relationship between customer satisfaction and organisational performance indicators, although the relationship is not very strong (*Wiele et al., 2002*).

The services provided also need to be communicated effectively so that customer use them, thereby maintaining customer relationship. Although a service provider's communication style significantly relates to customer satisfaction, the relationship is moderated by service criticality and service nature. Also the service firm managers need to train their employees to consider the criticalness and the nature of the services being sold and then how to adjust their communication style accordingly (*Webster & Sundaram, 2009*).

Over a period of time, the customer relations have infact become a business strategy for organisations, because customer relationship (and the benefits derived from them) are difficult to duplicate, these may be a source of competitive advantage for firms. Managing these relationships, as well as their quality, emerges as a point of competitive distinction (*Myhal et al., 2008*). This may hold true especially for service marketer's e.g health and beauty solutions. Intangibility is one of the distinctive characteristics of service (*Santos, 2002*). Since the relationship substance framework, composed of actor bonds, resource ties and activity links is built upon and expanded by adding four new dimensions: competitive positions, external association, relationship impact, and situational factors to gain customer satisfaction. Together, these dimensions successfully encapsulate the items that customers identify as important when evaluating the quality of their relationship with their service provider (*Myhal et al., 2008*).

Many types of services involve a sequence, in which customers choose a service provider followed by selection of service specifications, that is selecting when and how the service will be performed. For example, after choosing a cellular service provider, a customer chooses the plan either under pre-paid or post-paid. Specifications selection can be dominated by the provider, the customer or the customer and provider can jointly select specifications. Customer Satisfaction results if specifications selection meets customer expectations of the provider-customer role. Specifications selection unfolds as a process where information is exchanged between the customer and provider and the provider can be more or less customer oriented. Effective information exchange and a strong customer orientation by the provider contribute to customer satisfaction. Customers make attributions of provider or customer responsibility for specifications selection depending on the type of specifications selections that occurs and provider provision of specifications information. Customers who attribute specification selection to their decisions assume responsibility for the specifications selected (*Swan et al., 2002*). Two constructs Service quality and customer satisfaction are indeed independent but are closely related, implying that an increase in one is likely to lead to an increase in another (*Sureshchandar et al., 2002*). Another aspect i.e Commitment has a positive influence on customer satisfaction and diminishes risk perceptions. Customers with high commitment to an organization use satisfaction surveys to express their loyalty (*Johnson et al., 2008*).

Studies undertaken to identify the Customer satisfaction and the bouquet of services provided by the Marketers suggest that the providers may not always be able to delight the customers. Online service quality has no impact on customer delight, e-trust or the development of stronger relationships with customers. Online service quality is not enough to develop strong relationship. In one study it was found that Banks can achieve customer loyalty through attending to their personal needs in online situations as well as providing a well organized site. Alternatively, if banks wish to develop strong relationship with customers, they must provide user-friendly and efficient websites while also developing trust in the website (*Herington & Weaven, 2007*). Managing expectations is important since service quality and satisfaction result from how well the actual service performance, in other words, the service process and outcome, matches the expectations (*Ojasalo, 2001*). In a research study of on-line stores it was found that failure to institute adequate complaint management and service recovery system contributed to customer defection of online shops (*Ahmad, 2002*). Customer relationships were found to be more spurious than true in a car dealership. The study revealed that behavioural commitment to after-sales services was high, but that affective commitment was low to moderate (*Liljander & Roos 2002*). Customer Satisfaction with service companies is probably declining steadily across the developed world because it no longer matters to most people (*Williams & Visser, 2002*). But in developing countries like India, it is still important as it is only now that the customer has started getting a taste of customer relationship in the post liberalisation era of competitiveness.

Objectives of the Study

The study presented shall envisage the comparative analysis of the customer's response to the IVRS adopted by two of the leading telecom players (One in Public sector and the other in Private Sector) in the state of Haryana (India).

Hypothesis

H_0: $\mu_1 = \mu_2$ (i.e. Customer Satisfaction level of Airtel & BSNL respondents is same)

H_1: $\mu_1 > \mu_2$ (Satisfaction level of Airtel Subscriber is more than BSNL subscriber) (One tail test)

The Telecom Players Under Study

Airtel

Airtel comes to you from Bharti Tele-Ventures Limited - a part of the biggest private integrated telecom conglomerate, Bharti Enterprises. The Group's principal activity is to provide mobile telecommunication services. The Group also provides fixed-line, VSAT, Internet and broadband services and DTH TV service. It offers national and international long distance services. The Group operates in five segments namely Mobile Services, Telemedia Services, Enterprise Services Carriers, Enterprise Services Corporate and Passive Infrastructure Services.

Bharti Airtel Limited, India's largest integrated and the first private telecom services provider has footprint in all the 23 telecom circles of the country. The businesses at Bharti Airtel have been structured into three individual strategic business units (SBU's) - Mobile Services, Airtel Telemedia Services &

Enterprise Services. The mobile business provides mobile & fixed wireless services using GSM technology across 23 telecom circles while the Airtel Telemedia Services business offers broadband & telephone services in 95 cities. The Enterprise services provide end-to-end telecom solutions to corporate customers and national & international long distance services to carriers. All these services are provided under the Airtel brand.

CRM Initiative of Airtel

There are various methods adopted by Airtel for reaching out to its customers and ensuring service satisfaction like:

Airtel Bill Payments & Recharges

- Postpaid Bill Payment: Pay outstanding Airtel mobile bills.
- Prepaid Recharge: Recharge Airtel prepaid.
- Fixedline & Broadband Bill Payment: Pay Airtel Fixedline & Broadband bills.

Merchant Services

- *Utility Bill Payment:* Payment of utility bills for electricity, water and gas.
- *Insurance Premium Payment:* Payment of insurance premiums.
- *Air Tickets:* Booking through MakemyTrip.
- *Movie Tickets:* Booking through Bookmyshow or PVR Cinemas.
- *Recharges:* Recharge of Airtel digitalTv account, Delhi-Gurgaon Toll Tag and BigFlix or Seventymm movie rental accounts.
- *Shopping* Shopping for flowers through Ferns n Petals and for Team India T-shirts through Playground online.
- *Donations:* Donation to the needy through ISKCON society.

Other Services

- Sending SMS for Hello tunes, reminders and alerts, Cricket updates, Missed call alerts, Balance and recharge options.

- Call for assistance and feedback
- Toll free customer care number etc.

BSNL

Bharat Sanchar Nigam Ltd. BSNL formed in October, 2000, is World's 7th largest Telecommunications Company providing comprehensive range of telecom services in India: Wireline, CDMA mobile, GSM Mobile, Internet, Broadband, Carrier service, MPLS-VPN, VSAT, VoIP services, IN Services etc. Presently it is one of the largest & leading public sector unit in India.

BSNL has installed Quality Telecom Network in the country and is now focusing on improving it, expanding the network, introducing new telecom services in villages and wining customer's confidence. Today, it has about 46 million line basic telephone capacity, 8 million WLL capacity, 52 Million GSM Capacity, more than 38302 fixed exchanges, 46565 BTS, 3895 Node B (3G BTS), 287 Satellite Stations, 614755 Rkm of OFC Cable, 50430 Rkm of Microwave Network connecting 602 Districts, 7330 cities/towns and 5.6 Lakhs villages.

BSNL is the only service provider, making focused efforts and planned initiatives to bridge the Rural-Urban Digital Divide. In fact there is no telecom operator in the country to beat its reach with its wide network giving services in every nook & corner of country and operates across India except Delhi & Mumbai. Whether it is inaccessible areas of Siachen glacier and North-eastern region of the country. BSNL serves its customers with its wide bouquet of telecom services.

The turnover, nationwide coverage, reach, comprehensive range of telecom services and the desire to excel has made BSNL the No. 1 Telecom Company of India.

CRM Initiative of BSNL

BSNL Bill Payments & Recharges

- *Prepaid Recharge:* Recharge BSNL prepaid.
- *Fixedline & Broadband Bill Payment:* Pay BSNL Fixedline & Broadband bills.

Merchant Services

- Updates: Score Updates, Political News, Hollywood gossip, Movies & Reviews.
- Downloads: Wallpapers, Songs, and Movies.
- Social Initiative: Sending reminders for Pulse Polio day.

Value Added Services (VAS)

BSNL is focusing on provision of value added services/features to attract high end customers and to double its revenues from VAS.

Analysis & Interpretation

Table 1
Profile of Respondents

	Airtel (500)		*BSNL (500)*		*Total (1000)*	
Profile of Respondents						
Age (in yrs)	*N*	*Percent*	*N*	*Percent*	*N*	*Percent*
16-22	230	46	189	37.8	419	41.9
22-28	130	26	122	24.4	252	25.2
28-34	40	8	54	10.8	94	9.4
34-40	35	7	70	14	105	10.5
41-46	65	13	65	13	130	13
Location						
Urban	312	62.4	295	51	607	60.7
Rural	188	37.6	205	49	393	39.3
Occupation						
Students	112	22.4	125	25	237	23.7
Self-employed	134	26.8	129	25.8	263	26.3
Business	84	16.8	112	22.4	196	19.6
Housewives	95	19	82	16.4	177	17.7
Retired	75	15	52	10.4	127	12.7

a) Majority of Airtel Respondents (72%) are of the power age bracket of 16-28 years as against only (62.2%) of BSNL respondents in this segment. This indicates that Airtel is more popular amongst the youngsters.

b) While a bulk of Airtel respondents (62.4%) are of urban base, the subscriber of BSNL are almost equally divided in Urban (51%) and Rural (49%) areas. This is Also the reflection of the BSNL initiative of bridging the rural-urban divide

c) It has been observed that a majority of Airtel & BSNL respondent constituted of self- employed (26.8% & 25.8%) and students (22.4% & 25%) respectively.

However, BSNL seems to be more popular amongst the Business class with 22.4% as against 16.8% using Airtel.

Table 2
Satisfaction Indicators-Airtel vs BSNL

	AIRTEL (500)		BSNL (500)		TOTAL (1000)	
Satisfaction Indicators	*N*	*Percent*	*N*	*Percent*	*N*	*Percent*
Satisfaction with the overall CRM initiative of the cell operators	294	58.8	221	44.2	515	51.5
Satisfaction with the IVRS	253	50.6	209	41.8	462	46.2
Perception that transactions through IVR takes longer	417	83.4	371	74.2	788	78.8
IVR Transaction are less customizable	423	84.6	351	70.2	774	77.4
IVR benefits the customers	299	59.8	215	43	514	51.4
IVR benefits the company	417	83.4	371	74.2	788	78.8
Choice of human operator is given	103	20.6	83	16.6	186	18.6
Choice of a human operator should be the first step of IVR transaction	480	96	456	91.2	936	93.6
IVR's are Unfriendly	471	94.2	453	90.6	924	92.4
Difficult to operate for masses	417	83.4	371	74.2	788	78.8

$X_A = 40.06$ $X_B = 39.4$ $n_A = 500$

$S_A = 3.84$ $S_B = 4.05$ $n_B = 500$

$$|Z| = \frac{|\overline{X}_A - \overline{X}_B|}{SE_{\overline{X}_A - \overline{X}_B}}$$

$$SE_{\overline{X}_A - \overline{X}_B} = \sqrt{\frac{S_A^2}{n_A} + \frac{S_B^2}{n_B}} = .33$$

$$|Z| = 2$$

At 5% level of significance, the critical value of Z = 1.64 for one tail test. Since calculated value is greater than critical value (Table-value) of Z, we reject Hî in favour of H1 and conclude that Airtel respondents are more satisfied with the IVRS of Airtel as compared to the BSNL respondents.

- Though the overall percentage of respondents has shown dissatisfaction with the CRM initiative taken up by both the companies. Majority of Airtel respondents (58.8%) said that they were satisfied as compared to only (44.2%) respondent of BSNL.
- Despite the fact, that the cellular service providers aim to provide a better customer care with the use of IVRS; the respondents carry a different view. Only 50.6% of Airtel respondents and 44.2% BSNL respondents felt that they were satisfied with the IVRS installed by the organizations. Surprisingly, a major chunk of 83.4% of Airtel respondents and 74% of BSNL respondents felt that the transactions through the IVRS takes longer, is unfriendly to operate and it only benefits the respective company in filtering the incoming calls.
- 84.6 percent of Airtel respondents and 70.2 percent of BSNL respondents perceive the IVRS systems to be less customizable.Though it constitutes the bulk of respondents, the BSNL respondents found the IVRS customized as compared to Airtel respondents. However, on the contrary 59.8 percent of respondents held that the IVRS benefits the customers.
- A striking majority i.e 96 percent of Airtel respondents and 91.2 percent of BSNL respondents viewed that the choice of a human operatoer should be the first step of IVR transaction. The respondents opined that though the IVRS are complicated to operate for masses, yet the ones who can operate shall also know it use. Thus the choice of human operator can help solve most of the queries of the cellular subscriber.

Observations

While administering the Questionnaire the researchers come across several respondents who opined that while the services of their respective organization was satisfactory, it was IVRS which was causing the dissatisfaction among them. They held that the recorded options in IVRS gives information which could otherwise also be gathered from the dealers etc. It was only when they wanted to contact the company officials that they called the toll free no. for example, in case of mobile theft, Service break down, other complaints etc. On the contrary the toll free no. gives no option of a human operator. Calling different numbers for complaining for post-paid and pre-paid connections also was perceived to be highly irritable to most of the respondents. Many respondents felt that the attempts of cellular service providers to be in touch with the subscriber in the form of sending SMS or making calls cause lot of dissatisfaction and frustration rather than helping the company in information dissemination.

Conclusion

Though the study has been conducted in the state of Haryana only, the results may be generalized to the country since the IVRS operates on the same pattern throughout the country and the subscribers profile especially the level of technology compatibility is almost the same across most of the states in the country. Based on the above studies it is analyzed that the Telecom Players in a view of getting a major chunk of the market share are initiating new ways of Customer Relationship Management which they portray as User friendly, after studying Two Major telecom players of it was seen that the customers are not accepting this initiatives specially the IVR's. Customers have a common perception that transactions through IVR takes longer and if given an option they would prefer a human operator. After having a thorough study on this aspect it may be concluded that telecom players in future should be more customer centric and should customize their services especially at the first step itself of IVRS keeping in the mind the customers convenience.

References

Journal and Other Articles

Anand Kumar Jaiswal (2008), "*Customer Satisfaction and Service Quality Measurement in Indian Call Centres*" Managing service quality, Vol: 18, No. 4, pp. 405-416.

Carmel Herington, Scott Weaven (2007), "*Can Banks Improve Customer Relationships with High Quality Online Services*" Managing Service Quality, Vol: 17, No. 4, pp. 404-427.

Cynthia Webster, D.S Sundaram (2009), "*Effect of Service Provider's Communication Style on Customer Satisfaction in Professional Services Setting: The Moderating Role of Criticality and Service Nature*" Journal of services Marketing, Vol: 23, No. 2, pp. 103-113.

Dwane H. Dean (2002), "*What's Wrong with IVR self-service*" Managing service quality, Vol: 18, No. 6, pp. 594-609.

Genevieve Catherine Myhal, Jikyeong Kang, John A. Murphy (2008), "*Retaining Customers through Relationship Quality: A Services Business Marketing Case*" Journal of services Marketing, Vol: 22, No. 6, pp. 445-453.

G.S Sureshchandar, Chandrashekharan Rajendran, R.N Anantharaman (2002), "*The Relationship between Service Quality and Customer Satisfaction– A Factor Specific Approach*" Journal of services Marketing, Vol: 16, No. 4, pp. 363-379.

Jessica Santos (2002), "*From Intangibility to Tangibility on Service Quality Perceptions: A Comparison Study between Consumers and Service providers in Four Service Industries*" Managing Service Quality, Vol: 12, No. 5, pp. 292-302.

John E. Swan, Michael R. Bowers, Rajan Grover (2002), "*Customer Involvement in the Selection of Service Specifications*" Journal of Services Marketing Vol: 16, No. 1, pp. 88-103.

Jukka Ojasalo (2001), "*Managing Customer Expectations in Professional Services*" Managing Service Quality, Vol: 11, No. 3, pp. 200-212.

Lawrence A. Crosby (2002), "*Exploding Some Myths about Customer Relationship Management*" Managing Service Quality, Vol: 12, No. 5, pp. 271-277.

Mark S. Johnson, Eugene Sivadas, Ellen Garbarino (2008), "*Customer Satisfaction, Perceived Risk and Affective Commitment: An*

Investigation of Directions of Influence" Journal of Services Marketing, Vol: 22, No. 5, pp. 353-362.

Roger Williams, Rolf Visser (2002), *"Customer Satisfaction: It is Dead but it will not Lie Down"* Managing Service Quality, Vol: 12, No. 3, pp. 194-200.

Sergio Dimitriadis, Eric Stevens (2002), *"Integrated Customer Relationship Management for Service Activities: An Internal/External Gap Model"* Managing Service Quality, Vol: 18, No. 6, pp. 594-609.

Sohel Ahmad (2002), *"Service Failures and Customer Defection: A Closer look at Online Shopping Experiences"* Managing Service Quality, Vol: 12, No. 1, pp. 19-29.

Timothy L. Keningham, Bruce Cooil, Lerzan Aksoy, Tor W. Andreassen, Jay Weiner (2007), *"The Value of Different Customer Satisfaction and Loyalty Metrics in Predicting Customer Retention, Recommendation, and Share-of-wallet"* Managing Service Quality, Vol: 17, No. 4, pp. 361-384.

Ton Van Der Wiele, Paul Boselie, Martijn Hesselink (2002), *"Empirical Evidence for the Relationship between Customer Satisfaction and Business Performance"* Managing Service Quality, Vol: 12, No. 3, pp. 184-193.

Veronica Liljander, Inger roos (2002), *"Customer-Relationship Levels-from Spurious to True Relationships"* Journal of Services Marketing, Vol: 16, No. 7, pp. 593-614.

Websites

www.tataindicom.com, viewed on February 9, 2010

www.airtel.in, viewed on February 9, 2010

10

Customer Relation Management in Cellular Services

Arun Kumar, Emmanuel Joseph, Ranjit Singh

Introduction

CRM has become an integral part of any successful business strategy. Nowadays businesses are also becoming increasingly mobile and most of the economic activities and global workforce is using wireless devices. Mobile access to sales information, customer data, and online transactions like reservations and stock trading is an essential part of a wireless CRM system. Almost all the leading CRM solution providers have started supplying wireless solutions to survive in this highly competitive global market.

Today's workforce is more remote and mobile than ever before. The workforce is being provided with the options they want for access to critical information. Whether working from home, in a remote office, or on the road, mobile CRM provides your staff access to customer, sales, and service information

The most striking part in business context is how many business people depend on their wireless devices to stay connected to the office. More and more traveling business users are using their mobile phone to communicate with customers and the office. Email, tasks, appointments, and contacts - all of this information is critical for the mobile user. In years past laptop computers were the only way to stay connected to the corporate office. In a matter of a couple of years, PDA's and Smartphone's have revolutionized mobile computing.

Era of the Mobile Agent and CRM

The advent of cellular communications and wireless technologies such as Wireless Access Protocol (WAP) communications format as well as devices such as smart cell phones, Personal Digital Assistant (PDA), wireless LAN has changed the face of CRM. It offers several options for mobile devices and smartphones, to access the information that keeps business moving forward while on the road.

Customers today have greater expectations than ever for rapid response. People in one's organisation - field sales and service staff, mobile professionals and executives need the right information at all times to respond to these demands. Mobile devices, including BlackBerry®, Windows Mobile® and other popular smartphones, have become critical tools to compete effectively.

Now, with mobile CRM including *CRM for BlackBerry, CRM for Windows Mobile* and *CRM for iPhone®*, one can go beyond reading and reacting to email-and be proactive about managing one's customers and winning more deals. One's laptop or Internet connection is not always available when one needs to look-up the latest status of an account's last service call, review the latest proposal, or check notes for the last phone call with a prospect.

Equipping one's staff with mobile CRM software gives them the edge over your competitors with access to accounts, sales deals, service cases, and schedules while on the road. No more waiting for a laptop to boot up, or fumbling through account notes before an important sales call. *Get the staff using Mobile CRM today to:*

- Get the edge on your competitors to win more deals.
- Reduce staff downtime and increase field productivity with access to customer information at all times.

- Increase customer face time by reducing time spent on administration in the office.
- Build customer intimacy by reviewing up-to-date customer details before a meeting.
- One-click access to maps and directions from customer records.
- Improve sales forecast accuracy through real-time updates from the field.
- Increase CRM data accuracy: an easy-to-use interface on a familiar mobile device increases the likelihood that sales representative will update customer information.

Major Leaders of CRM

Oracle

Oracle is the leader in the CRM field. The company currently offers 50 CRM applications that are able to provide for all the customer service requirements of small, medium and large industries. Oracle provides CRM applications that aid the organization through improved business processes.

SAP

SAP was established in 1972 and is now a leader in the provision of business solutions for all types of industries. It is a CRM software vendor that caters to businesses worldwide and currently serves more than 32,000 customers. SAP has a presence in more than 50 countries. It is the world's largest business software company. It is the world's third-largest independent software provider overall and employs more than 35,000 people.

Sales Force

This unique provider manages to provide simple yet effective customer relationship management products that equip the business with the capacity to increase its effectiveness. It offers a wide range of solutions from marketing to sales force automation to customer service and support.

Maximizer

Maximizer Software are the leading provider of simple and affordable Customer Relationship Management (CRM) to small and medium sized businesses, and the number one player in the Mobile CRM market niche. Maximizer CRM offers sales, marketing, customer service staff and managers their choice of access to customer information–through mobile devices, online, or the desktop.

Mobile CRM on the go in India

If we look at the global market, CRM applications are fast catching up on the mobile side, complementing front-end software on laptops/PCs. Indian companies need to gear up for such solutions to gain a competitive edge and push their marketing, sales force and CRM to the phone.

More Indians use mobile phones every year. The country witnessed a 54% y-o-y growth in subscriber base, adding over 100 million new users. With the mobile penetration level having exceeded 25%, considerable growth potential still remains.

There is a tremendous potential for mCRM in India and all major CRM players have started offering mCRM products in the market. More businesses across industries are reaching out to more than nine million SMBs in India, increasing the need for salespeople, service representatives, and managers to be on the road and all of them have phones.

Salesforce Eyes Indian SMBs for Mobile CRM Market

Mobile based CRM market mCRM is already flourishing in other countries like U.S. and U.K. As compared to them India's mCRM market is still nascent. But India is fast catching up, as it continues to add more and more mobile subscribers every month. India being the second largest mobile market in the world provides lot of opportunities for mCRM market to grow. With 3G auction around the corner in November this year in India, there are many companies who are looking to expand their businesses with the expanding mobile internet market and their target would be the nine million SMB market in India

One of the companies which is trying to expand its mCRM market in India is Salesforce. The company has been in India for two years. They already have many clients in India including few SMBs. "We provide solution that is scalable to any organization in size. Even the smallest organizations that have internet connectivity can use Salesforce".

Nowadays, sales representatives need to perform many tasks such as managing appointments, collaborating with sales team members, and connecting with customer contacts and that too punctually. To serve their need companies like Salesforce are offering their product called Mobile Lite, which enables users to access the Sales Cloud and Service Cloud from their mobile devices. The Mobile Lite service allows end users to log calls and emails, update activities and tasks as well as view account and contact details, leads, opportunities, cases, solutions, assets, all from their mobile device. Mobile Lite offers a subset of the features available in the full mobile version, and with just a few clicks, customers can upgrade to the full functionality.

Even though, mCRM only works on smartphones like Apple, Blackberry or the ones using Windows mobile, the market for mCRM continues to expand. India is the third fastest growing smartphone market in the world. According to Gartner, Asia Pacific recorded a 2.3 percent sequential growth, reaching 7.5 million unit sales, whiles the overall device sales dropped by 9.2 percent. 19 million smartphones are expected to be shipped into India over the next three years, as against a global forecast of a billion by 2011.

There are many barriers to mCRM in India, but one of the most crucial one is security. A mobile theft will also mean theft of crucial information of the company. There are other critical security concerns like handset security, transmission security, backend security, etc. Also GPRS has to be affordable for the companies to provide that to its employees for free.

Vendors Luring SMBs

When it comes to an IT implementation, small businesses often question the benefits of CRM. Although SMBs have a limited workforce and lesser business volumes than large enterprises, they often have the same business processes and even face the same complexities. SMBs have begun to realize that they can no longer sustain the informal approach of interaction with their customers if business has to grow. Today, SMBs are going in for CRM systems and agree that a proper *CRM plan has helped them increase customer retention, company profits and offer better service to customers.*

Best Practices and Process for Mobile CRM

CRM implementations should have executive commitment and focus on practical business result and internal processes to be successful. While companies invest in best to streamline critical business processes for a particular function, if these offerings operate in their own silos, there will be productivity issues, data quality problems, and reduced business effectiveness.

Here are some considerations:

- What devices are my employees currently using?
- What few things do my employees need to be able to do while mobile?
- How do mobile employees need to collaborate?

Best practices include:

- Keep it simple: focus on top few processes that will bring greatest value.
- Don't over customize in order to avoid high complexity and cost, and low adoption.
- Use a mobile solution provided by same CRM vendor or standards based to ensure interoperability, consistent UI/standards, vendor accountability and investment protection.
- Blend in collaborative and other third party mobile services for expanded value.

Points to be considered when going for wire less CRM systems:

- There are different wireless networks that have to work with the proposed CRM system

- There are a suite of different wireless devices such as smart phones, PDAs, pagers, and portable devices such as laptops being used mainly by mobile sales force in the enterprise. These devices can be controlled by the industry CRM solution but the enterprise's customers and partners may not have such a facility.
- There are also wireless technologies such as Wireless Application Protocol (WAP) and services such as i-mode, SMS and also client/server applications based on Java 2 Micro Edition (J2ME). Voice synthesis technologies have also come to provide a fine wireless user interface. There are applications that support text-to-voice and voice-to-text conversions.

Hinderances to Adoption

With the numerous benefits that mobile CRM brings to the table, there are many inhibitors for the large-scale adoption of this technology.

- The first inhibitor as in the case of most technologies is, cost.
- The other major concern for most organizations is security—this includes handset security, transmission security, backend security etc. Issues like device theft can jeopardize any organization's crucial information residing on the mobile phone.
- In a retail market like India where the number of feet on street is high and the transaction volumes are high and the margin per transaction low, considering an investment in such devices does not make business sense for most enterprises.
- The handsets that are optimized for Mobile CRM are relatively expensive. In addition, GPRS connectivity needs to be more affordable for organizations to give free access to their employees. Therefore the cost factor comes into play in India.

Emerging Trends

We are witnessing a significant adoption of CRM amongst large enterprises especially in industries like Communications (Telco), Automotive OEMs, Insurance Companies, Pharmaceutical companies etc. and, very interestingly, a similar demand for CRM coming from mid-sized businesses that look for quick deployments on smaller budgets. Today, any company looking to take its customer interaction to the next level should look at investing in mobile CRM solutions.

The emerging platforms form CRM are based on technologies such as J2ME and communication platforms based on USSD (which is very cost-effective) combined with SMS.

With the increasing innovation in the mobile CRM market, there is something for both enterprises and SMBs. Although mobile CRM is relatively new in India, it is a mature technology worldwide and poses fewer risks, when it comes to investing in it. Therefore, even if one does not have a CRM application in place, mobile CRM can help you achieve the competitive advantage that you were looking for.

Conclusion

Mobile CRM (mCRM) can be defined as adding a mobile, remote access or wireless component and applications to the traditional CRM system. By itself, mCRM cannot exist without traditional, 'non-mobile CRM because mCRM relies upon the underlying CRM database. mCRM makes it more convenient and efficient for mobile field forces such as sales, service, and technicians to interact with the customers in the field and to take what was previously desktop applications.

Adopting a CRM strategy means retooling all of the company's customer-facing activities so that the consumer's interaction with the brand is consistent and the experience is consistently good. It means starting to think more in terms of customer retention than customer acquisition, personalized service rather than mass marketing and growing the brand's share of customer rather than its market share. It's up to a company to determine its role in the total experience that's its customer wants to have.

Time is precious in a sales cycle. Today's sales professionals spend an ever-increasing amount of time away from the office while juggling multiple deals. Sales users need to complete frequent tasks involving customer information in CRM, for that they need an application that is designed specifically for a mobile device and for their mobile work style where information is just a click away. Work styles on the mobile are different from those when in front of a desk, yet many mobile solutions today mimic desktop counterparts.

In India's context mCRM is based on internet and that can be one of its biggest disadvantages. India does not have a good mobile internet penetration. Currently most of those who have internet use GPRS and Edge technology. But Knott says that internet speed is not that critical to run mCRM. "For Salesforce, you are accessing applications on the internet. So it does not matter what network you use. All you need is GPRS in a mobile device to access it. Of course, it will run better on 3G broadband but it runs smoothly on GPRS as well," he added. He is optimistic that the availability of 3G will definitely change the internet scenario in India.

References

Article entitled-Corporate Data Priming Mobile CRM for the Big Leagues, *By Prasad Rai, Senior Director CRM on Demand, ASEAN and India Oracle Asia-Pacific*

Article entitled CRM on the go by *Varun Aggarwal,* 2 March 2009.

Article entitled Mobile CRM Trends by Elisabeth Rainer (Project Manager/Strategic Planning)

Article entitled- Salesforce Eyes Indian SMBs for Mobile CRM Market by Ojas Sharma, Monday, 13 July, 2009, 16:23 hours.

Article entitled- Welcome to the Era of the Mobile Agent and CRM by Ran Reichberg, Manager of Mobile Data, Technology Division of Matrix

Article on CRM by Gaurav Patra

CIOL News. *Making it Your Advantage*

www.crminfonline.com

www.peterindia.net/wirelessCRMoverview.html

www.salesforce.com

www.max.co.uk

11

Impact of CRM in Hotel Business

Sayeda Meharunisa

Introduction

CRM is a business model that aligns product and sales strategies with customer requirements and preferences. Services are then provided in a timely manner using the channels that are preferred by the customers. Effective CRM starts by focusing on the development of business strategies and by aligning an organization to serve customers. These business strategies are then executed using CRM technology solutions. The most successful business strategies are developed only after an organization learns about customers' behavior patterns and attitudes.

This report on Indian Hotel Industry provides an in-depth view of the sector in general and important aspects of the sector. The report starts with the global hotel industry to give a perspective of the Indian hotel industry in the global context. The report covers the hotels industry structure, major players, regulations, growth drivers, issues and challenges, critical success factors and foreign direct investment trends.

Customer Relationship Management is defined by four elements of a simple framework: Know, Target, Sell, and

Service. CRM requires the firm to know and understand its markets and customers. This involves detailed customer intelligence in order to select the most profitable customers and identify those no longer worth targeting.

CRM also entails development of the offer: which products to sell to which customers and through which channel. In selling, firms use campaign management to increase the marketing department's effectiveness. Finally, CRM seeks to retain its customers through services.

As customers and businesses interact more frequently, businesses will have to leverage on CRM and related technologies to capture and analyze massive amounts of customer information. Businesses that use customer data and personal information resources effectively will have an advantage in becoming successful. Different technologies vary in terms of effectiveness and ease of use. It is businesses and managers who determine how to exploit collected data, in other words, more of a policy issue than a technology issue.

Customer Relationship Management- An Overview

CRM is a business model that aligns product and sales strategies with customer requirements and preferences. Services are then provided in a timely manner using the channels that are preferred by the customers. Effective CRM starts by focusing on the development of business strategies and by aligning an organization to serve customers. These business strategies are then executed using CRM technology solutions. The most successful business strategies are developed only after an organization learns about customers 'behavior patterns and attitudes. CRM is essentially a two-stage concept. The task of the first stage is to master the basics of building customer focus. This means moving from a product orientation to a customer orientation and defining market strategy from outside-in and not from inside-out. The focus should be on customer needs rather than product features. Companies In the second stage are moving beyond the basics; they do not rest on their laurels but push their development of customer orientation by integrating CRM across the entire customer experience chain, by leveraging technology to achieve real-time customer management and by constantly innovating their value proposition to customers.

Implementation of Customer Relationship Management

In today's global environment the two key areas of CRM are to plan revenue growth and to optimize the customer profit. The revenue growth planning can be illustrated from two dimensions: customers and products. The revenue will grow when promote the existing products to new customers, or when new products are developed and sell to the existing customer.

Due to the adoption of customer relationship management throughout industry, there are several factors towards the objective of optimizing customers profit: Industry has discovered the value of loyal customers: they buy more, buy more often are cheaper to serve, have higher retention rates, and are more profitable than newly acquired customers.

Marketers have discovered that it is possible to influence the level of customer loyalty through two methods: recruit the right kind of customers to begin with, and treat them very well once acquired excellent customer care is the most important method for improving customer loyalty. Customer service personnel are the front line troops in the battle to win customer loyalty. To provide good customer care, customer contact personnel have to be empowered with information and the authority to make decisions and to act in the customer behalf.

By means of building up a data warehouse and conducting data mining techniques to manage customer relationship, there are several issues about customers need to be addressed when design campaigns for banking industry: understanding customers, avoiding high-risk customers, retaining profitable customers, and targeting profitable customers.

Genesis of Customer Relationship Management

- Increasingly competitive environment in global market.
- Rapid advances in the customer intelligence.
- Shift revolution is held in Marketing philosophy.

- CRM concept is developed.
- Retail companies look for new business and marketing models.
- Idea of a more customer oriented strategy is developed.

Secrets of Customer Relationship Management

Understanding Customers: it is the first and important step to successful customer relationship management. Once the banks know what customer attributes and behaviors are currently driving the profitability, they can use these to direct the prospecting efforts as well. The first step in effective prospecting is learning how to find prospects that look like your customers. It is useful to segment and profile the prospect base to assist acquisition efforts. The goal is to identify what drives customer profitability.

Avoiding high-risk Customers: most businesses are interested in knowing who will respond, activate, purchase or use their services. services. Business is concerned with the amount of risk they are taking by accepting someone as a customer. They assume risk through loans and credit cards. Virtually any company delivering a product or service with the promise of future payment takes a financial risk.

Retaining Profitable Customers: Business are focusing more on retention because it costs much less to keep a current customer than to acquire a new one. One way to improve retention is to take action before the customer churns. Churn models, also known as retention or attrition models, predict the probability of customer attrition. Because attrition has a powerful impact on profitability, many companies are making these models the main focus of their customer loyalty program.

Targeting Profitable Customers: in the early years of direct marketing, much of the growth in revenue took place through the acquisition of new customers. . This makes it more difficult and expensive to acquire new customers. To compensate, many companies are relying on their current customer base to generate the bulk of their profits.

Incorporating Customer Relationship Management

The effective use of CRM principles requires a three-pronged approach. First, all CRM efforts should begin with a well-defined strategy. Second, an infrastructure must be developed to achieve appropriate objectives. Specifically, the infrastructure should align product and sales goals to meet customer needs, according to their preferences, and taste. Third, continuous analytic intelligence should be used to determine and modify customer interaction. In addition to the above approach, implementing CRM involves collecting and reviewing the most relevant customer data.

Relevant customer data can uncover needed information about behavior patterns and attitudes. Once identified, the customer data should be incorporated into the infrastructure so that effective marketing plans can be developed. The execution of marketing plans is driven both by analytic insights obtained about customers and by any existing marketing communication plans. These 'drivers' can be used to place customers in pre-identified groups or to support triggers and scores that identify specific individual behavior patterns. After appropriate customer data analysis and marketing plan development is complete, the multi-channel customer .contact strategies can be implemented within the CRM technology infrastructure.

Customer Relationship and Hotel Management Business

India's hospitality industry is booming. Hundreds of hotels are expected to open in the next few years. Major U.S.-based international brands, such as Hilton and Marriott, have announced plans to invest in India. But they may discover good help is hard to find. As Nilanjana Bhowmick reports from Kolkata, the industry is facing a severe shortage of skilled manpower.

The Indian travel and tourism sector is currently a $100 billion industry. The World Travel and Tourism Council says that over the next decade the size of the industry will nearly triple. Business visitors and tourists to India are surprised to frequently find no room at the inn. And when there are vacancies, the rates at the better hotels rival or exceed those found in New York, London or Tokyo. That is because there is typically a demand nationwide for nearly a quarter of a million rooms, far beyond the 90,000 currently available.

Staffing those hotels is a constant challenge for hoteliers. India's government-run and private Nector hotel management institutes each year graduate more than 10,000 students. But the supply can hardly keep pace with the demand. Industry analysts estimate that by 2012, just the premium slice of the hospitality industry in India will require more than 50,000 trained employees. Natwar Nagar, of HVS International, an organization that predicts hospitality industry trends, says India lacks the personnel to meet the high demand. The bright and educated younger generation of the country has never considered [the] hotel industry as a future employment option," said Nagar. "Trained hospitality workers are also in demand overseas, making it even more difficult for the domestic hotels to find enough qualified clerks, bellhops, waiters and maids. An operator of one placement agency in Mumbai, reports that they send more than 1,000 candidates abroad every year.

"The hotel industry is the most poorly paid industry in India," he said. "As such, skilled people often prefer to work abroad. Apart from the money, the growth opportunity is also greater." Anirban Shimlai of the upscale Park Hotel in Kolkata says even when he is able to find newly-graduated chefs they are frequently lacking in the basic skills.

"There have been hotel management institutes mushrooming all over the country," he said. "However, they somehow get affiliation with foreign universities and top notch catering colleges and go about the course in a short-cut way." "There is no proper training or induction or a proper understanding of the hotel industry. As a result there is faster burn out as people are clueless about what to expect, leading to a high rate of attrition," he added. The Indian government plans to declare the hospitality industry a priority sector, which would allow for 100 per cent foreign direct investment. But that still will not solve the biggest challenge facing the industry: how to find and retain enough qualified staff in the years ahead.

Operational Factors in Hotels in Indian Scenario

Mumbai has traditionally been a very good market for hotels. Our research into the city indicates that demand grows by approximately 1,000 room nights per day every year. We believe the proposed new supply–which would equal about 36% of the existing 9,000-odd rooms–will not be inadequate to meet the city's requirements and we think the market is ripe for more supply.

Bangalore has been on the radar of quite a few developers mainly due to the spectacular performance of the city over the past 2-3 years. However, we must realise that the performance is due to the historical low supply of quality hotels. Once the supply–demand equilibrium is reached (around 2009/10), HVS predicts that there will be sharp rate correction in the Bangalore market. Therefore, having the right location, operator or a unique USP for the market is of utmost importance.

Hyderabad is a relative newcomer and is fast becoming an important hotel market. It enjoys the highest occupancies amongst the major cities and has seen huge rate improvements in the current year.

Another market we are extremely confident of is Chennai, which historically has performed very steadily. While Chennai expects a 212.4% increase in its room supply only 36% of this is likely to be developed in the next few years, and this therefore offers good opportunities for investors to look at. Chennai enjoys the advantage of strong growth in the IT/ITES sector coupled with good demand from the automobile sector, which has a strong manufacturing base in the city.

Future Trends in Hotel Management

With most cities showing impressive demand for hotel rooms, we believe that operators will try and optimise demand and put in place proactive rate management strategies. This year we expect many hotels to increase their annual rates (typically done in October before the peak season). With demand projected to remain strong for the next two three years and with hardly any new supply entering the various markets, we expect the rates to continue to go up annually by 20-25%. There is not much potential for increase in occupancy, as mentioned before, as most cities are driven by commercial demand, with occupancies already in the high 70s or low 80s. Due to low weekend traffic these markets cannot improve their occupancies much further.

In most hotel markets during the past 12 months, insufficient availability and high room rates create conditions that are not conducive for large international conferences to be held. Logistical bottlenecks in these markets also pose a problem. Post 2009, once several markets see an increase in supply, most hotels would adopt an aggressive marketing strategy for the MICE segment and demand from this category is likely to rebound strongly.

India's hotel industry is increasingly being viewed as investment-worthy, both within the country and outside, and several international chains are keen to establish or enhance their presence here. We anticipate that, over the next three to five years India will remain as one of the world's fastest growing tourism markets and will be hard to ignore.

Customer Centered Features

- *Centralize Customer Information.* Establish a single view of customer relationships across your hotel organization.
- *Schedule Appointments and Meetings.* Access sales opportunities, campaign offers, and account sales history within each appointment.
- *Unify Customer Email and Responses.* Automatically capture entire discussion threads within your customer history.
- *Configure My Workplace.* Select the workplace profile that delivers instant access to your customer information and activities.
- *Take your Customers Everywhere.* Get full access to your sales and marketing information on your laptop or mobile device with offline availability and enhanced data synchronization.

Scope for Future Efficiency

Technological Intervention– The industry needs to wake up to the benefits of superior technology to achieve a higher operational efficiency. The luxury and first class hotel segment could focus towards standardization and product enhancement via technology. The mid-market and budget segment needs to reduce the ratio of employee to room by the innovative use of technology.

Improving Industry Interface with Academia- It is a common knowledge that the best MBA schools regularly use the services of practicing industry experts as guest/visiting faculty. However, even the relatively well-known hotel schools of India witness negligible involvement from the industry. Complaints about the bad quality and low employability factor of fresh hotel school graduates need to be addressed holistically.

Outsourcing- Hotels need to learn to outsource areas of operation where they do not possess key competence. Internationally, hotels manage to save millions of dollars per year by outsourcing activities like restaurants, security, accounting, housekeeping, amenities, maintenance etc. This has to be complemented by a comprehensive Quality Control mechanism to ensure the outsourced function conforms to the brand standards.

Conducive Work Environment- In order to attract quality talent, hotels need to be seen as fun places to work in by today's generation. The stiff, hierarchal set-up is passé. Transparency and communication can be used effectively to get the employees involved with the growth of the company. It is appalling to understand that a significant number of employees in some of the top hotel companies wish to have an improved performance management system and H R participation.

Work-Life Balance- This is the soft underbelly of hotels. A majority of hoteliers looking out of this sector mention work-life balance as the main reason. The fast-changing family system in India and increased responsibility of both sexes has made it difficult for even die-hard hoteliers to ignore the social and personal aspects of their lives. Haphazard steps have been taken in this direction but they are certainly not adequate.

Technological Intervention - The industry needs to wake up to the benefits of superior technology to achieve a higher operational efficiency. The luxury and first class hotel segment could focus towards standardization and product enhancement via technology. The mid-market and budget segment needs to reduce the ratio of employee to room by the innovative use of technology.

Conclusion

As customers and businesses interact more frequently, businesses will have to leverage on CRM and related technologies to capture and analyze massive amounts of customer information. Businesses that use customer data and personal information resources effectively will have an advantage in becoming successful. Different technologies vary in terms of effectiveness and ease of use. It is businesses and managers who determine how to exploit collected data, in other words, more of a policy issue than a technology issue.

Hotels need to learn to outsource areas of operation where they do not possess key competence. Internationally, hotels manage to save millions of dollars per year by outsourcing activities like restaurants, security, accounting, housekeeping, amenities, maintenance etc. This has to be complemented by a comprehensive Quality Control mechanism to ensure the outsourced function conforms to the brand standards.

References

Bligh, Philip; Douglas Turk (2004), CRM Unplugged- Releasing CRM's Strategic Value. Hoboken: John Wiley & Sons. ISBN 0-471-48304-4.

Gartner, Inc (2008-09-12), "Gartner Says Worldwide Customer Relationship Management Market. Press release. Retrieved on 2008-08-15.

Gartner, Inc. (22 June 2007), Commonly Deployed CRM Application Vendors in 2006.

http: / / en.wikipedia.org/ wiki / Customer_relationship management"

12

Role of Internet in Customer Relationship Management

S. Jeyalakshmi, G. R. Gayathiri

Introduction

In the early 20th century, in the United States, the suppliers focused on product development, manufacturing capacity, and securing distribution outlets without considering their consumers. They did not pay much attention on customers needs also. They used only mass marketing.

By the middle of the 20th century, all the companies began to find out who their customers were, what they wanted, and how they could be satisfied. They collected and analysed data about their customers and segmented them based on their demographics, such as age, gender, and other personal information. Then, they took steps to promote their product or service to the specific set of customers and their prospects. This was called target marketing. Each company started to concentrate on 4 Ps, (Price, promotion, product, and placement.) which was first suggested by the marketing expert, Jerome McCarthy, in 1960.

By the middle of the 1980's, the traditional target marketing was not so gratifying under circumstances in which it was so difficult to cultivate new customers that this tactic could not sustain cost efficiency. At this point only, the idea of "customer relationship management' gained the confidence of the business sector. The main aim of this concept was building a long term relationships with customers in order to retain them.

Birth of CRM

The concept CRM came into existence in the late 1990's. This term, does not have any clear definition also. Jeffrey Peel, CEO of Quadriga Consulting, defined this term as follows:

"CRM is about understanding the nature of the exchange between customer and supplier and managing it appropriately. The exchange contains monetary considerations between supplier and customer – but also communication. The challenge to all supplier organizations is to optimize communications between parties to ensure profitable long term relationships. CRM is a key focus for many organizations now as a shift away from customer acquisition toward customer retention and churn reduction strategies dictates a need for best practice CRM processes".

Meaning of CRM

Customer relationship management is a management strategy that unites information technology with marketing. It originated in the United States in the late 1990's and a number of companies accepted this worldwide.

CRM is short for Customer Relationship Management. It is the industry term for the set of methodologies and tools that help an enterprise to manage customer relationships in an organized way. (Strategic management website – 2005)

Customer relationship management has been defined narrowly as a customer database management activity. It involves managing detailed information about individual customers and carefully managing customer touch points in order to maximize customer loyalty.

Customer relationship management is the overall process of building and maintaining profitable customer relationship by delivering superior customer value and satisfaction. So, now a day's companies are going beyond designing strategies to attract new customer and to create transactions with them. They are using customer relationship management to retain current customers to earn profits and to maintain long-term relationships with them. The new idea is that marketing is the science and art of finding, retaining, and growing profitable customers.

The key to build customer relationships is to create superior customer value and satisfaction. Satisfied customers are more likely to be loyal customers and loyal customers are more likely to give the company a larger share of their business. We now look more closely at the concepts of customer value and satisfaction, loyalty and retention, and share of customer. Attracting and retaining customers can be a difficult task.

CRM software is fast becoming very popular. The main reason for this is that more people know what CRM is for? And are deciding to use it for customer's support. It is also becoming more popular because of its increased ease of use. Web based CRM software offers companies tons of features and benefits that were not offered in the past. As more companies requires call centre software to run their businesses, this type of software will only continue to grow in popularity.

It helps companies to find the customer needs and also helps to the companies to manage the relationships more intelligently and also helps to the predict the future.

Actually, it is a process or methodology used to learn more about customers' needs and behaviors in order to develop stronger relationships with them.

Customers often face a bewildering array of product and services from which to choose. To attract and to keep customers, a company must constantly seek ways to deliver superior customer value and satisfaction. Companies can build customer relationships at many levels, depending on the nature of the target market.

The choice of routes to customer relationship management is dependent upon the following factors such as nature of business, size of organization, number of customers, types of customers, geographical spread of customers, frequency of contact, type of product, technical support available, presales interaction required, after sales interaction required, competitor's practice of interaction, extent of loyalty, status of customers in the relationship process and life cycle of customers.

The companies can create customer delight by adding social benefits and financial benefits, adding structural ties and holding basic relationship with customers. Satisfaction of customer needs and holding good relationship with customers may leads to innovations in many firms. Thus attracting and retaining customers is vital for all types of organizations. The following picture shows the various process which involved with CRM.

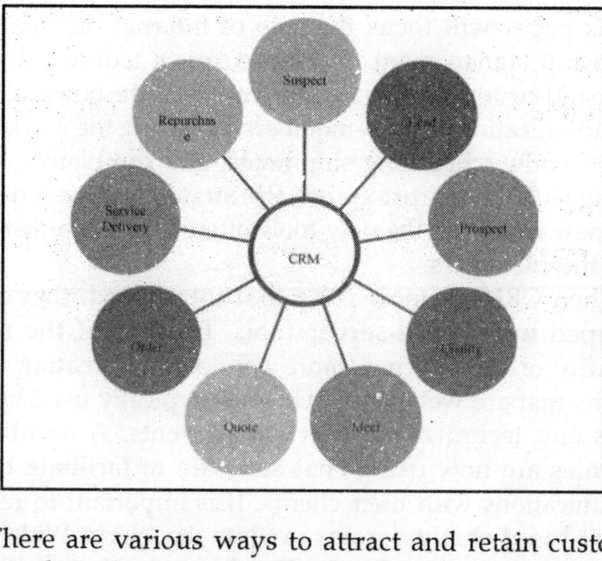

There are various ways to attract and retain customers. Among these Customer loyalty and retention is the new trend in customer loyalty programme. Customer retention is the maintenance of continuous trading relationships with customers over the long term. Customer retention is the mirror image of customer defection or churn. High retention is equivalent to low defection. The leading CRM includes SIEBEL, PEOPLE SOFT, ORACLE, CORE CRM, MySAP, MSCRM, ONYX etc.

The following are the top ten companies providing CRM soft ware

Sl. No.	*Name of the Companies*
1	Siebel
2	Amdocs
3	People Soft
4	Oracle
5	SAP
6	EDS
7	Avaya
8	Baan
9	Aspect
10	E.phany

Source: secondary data

This paper will focus the role of internet on customer relationship management. E-commerce is a tool to maintain and expand customer relationship. Internet is the powerful tool for communicating with co-members, watching the market for pricing trends, scheduling shipments, and completing sales. Working with the touchstone of CRM strategy, one will be able to use new rules and the new tools offered by e-commerce to satisfy the customers.

When CRM systems were first introduced, they were developed with client-server tools. Because of the rapid popularity of the internet, more vendors are creating CRM solutions that are web based. They are typically used by call centers and technical support departments. A number of companies are now using chat software to facilitate better communications with their clients. It is important to realize that text based chat programs predate the World Wide Web by a number of years. Combining this technology with the internet has allowed being user-friendly.

In common, newly acquired buyers are often unprofitable. The profits come from repeat business of loyal customers. Such customers usually:

- Buy more per year.
- Buy higher-priced options.

- Buy more often.
- Are less price sensitive.
- Are less costly to serve.
- Are more loyal.
- Have a higher lifetime value.

So how can attract and retain long-term loyal customers? Using a customer marketing database, a number of tried and true methods really work and pay for themselves many times over.

The first step is to recruit the right kind of customers to begin with. According to Frederick Reichheld[2] 'some people are inherently loyal and some are not'. Customers acquired by low-ball offers are seldom loyal. To attract the right kind of customer, the service can be sale at its value. It makes them to think about what they are getting rather than what they are paying. To keep loyal customers, once acquired, the organiasation must communicate with them often. For example, Travelers created a one-to-one customer contact system consisting of:

- A letter 60 days before annual renewal.
- Annual review.
- Thank-you card in first quarter.
- Cross-sell postcard in second quarter.
- Newsletter in third quarter.
- Seasonal card in fourth quarter.

A study revealed that, the result of agents using this system was to raise the customer retention rate from 85.1 percent to 90.5 percent. To create loyalty and retention internet is the powerful tool. It provides a means to find out interest information directly from the contact.

Modes of CRM in Internet

The Internet enable customer relationship management in three ways, they are,

- Getting information out to customers.

- Getting information back from customers.
- E-commerce sales.

Getting Information Out to Customers

The Internet can provide an avenue for getting information about business and products and services to current and potential customers. From CRM standpoint, it's helpful to think about the level of Internet activity in two ways, passive and active.

A search of the Internet may reveal passive presence in any number of ways. Just as,

- Electronic Yellow Pages.
- Conversations in an online chat or on an industry or association based bulletin board.
- References in articles.

Active Internet presence can put up a simple, information-based Web page or by placing articles on sites of customers and potential customer may attract them to visit.

Getting Information Back from Customers

The next level is to use the internet to get information back from the customers. It involves three general ways to do this. The first way to motivate the customers is making availability of e-mail address to them. For example, an advertisement like, cast your votes to Madurai Meenakshi Amman Kovil at *www.meenakshiammam.org* to select it as one of the wonders of the world. This will directly motivate the customers for active participation.

Secondly, by collecting information from the customer by asking them to register at the site. The registration process allows to collect general information and customer log in on subsequent visits, web-based software can track the way they use the site so one can learn about what information they seek out first and most often, what areas they don't bother to visit and how frequently they stop off .

In the third way to collect data from the customers, putting surveys or question of the day on site is useful. It also encourages them to actively engage in the site. Offering result in their e-mail and post the results in the web page provide another opportunity to communicate with the customers.

E-commerce Sales

This level encourages an organization to walk before run or drive on e-commerce in highway. Launching the three levels at the same time, will help to consider the customers in a linear fashion. There are two parts in the third level. They are, actual sales of products and services and real-time customer service support. The former term refers, what comes to mind when we here the term e-commerce. It highly used by the large-scale retailers for sophisticated applications to manage online sales. But it requires a large investment and requires high-volume sales to make it pay off. The later term save money. Because under this, one can use online help instead of calling customers. The online customer service can be provide through the following means, search engines, frequently asked questions, live help and online order tracking.

Three Rules

The following three rules should be implemented to manage the customer relationship management in a successful manner through internet:

- E-commerce doesn't need to cost big bucks.
- Keep it current. Customers expect internet data to be more current and up to date.
- Strive to keep is personal

Future Prospects of Internet in CRM

Internet can not be replaced by any other technique and there is no substitute for it. Today many stores are converted into bricks-and-clicks entities at an amazing pace. Number of departmental stores that offer online shopping inside the store. Almost all companies and organization will need to create and manage the lectronic contacts with customers. In a recent start the week inspiration pack, e - customer-service world.com are also developed. E-customer service world.com invited the customer for the future of wire communication. Like all other IT enabled services, CRM will also grow with the help of internet and e-commerce.

Conclusion

The internet allows a company to follow new ways to become more effective with its customers and sales prospects. The approaches used under internet and e-commerce will help the organization to develop customer relationship management. Thus this Internet facility has become a common necessity all types of business concerns. It is helpful to E-CRM which maintains the customer relationships effectively and also offer support via the internet 24 hours a day and 7 days a week.

References

Books

Kristin Anderson and Carol Kerr (2002), *Customer Relationship Management*, New Delhi, Tata McGraw Hill Publishing Company Ltd.

H.Peeru Mohamed and S. Agadevan (2003), *Customer Relationship Management*, A Step-by-Step Approach, New Delhi, Vikas Publishing House Pvt. Ltd..

Philip Kotler and Kevin Lane Keller (2008), *Marketing Management,* New Delhi Prentice - Hall of India Private Limited.

V S Ramaswamy and Namakumari (2005), *Marketing Management – Planning, Implementation and Control*, New Delhi, Macmillan India Ltd.

Websites

Viewed on 15.02.2010-http://resources.bnet.com\topic\crm and internet

Viewed on 15.02.2010-http://www.exforsys.com\crm with internet chat

Viewed on 17.02.2010-http://www.toptenlinks.com/cat.php/businee:E+Commerce:crm

13

CRM Practices by Cellular Services Provider- A Select Study of BSNL

Byram Anand, P. Varalaxmi

Introduction

Service dominates the development of any economy. The history of developed economies shows that services played major role in their economic development. Approximately 70% of the GNP is from the services.

Services act as catalyst in the generation of income and employment. This in turn leads to expansion of market for several product and services. Services are no longer an industrial by-product. But has become a powerful economic engine where the jobs are created and the energy for gaining accelerations for economic growth is provided.

Marketing Orientation for services is the need of present day business. Services' marketing plays a crucial role in the creation and delivery of customer focused services. Organizations that are engaged in any line of business including specialized services have to lay major emphasis on services marketing.

A major shift from product oriented to customer orientation compelled organization to get into Customer Relationship Management (CRM), Supply Chain Management (SCM), presales services, post sales services and a set of interactive customer care services. Also a major shift in the life styles necessitated the business to offer specialized services, such as Financial Services, Money Management Services, Insurance Product services, Personal Care services, Telecom services, and a whole gamout of services, which are not Linked to this product, but to the customer needs. As such marketing of services play a strategic role in the survival and success of business entities.

Need of the Study

The changing competitive structure brought in by the liberalization of Telecom Industry necessitates that any enterprises engaged in providing telecom services need to adopt marketing orientation in providing telecom services. The adoption of services marketing concepts is a precondition for the survival and growth of enterprises engaged in this sector. Keeping the strategic nature of Telecom Industry in view and the adoption of marketing concepts to provide effective services as a means to create and expand markets, it is proposed to undertake the research study into services marketing in telecom industry with the particular emphasizes on ""CRM practices by cellular services provider -A select study of BSNL".

Methodology

For the purpose of this paper, a descript research deigns was adopted since the study covered the services with reference to Telecom Sector, an attempt has been made to study the BSNL the Basic services provided such as area of operation.

Data Sources and Methodology

For the purpose of the research study, both the primary and secondary data is collected.

Primary data is collected through comprehensive questionnaire administered to the executives of the selected enterprises as well as their customers.

Secondary data is collected from the various research publications, journal, magazines, employment news, reports of center for monitoring the Indian Economy (CMIE), daily news papers, pamphlets, published reports and as well as published and unpublished literature related to the telecom industry.

The collected data on customer services in telecommunications of the selected enterprises is classified, analyzed and tabulated in systematic manner. For the data analysis various statically techniques such as average, percentage, graphs, diagrams, standard deviation, standard error and coefficient of variation and other appropriate tests i.e., Chi square test has been employed depending upon the requirements

The data collected was examined for competence, consistence and reliability; hence the data collected for this study is secondary in nature.

Objective of the Paper

The present paper focuses on the following objectives.

1. Customer Relation ship Management need
2. Relationship Marketing.
3. Dimensions of CRM in Telecom Services.
4. Segmentation of customers in the telecom sector.
5. Development in the telecom sector.
6. Conclusions.
7. Suggestions

Scope of the Study

The scope of the study is related to the services rendered by different service provider in the state viz. the public sector enterprises and the private sector enterprises. The public sector enterprises are Bharat Sanchar Nigam Limited (BSNL) and the private sector enterprises comprising of Reliance Info Com (RIM), Airtel, Tata Indicom, Vodafone (Hutch), Idea. Further, the area of the study is restricted to Telenagana region in the state of Andhra Pradesh.

Sample of the Study

The enterprises for the study in chose at least one from the public sector and others from the private sectors enterprises. The area of the study is restricted to the Telecom Enterprises operating in Andhra Pradesh. The customer sample size is taken as four hundred and eighty. The customer sample is based on randomized cluster sampling technique. For this present paper a sample of sixty is taken

Time Span

Taking the financial resources and problems into consideration and the telecommunications in India are about 150 years old, for the purpose of the research study only fifteen years of data is taken from 1991 to 2010, i.e., covering the pre-liberalization period. Since, the Telecom industry is of 150 years old in India the time span of the research study is limited to 10 years i.e. from 2000 to 2010 including covering the pre-liberalization period.

Limitations

1. As the Telecommunications in India are about 150 years it is difficult to study for 150 years of the industry. Hence only 10 years are taken for this purpose.
2. As the research is confirmed to only the state of Andhra Pradesh, Telengana region only.
3. As the sample size is taken is very small and its does not represents the universe, the conclusion drawn for the study may be biased.

Review of Literature

After going through the published and unpublished literature relating to the customer relationship management the following authors have given their views on customer relation ship management (CRM) in their articles.

......M. Veerabhadraiahin, IAS, Managing Director, A.P state co-operative Bank, in his article "Customer relation ship management in services sector" he emphasized the importance of CRM in public sector enterprises ,he says that CRM is in high gear as telecommunications carriers struggle to identify, retain and grow their business with profitable customers.

.....Dr. G. Bhaskar Rao, Chandra shekar and Venkateshwar Chavan in their article "customer relation ship management - its dimensions in telecommunication sector" they said a successful CRM implementation will allow customer services, scale and marketing people to have a holistic view of each and everyone customer and have given the dimensions in telecommunication

......Prof. K. Sayalu and Ch.Vijay Bhaskar Reddy in their article "Customer relationship management in telecom sector -A study of BSNL" has emphasized on implementation of CRM on the BSNL Organisation they say the major thrust areas of concern in the CRM policy of a company are services by the company, customer acquisition is more important they say retention strategies for potential defectors, retention strategies for loyal customers, measurement system for customer value ,implementing retention plans.

......R.. Ashok Babu in his article "e-CRM -A 'Must Need' tool for the services sector edited by V.Venkat ramana and G.Somayajulu in his article he says that the role of then customer is becoming increasingly important in the telecom sector. Customer retention and customer communication programs play a key role in the profitability of all telecom companies.

– – –A study By Reichheld and Sasser[1] explored the relation ship between customer retention and profits .This study covered four services industries: credit card ,industrial laundry , industrial distribution and auto servicing. The study calculated the impact of five point customer retention rate on the profits. Reducing the customer defection by five percent can lead to dramatic rise in the profit per customer. Firms in different industries could gain profit increase of different order simply by increasing the retention rate by five percent.

– Reichheld and Sasser in an another paper threw light upon the important of customer defection they revealed that reducing customer defection by just five percent is capable of boosting profits anywhere in the range of 25-85 percent. No impact of reduction in customer defection could have been more dramatic than the experienced by MBNA.

Are the few review of literature on CRM

CRM Introduction

Customer Relationship Management (CRM) is becoming complex in the context of present day due to increasing customer expectations and growing shift from mass production to mass customerization. Customers care recognition, but not freebies, shows that one should recognize him/her and value of his custom. Get to know him better, specially in terms of the consumption patterns of the product or service is gaining importance. To preempt his future needs by building on the understanding to suggest relevant offers about the product is the key.

CRM seamlessly links customers with the organization, keeps information consistent across all customer contact points, and helps provide individualized or personalized service by integrating all other business processes. The results is "sales cycles" are shortened with increase in productivity. This paper studies the concept of CRM and how it is beneficial to the organizations in improving bottom line.

Need for CRM

Customer relationship management is very much vital for companies in the present highly competitive scenario. The organizations attitude towards customer service should be inculcated and this should be driven from the top most downwards.

Customer Centric: Two trends have brought CRM to the forefront. First, with increased global competition and easy access to the latest technology, products have become harder to differentiate; hence companies are increasingly pursuing a customer-centric competitive strategy rather than a product centric. Second, it is possible to put customer information from all over the enterprise into a single system rather than a no different systems and access it from anywhere in the world through the internet.

Customer Demand: Customers in the e-business age expect constant access to a company, through e-mils; call centers, faxes and websites. They demand immediate response and a personalized touch meeting their needs, placing new demands on the enterprise, which CRM alone can satisfy.

Effectiveness: With the product quality at all time highs, manufacturers find it increasingly difficult to gain competitive advantage based solely on product attributes. There the focus now is on channel operations and customer relationships, when there is great potential for adding value and differentiating the offerings. Increasingly companies are applying sophisticated information technology to identify, acquire and retain the most profitable customers by continuously improving the highest levels of customer experience, and creating and sustaining the highest levels of customer satisfaction. The focus on demand chain effectiveness to continuously improving their ability to identify, acquire and retain profitable customers.

Intelligent Management: The effect of increased commoditization of products and production process is that customers now have more and more choices giving them better, more personalized product offerings and services is the only real way to make a difference winning depends on the understanding and intelligently managing relationships with customers.

Principles of Relationship Marketing

To understand customer relationship marketing, we must first examine the process involved in attracting and keeping customers.

Figure 1

Category	*Past*	*Present*	*Future*
Item	Product	Augmented Product	System contract
State	Unit	System	System / time
Value	Feature	Technology	System
Lead time	Short	Long	Lengthy
Service	Modest	Important	Vital
Delivery place	Once	Frequently	Continuous
Strategy	Sales	Marketing	Relationship

Source: Theodore Levitt; The *Marketing Imagination,* Free Press, New York, p.116.

Figure 1 shows the main steps in the customer-development process. The starting point is suspects, everyone who might conceivably buy the product or service. The company looks hard at the suspects to determine who are the most likely prospects–the people who have a strong potential interest in the product and the ability to pay for it. *Disqualified prospects* are those whom the company rejects because they have poor credit or would be unprofitable. The company hopes to convert many of its *qualified prospects* and *first time customers,* and then convert those satisfied first-time customers into *repeat customers.* Both first-time and repeat customers may continue to buy from competitors as well. The company then acts to convert repeat customers into clients - people who buy only from the company in the relevant product categories. The next challenge is to turn clients into *advocates,* customers who praise the company and encourage others to buy from it. The ultimate challenge is to turn advocates into partners, where the customer and the company work actively together. At the same time, it must be recognized that some customers will inevitably become inactive or drop out, for reasons of bankruptcy, moves to other locations, dissatisfaction, and so on. The company's challenge is to reactivate dissatisfied customers through customer win-back strategies. It is often easier to re-attract ex-customers than to find ones.

Developing more loyal customers increases the company's revenue. However, the company has to spend more to build greater customer loyalty. Development of customer loyalty will be more profitable in some business than in others.. Five different levels of company investment in customer-relationship building:[2]

Basic Marketing: The salesperson simply sells the product.

Reactive Marketing: The salesperson sells the product and encourages the customer to call if he or she has any questions, comments, or complaints.

Accountable Marketing: The salesperson phones the customer a short time after the sale to check whether the product is meeting the customer's expectations.

Proactive Marketing: The company salesperson contacts the customer from time to time with suggestions about improved product uses or helpful new products.

Partnership Marketing: The Company works continuously with the customer to discover ways to effect customer savings or help the customer perform better.

Levels of Relationship Marketing

Levels of relationship marketing is given in Figure 2 below.

The levels of relationship marketing are High Margin, Medium Margin and low Margin. From the above above table it is seen that the Accountable is common and important in High, low, medium level of relation ship a Marketing.[3]

Figure 2: Levels of Relationship Marketing

	High Margin	*Medium Margin*	*Low Margin*
Many Customers/ Distributors	Accountable	Reactive	Basic or Reactive
Medium no. of customers/distributors	Proactive	Accountable	Reactive
Few Customers/ Distributors	Partnership	Proactive	Accountable

Source: Philip Kotler, Marketing Management, p.50.

Call Centre

A call centre is a group of agents and or/ automated voice response units that support customer contacts function over the telephone. They are assisted by computers. A call center must anticipate and accumulate customer needs by delivering the right information, at the right time in the right way, with the right quality.

Call centre features and their functionalities are Contact Management, Opportunity Management, Activity Management, customer Management, Workshop Management, Knowledge Management.[4]

Contact Management: improves the quality of customer services by providing the information on the agents screen. Delivery prompt refined and a Knowledge able service that does not requires callers to repeat their questions as they are routed through the organisation. Maintain a data base of all customers contact persons with details as apart of knowledge base.

Customer Managent provides single contact point for any customer query. Identify and track loyal customers based on pre defined parameters and focus on profitable customers, attracts new customers nurture and them for high profitability.[5]

Incoming Calls Management

Agents - available on line to take calls.

ASA - average speed of answer

SL (%) = Service level (% answered with in started objective)

OCC = Occupancy (% of time agents speed in talk of work).

Use a talk time of 220 seconds, after call work of 30 seconds, 150 calls in the half hour and service level objectives of 20 seconds. For a service level of at least 80 % we would require 26 people to be available to answer calls .We would expect an average speed of answer of 10 seconds and an occupancy rate of 80%.[6]

Computer Telephone Integration (CTI)

With global competition growing, out standing customer services is becoming an increasingly important business of competitive advantage for many Organisations. Call centers or customer contact centre have long played a critical role on the customer interaction front compared with other forms of customers interactions, call centers provide a highly efficient and effective medium for serving customers.[7]

Competitive telephony integration technology (CTI) can play a critical role in helping call centers achieve their competitive and effective goals. CTI can be defined as the application of computer based intelligence to telecommunication device. CTI can also defined as the process of blending the functionality of computers and computer networks with the features and capabilities of sophisticated telephone system over an intelligent data link to gain in agent productivity , customer satisfaction and enterprise cost savings.

The advantages of CTI are:

CTI functionality (Screen pop, Call -data transfer and IVRT integration) has four principal benefits.

- Increased agent productivity.
- More competent customer services.
- Faster access to customer information.
- Long distance cost savings.

PC–Based Technology

The main benefit associated with PC based telephony is increased Agent productivity agents are able to make calls, transfer callas etc. Additionally agent productivity is improved by removing the necessary of having to deal with two different interfaces[8](i,e, the telephone and the computer)

Measured Computer Levels by Customer

Many Organisations are obliged to provide minimum services levels to certain groups of customers. Often Organisations will want to ensure that their most valued customers receive the highest level of services with reporting, customer contact centre managers have access to the information they need to ensure that the required services levels.

Data Ware House–Customer Retention

Integration of CRM with Data ware house:

Data mining is the process of extracting and presenting a new knowledge, previously undetectable, selected from data base for actionable decision.

Data Ware House/Data Mining–Customer Retention

Customer retention is a similar business problem as target marketing is both involved building propensity models, predictive models indicating a customer propensity.

In this case the model identifies customers with a propensity to switch to a competition who have recently defected and others who have not campaigns would be targeted at those customers who are likely to be detected. If customers profitability information were available, only customer above a certain profitability level would be targated.[9]

Customers retention also benefited from customers segmentation to develop tailored campaigns for each segment with differing assumptions regarding cost of defection (lost profitability 'X' estimated continuing longevity) and with separation predictive models development for each segments.

Customer retention that is well suited to data mining includes:

- Identifying key factors activity pattern in winning back customers.
- Data mining characteristics of loyal customers
- Data mining can be applied to the problems of Fraud analysis and detection in several ways similar to target marketing and customer retention. It involves developing a predictive model indicating customer propensity to fraud. Data is analyzed relating to sample of known previous fraudulent customers and not fraudulent customers.

Customer Centric Information and Application System

Managing customer and channels is to increase profitability services, marketing business velocity and long term growth.[10]

The integrate CRM flow and process include

- Knowledge discovery
- Market planning
- Customer interaction
- Analysis and refinement.

The function and analysis into the process, then integrate an ongoing process:

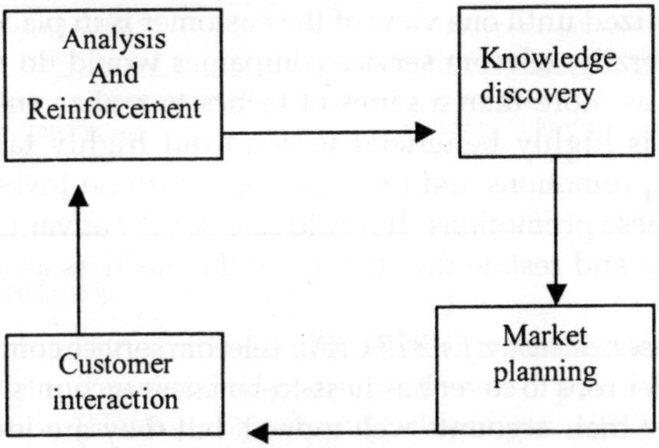

Source: CRM H.Peeru Mohamed & Asagadevan

Figure 3: The CRM Iterative Learning Process

Dimensions of CRM in Telecom Services

Telecom companies have moved quickly to adopt CRM principles. A number of issues which can challenge CRM adoption, including the vision and commitment of senior management, choosing customers, creating new value, overcoming legacy investments and developing meaningful e-CRM strategies. These issues are barriers in the telecommunications service arena, too, although not always of equal significance. The following are some of the dimensions that merit special mention in the telecom sector[11]:

Single View of the Customer: Companies with a single view of the customer are able to link call centre databases, Internet orders and inquiries, customer prospect lists, accounting files, and other databases so they have but one view of the customer. They are able to update this in real time and ensure that a customer accessing the company through the Internet. For telecom service companies, a single and comprehensive view of the customer, while a sought after objective, is not yet in place. For several firms, there remains an opportunity to further develop the customer data warehouse and knowledge management, and deploy software to manage all inbound and outbound customer interactions.

CRM as a Series of Tactics: The full potential of CRM will not be realized until one view of the customer is in place. But, more generally, telecom service companies would do well to see CRM as more than a series of tactics to realize customer value. It is highly beneficial to send out highly targeted customer promotions and measure the Return on Investment (ROI) of these promotions. It would also be very advantageous to redefine and restate the strategy of the business as a CRM strategy.

Business well known for B2B CRM: Telecom service companies deploy sales reps to cover business-to-business accounts. These reps know their accounts well indeed, but they are less well supported by CRM technology than they might be have opportunities exist and selecting personalized and customized communications solutions to drive this behavior, all at a distance, on-line. Software exists to ease this task.

Customers Triaged According to their Value: Telecom companies have already assessed the value of their customers to the company and have triaged customers by this value- "Best", "Average" and "Worst" or according to their profitability and potential for growth. Some telecom service companies have used this triage as a basis to organize their companies according to the value of the customer. They often have the processes in place to address each type of customer efficiently and effectively.

Excellent Use of People to Respond to E- mails and SMS: From personal experience, telecom service companies do a great job of personally responding to e-mails but might do more with technology to handle the flood of e-mail. There is not only a need to intelligently manage the flood of inbound e-mails that many companies are experiencing but to tie in a corresponding outbound management system, ideally with a single solution. Companies can do much more than simply automate the response. It is no longer acceptable to many customers to receive a timely but irrelevant or impersonal response, which has obviously been sent by an automated system. Software and service bureaus are available to manage responses, analyze content in e-mails to auto-reply in context with personalized messages. Without technology intervention, telecom service companies will have to scale up or refocus some among their human resources to meet the challenge, not quite what their shareholders have in mind.

Technology enables companies to automate, personalize and customize interactions, with minimum human intervention. The right technology can provide an intelligent response to every customer.

Telecom service companies want to forge close and enduring customer relationships and many have taken important steps to ensure that they do precisely this. Yet it still appears to some businesses and consumers as though additional value remains to be unlocked from the customer data the telecom companies have and the knowledge and insight they could create and use.

Segmentation of Customers in the Telecom Sector

Customer segmentation is really a continuation of understanding lifetime value. Once customer lifetime value has been established, companies can determine how much service and support to provide each customer, and differ communication and promotional programs, based on how customers are then segment. This is also where advanced churn and CRM program modeling come into play, where companies can select the most appropriate programs based on the customer's value to the company, likelihood to defect, and probability of positive response to the program.

Determining both the lifetime value of each customer–their revenue minus their costs - and the 'second lifetime' value of a recovered customer, are perhaps the most important considerations in decisions regarding what resources to invest, and where, we believe that a company will want to determine.

- Cost to acquire a customer
- Average amount each customer spends per period (month, quarter, year)

- Products and services purchased
- Average time with supplier
- Time remaining in the customer's life cycle
- Costs to retain each customer, i.e., ongoing relationship expenses, such as customer service.
- Profit from average customer (sales, minus fixed and variable costs)
- Referral and information value attributed to each customer.

Current Developments in the Telecom Sector

The telecommunications industry faces a particularly daunting challenge in its efforts to prevent customers from defecting to the competition. With new providers, services, rates and incentives seemingly multiplying faster than rabbits, carriers are engaged in a perennial struggle against the revolving door and the financial complications caused by this subscriber "churn". New tools are now combating the problem with sophisticated technologies for predicting customer behavior.[12]

Critical CRM

Customer relationship management is important for every business, but in the telecom world it is truly a matter of survival. Internet service providers grapple with a comparable set of scenarios.

Traditionally, telecom companies and other churn-plagued industries have responded to these business realities by luring new customers with deals. Unfortunately, this has resulted in squeezed profit margins, a perpetual cycle of competitive discounts, and more of the churn that companies were trying to combat in the first place. In response, the industry is turning to CRM.

One-On-One Marketing

Conventional CRM database analysis techniques that group customers into clusters or segments do not adequately address the needs of telecom companies and other subscription-based enterprises. Traditional CRM applications produce detailed profiles on groups of at-risk accounts, but they fail to the answer to why customers are likely to leave, and what can be done to make them retain.

Currently, some of the CRM providers are applying some of the world's most advanced predictive technologies to answer these questions. Utilizing sophisticated computational models with names like neural networks, logic regression and decision three analysis, these applications make it possible to predict behavior on a customer-by-customer basis and use that data to determine which incentive offers are likely to keep individual subscribers on the company roster. The best of these CRM technologies learn over time, so that a company's knowledge of an individual customer grows with every conversation or interaction. Combine that with the ability to automatically customize individual or batch e-mails with the best offer for each subscriber, and the result is the ability to treat customers as individually as the store clerks of yesteryears.

Predictive Modelling

At the heart of these new-generation CRM solutions are artificial intelligence systems that track and map subscriber attributes such as purchasing behavior, the types of calls made to customer support, the length of time the subscriber has been with the company, and so on. The actual variables are customized to the company's product offerings and unique circumstances. Every time the subscriber interacts with the company, the system adds information to the mapping.

This has two important effects. First, at each customer touch point, the company can have an intelligent conversation reflecting an understanding of the customer's experience to date and some computer-generated insight into his or her satisfaction level. This focus on the consumer's needs rather than the company's agenda is an important step toward increasing customer retention. Second, the data gathered by these artificial intelligence systems is used to assign "church scores" that predict whether that individual is likely to cancel and why, and to recommend the most effective, cost-efficient response to retain that subscriber. Instead of offering every disgruntled subscriber the same incentive to stay, each subscriber can be offered the incentive, loyalty reward, or up-sell or cross-sell offer best suited to his or her individual circumstances.[13]

Targeted Incentives

For a subscriber, the incentive may be one month of free service. For another, it may be enhanced functionality. Today's systems can not only intelligently match each customer with the offer they will most likely accept and list the offers in order of their likely acceptance and highest revenue, but also filter out unlikely prospects to avoid wasting time and creating customer ill-will.[14]

This information can be used for highly targeted outbound calling or e-mail campaigns as well as for fielding incoming calls and making cross-sell/up-sell recommendations in real time. Personalized e-mail messages can be mass-generated to appeal to different subscribers with different offers, yielding one-on-one marketing campaigns with the efficiency of mass mailings.

The newest of these systems also enable companies to predict how much an individual customer is worth in the future with and without incentive offers. By analyzing the inter-relationship between revenue potential, churn risk and other factors, these solutions can help companies.

Table 1
Age of the Respondent

Age of the Respondent in Years	*No. of Respondent*	*% of the Total*
<15	3	5
15-25	13	22
25-35	32	53
35-45	7	11
45 & above	5	9
Total	60	100

Source: Primary Data

It is well know fact CRM is critical for the success of services sector. In order to understand the effectiveness CRM practices followed by BSNL the study was conducted on Customer Perceptions and CRM practices of BSNL in Andhra Pradesh. The data is presented in the following tables.

From the above Table 1 it is infered that the majority 53% of the respondents age falls in the age group of 25-35 years and that of 22% ate between 15-25 years and the least 5% of the respondents falls under the age group of less than 5 years.

Table 2
Area of the Respondents

Area of the Respondents	*No. of Respondents*	*% of the Total*
Urban	47	78
Semi urban	9	15
Rural	4	7
Total	60	100

Source: Primary Data

From the above Table 2 it is observed that majority 78% of the respondents are from the urban area and that of 15% are from semi urban and the least 7% of the respondent are from the rural areas.

Table 3
Income of the Respondents

Income Per Month	*No. of Respondents*	*% of the Total*
< 5000	11	18
5000-10000	30	50
10000-20000	14	23
20000-30000	4	7
More than 30000	1	2
Total	60	100

Source: Primary Data

From the above Table 3 it is observed that majority 50% of the respondents income is between Rs 5000-10000, 23% of the respondents income is between Rs 10,000-20000 and the least is 2% of the respondents income is more than Rs 30000.

Table 4
Primary Use of the Telephone

Primary Purpose	*No .of Respondent*	*% of the Total*
Residential purpose	40	66
Business use & commercial	14	23
Office	2	4
Public call office use & fax use	3	5
Internet use	1	2
For other purpose	0	0
Total	60	100

Source: Primary Data

From the Table 4 it is infered that the majority 66% of the respondents the primary use of the telephone is for the residential purpose, 23% use for the business and commercial purpose and that of the least 2% of the respondents use telephone for the internet purpose.

Table 5
How Long You are Using the Telephone

No. of Years	*No. of Respondent*	*% of the Total*
< one year.	20	33
1-2 years	20	33
2-4 years	18	30
4-6 years	1	2
Above 6 years	1	2
Total	60	100

Source: Primary Data

From the above Table 5 it is infered that majority 33% of the respondent are using the telephone less than one year and one to two years and the least of the respondents are using the telephone from 4-6 years and above 6 years.

From the Table 6 it is infered that majority of the respondents average monthly bill is less than 300 rupees ,30% respondents average monthly bill is between 600-900 rupees and the least is 10% of the respondents average monthly bill is between 300-600,900-12000 ad 2500-3000 respectively per month.

Table 6
Average Monthly Bills

Amount of Rs per month	*No. of Respondents*	*% of the Total*
< 300	24	40
300-600	6	10
600-900	18	30
900-1200	6	10
1200-1500	0.0	
1500-2000	0.0	
2000-2500	0.0	
2500-3000	6	10
3000 & above	0.0	
Total	60	100

Source: Primary Data

Table 7
Penalty /Surcharge after Pay by Date

Surcharge /Penalty	*No. of Respondent*	*% of the total*
Rs 10/-	7	12
Rs 20/-	4	7
Rs 60/-	6	10
Rs 100/-	3	5
More than 100/-	3	5
Non	37	61
Total	60	100

Source: Primary Data

From the above Table 7 it is infered that majority 61% of the respondents says that they have not paid any surcharge. 12% of the respondents say that they have paid 10 rupees as surcharge after pay by date, 10% of the respondents say that they have paid 60 rupee sand that of the least 5% of the respondent says that they have paid 100 rupees and more than 100 rupees as penalty/surcharge.

From the Table 8 it is observed that 68% of the respondents are not aware of the toll free numbers, 32% of the respondents are aware of toll free numbers of them majority 185 of the respondents says that they have dialed the toll free number 2-3 times and that of the least 4% of the respondents says that they have dialed the toll free more than 5-8 times

Table 8
Toll Free Numbers Awareness and Dialed the Toll Free Numbers

Toll Free Numbers Dialed	*No. of Respondent*	*% of the Total*
2-3 times	11	18
3-5 times	6	10
5-8 times	2	04
Not at all dialed	41	68
Total	60	100

Source: Primary Data

Table 9
Attended Telephone Adalath/Open House Session

Yes 20 No 40

Attended Telephone Adalath/ Open House Session	*No.of Respondent*	*% of the Total*
Attended 1-3 times	112	18
Attended 3-5 times	5	8.33
Attended 5-8 times	4	6.67
Noi at all attended	40	67
Total	60	100

Source: Primary Data

From the above Table 9 it is observed that 67% of the respondents says that they have not attended the telephone adalath and 33% of the respondents says that they have attended the telephone adalath/open house session, of them majority 18% of they respondent says tat they have attended the open house session 1-3 times and that of the least 6.67% of the respondent says they have attended 5-8 times

Table 10
Place of Payment of Bills

Place	*No.of Respondents*	*% of the Total*
At customer center	20	40
At post office	4	8
At telegraph office	10	20
At on-line billing service counters	15	30
e-seva	0	0
Bank	1	2
Total	60	100

Source : Primary Data

From the above Table 10 it is observed that majority 40% of the respondents says that they pay the monthly bills at the customer service centers and,30% of the respondent says that they pay the monthly bills at the on line billing service counters and the least they pay at the bank.

Table 11
Distance of the Service Center

Residential Place to the Customer Service Center	*No. of Respondents*	*% of the Total*
½ km	16	27
1-3 km	28	46
3-5km	13	22
Above 5 km	3	5
Total	60	100

Source: Primary Data

From the above Table 11 it is observed that majority 46% of the respondents say that the distance between the residential place to customer service center is 1-3 km ,22% of the respondents says it is 3-5 km and the least 5% of the respondents says the distance is above 5 km.

Table 12
Promptness in Attending the Customer Request

Promptness in Attending the Customer Request	*No. of Resondents*	*% of the Total*
a) phone shift		
1-2 days	5	8
2-4 days	6	10
4-5 days	4	7
none	45	75
Total	60	100
b) clip facility		
8 hours	17	28
12 hours	6	10
1-2 days	21	35
More than 2 days	3	5
none	21	35
Total	60	100

Contd.

Promptness in Attending the Customer Request	*No. of Resondents*	*% of the Total*
c) change of plan		
1-2 days	21	35
2-4 days	16	26
4-5 days	11	18
More than 5 days	10	16
none	2	4
Total	60	100
d) Excess meter reading		
1-2 days	19	32
2-4 days	11	18
4-5 days	14	23
More than 5 days	04	7
none	12	20
Total	60	100
e) refund of deposits		
1-3 months	21	36
3-6 months	17	28
6-9 months	5	8
One year	12	20
None	5	8
Total	60	100
Restoration of connection		
1-2 days	24	41
3-4 days	12	20
4-5 days	8	13
More than 5 days	13	21
none	3	5
Total	60	100

Source: Primary Data

From the above Table 12 it is observed that 75% of the respondents have not shifted the telephone and 25% of the respondent says that they have shifted the telephone of them majority 10% of the respondents says the promptness in attending the customer request for telephone shifting is 2-4 days and that of least is 7% says it is 4-5 days.

Regarding CLIP facility majority 35% of the respondent says that promptness in attending the customer request for clip facility is 1-2 days and that of least 25% says it is 8 hours and the least 5% of the respondent says it is more than 2 days to provide clip facility.

Regarding change of plan majority 35% of the respondents says that customer request for change of plan is 1-2 days and that of 26% of the respondent says it is 2-4 days and the least 4% of the respondents says there is no change in the plan.

Regarding excess meter reading the promptness in attending the customer request is majority 32% of the respondent says it is 1-2 days and that of 23% of the says it is 4-5 days and that of the least 7% of the respondent says it is more than 5 days.

Regarding refund of the deposits the promptness in attending the customer request majority 36% of the respondents says the refund of the deposits is 1-3 month and that of 28% says it is 3-6 months and that of least 8% says it is 3-9 months to refund the deposits

Regarding restoration of connection the promptness in attending the customer request majority 41% of the respondent says it is 1-2 days to restoration of the connection ,21% says it is more than 5 days and the least is 4-5 days for the restoration of the connection .

Table 13
Exempted from Payment of Rentals for the Disconnected Period

Amount Exempted	*No. of Respondent*	*% of the Total*
500-1000	13	22
1000-1500	8	13
1500-2000	2	3
2000-2500	2	3
If any other amount pl.spy	0	0
none	35	59
Total	60	100

Source: Primary Data

From the above Table 13 it is observed that majority 59% of the respondent says that their is no exemption of payment of rental for the disconnected period, 22% of the respondent says they are exempted from 500-1000 rupees rental, 13% of

Table 14

Customer Satisfaction Levels with respect to BSNL Telecom Services

Satisfaction Levels	*Billing Performance*	*Network Performance*	*Instrument Provided*	*Customer Services*	*Telephone Availability*	*SIM Card Availability*	*Recharge Coupon Availability*	*Voice Quality*
H.S	9(15)	2(4)	4(12)	4(7)	7(12)	7(12)	10(17)	10(17)
S	30(50	28(47)	30(50)	25(42)	33(54)	34(56)	34(56)	31(52)
NSNDS	15(25)	21(36)	17(28)	16(27)	12(20)	10(17)	10(17)	8(12)
D.S	4(7)	5(8)	6(10)	7(12)	4(7)	6(10)	4(7)	7(12)
H.D.S	2(3)	3(5)	3(5)	6(12)	4(7)	3(5)	2(3)	4(7)
Total	60(100)	60(100)	60(100)	60(100)	60(100)	60(100)	60(100)	60(100)

Source: Primary Data

H.S = highly satisfied
S = satisfied
NSNDS = neither satisfied nor dissatisfied
D.S = dissatisfied
H.D.S = highly dissatisfied.

the respondents says they are exempted form 1000-1500 rupees and the least 3% of the respondents says they are exempted from 1500-2000 & 2000-25000 monthly rentals for the disconnected period

From the Table 14 it is observe that customer satisfaction levels of the customers regarding billing performance is that 50 % of the respondents are satisfied, 25% are neither satisfied nor dissatisfied and the least 3% of the respondents are highly dissatisfied with the billing performance.

Regarding network performance 50% of the respondents are satisfied, 28% are neither satisfied nor dissatisfied and the least 5% of the respondents are highly dissatisfied with respect to network performance

Regarding instrument provided by the service provider 36% of the respondents are neither satisfied nor dissatisfied and the least 10% of the respondents are highly dissatisfied.

Regarding customer services 42% of the respondents are satisfied and the least 7% of the respondents are highly satisfied. And 8% of the respondents are highly dissatisfied with the customer services

Regarding telephone availability 54% of the respondents are satisfied and the least 7% of the respondents are dissatisfied and highly satisfied with the telephone availability

Regarding SIM card availability 56% of the respondents says they are satisfied with the availability of the SIM cards and the least 5 % of the respondents are highly dissatisfied

Regarding availability recharge coupons/top up cards 56% of the respondents are satisfied with availability of recharge coupons and that of 3% of the respondents are highly dissatisfied with the availability of recharge coupons/top up cards.

Regarding voice quality of services 52% of the respondents are satisfied with the voice quality and that of 7% of the respondents are dissatisfied with the voice quality of the services.

Findings of the Study

1. The customers mainly belong to the age grouped 25-35 years; have average income of 5000-10,000 and mostly from urban population.

2. Majority of the telephone users are from residential sector followed by Business & Commercial sector.
3. The average time span for the usage of telephone is between 1-2 years with monthly bill of Rs.300/- per month.
4. 66% of the respondent's user the telephone for the Residential / personal use and 23% user for business and commercial purpose, and for least 2% of the user telephone for Internet purpose.
5. 33% of the respondents are using the telephone for less than one year and + 2 years respectively and 2% are using the telephone 4-6 years and above 6 years respectively.
6. 40% of the respondent's monthly telephone bills in less than 300 per month and that of 600-900 per month and the least 900-1200 per month.
7. 12% of the respondents says that they have paid Rs.10/- as a surcharge/penalty after pay by date and 5% of the respondents says they paid Rs.100/- and more than 100 rupees as a penalty. This is due to the telephone bills receiving after last date by the postal delay.

   To over come the problem of postal delay to maintain the relationship with the customer BSNL has provided a toll free numbers 1501 or 1502 or 1503 to know the latest payment of telephone bills. More over it is sending the voice mail to the customers saying the telephone bills details and the last date of payments and kio's are provided at customer service centers.
8. 18% of the respondents say that they have dialed the toll free numbers 2-3 times and 4% says they have dialed the toll free numbers more then 5-8 times.
9. 18% of the respondents say they have attended the telephone adalath / open house session 1-3 times and 6.67% says they have attended the telephone adalath 5-8 times.
10. 40% of the respondents says that they will pay the telephone bills at the customer centers and 2% says they will pay at the Bank i.e., through salary account payment.

11. 46% of the respondents say that the distance of service center is 1-3 km's and 5% of them say it is above 5 kms from the residential place to the customer service center.
12. 10% of the respondents say it has taken 2-4 days and 7% says it has taken 4-5 days to shift the phone from once place to another place. 32% of the respondents says it has taken 1-2 days, 7% says it has taken 4-5 days for attending the excess meter reading request. 36% of the respondent says 1-3 months, 8% says 6-9 months for the refund of deposits after the surrender of the telephone. 41% of the respondents say it has taken 1-2 days and 13% of the respondent says it has taken 4-5 days for the restoration of the connection after disconnection.
13. 22% of the respondents say they are exempted from 500-1000 and 3% of the respondent says they are exempted from 1500-2000, 2000-2500 rupees simultaneously from payment of rentals for the disconnected period.

Suggestions

1. In this growing young generation there are more number of youngsters. The telephone service providers can tap the youngsters less than 15 years and between 15-25 years.
2. All most all the urban area is saturated with the telephones. Now the telecom service provider should focus on the rural area which is untapped. BSNL all most all covers the rural areas by providing VPT's in every village with out any payment of rentals for 2 years and with less installation charges to have the relation with the rural customers.
3. The income of the customers/consumers plays a major role in buying decision. Now telephone has become necessary thing in the daily life. Irrespective of income every one in buying a telephone. (Ex: Rikshapuller, banana Seller, Broom stick seller also using the mobile phones now a days).
4. The telephone can by used different ways i.e., for the personal use/business use, fax use, internet BSNL is providing separate phone for the internet users already

having the landline phone. As the tariff has cut down now every one is coming forward to use for internet purpose.

5. To get a telephone 10 years back it is very difficulty. But due to entry of private telephone service providers (operators) now the customers are getting the telephone at any time i.e., now there is no waiting list in BSNL. BSNL is giving connections by providing a telephone by dialing a phone call telephone at your door steps.
6. Many of the respondents feel that they should not get more monthly bills to control the monthly bills the customer use going for prepaid mobile (or) life-time connection or sulab plan.
7. To over come the payment of surcharge customer can dial the toll free numbers and get the details and pay the bill in due date.
8. The toll free numbers are free to dial by the customers to any where in the country. But it is observed that toll free numbers can be dialed only through the land line phone, but it is not possible to dial through mobile phones. BSNL should make a provision to the customers that toll free numbers can be dialed from the cellular mobile phone also. (Ex: 198). More over the toll free number 1800 - XXXX numbers can be dialed only in the major cities and towns like Hyderabad.
9. To have the relationship with the customers and to solve the problems of the customers relating to the telecom services, customer redressal adalath / open house session is conducted once in 3 month at the district level and once in 6 months at the state level and the problems are solved in the telephone adalath on the same day.

   The company has to inform the customers well in advance the importance of telephone adalath / open house session, so that customer can attend in very large number. If the customers are unable to attend the session it should make possible to receive complaints through a phone or through email or through a post card. So that relevant action can be taken and the problem is solved.

10. To have the customer relation and for the convenience of the people the BSNL have made a provision of payment of telephone bills at prescribed post offices, telegraph offices, on-line billing service centers. But at the post office the telephone bills are collected only up to the due date i.e., pay by date and after wards they won't take the telephone bills at the post offices. It in inconvenient for the customer to go to the customer service centers and pay the bills (in rural areas). As the technology is developed and more over telephone bills are not paid at e-seva centers, make e-seva centers as one of the point of collection of telephone bills like that of payment of house tax, water tax, electricity bills, paid at e-seva centers.
11. To maintain the relationship the BSNL should provided customer service centers at every one km or in places where ever it is possible.
12. Shifting of phone should be done on the same day within the same SDCA/same exchange, 1-2 days to others SDCA's/other exchange and with in 2-3 days to the other districts with the same universal access number.
    Change of plan should be done on the same day of the request. Service provides should see whether there is any meter fault in the system and also customer should use dynamic locking system for unauthorized used by other persons so as not to exceed the telephone bill. After settling the due bills if any the refund of deposits should be done immediately. To maintain the relationship of the customer provide the telephone services immediately after the customer request.
13. To maintain the customer relationship and to retain the existing customer or out going customer the company is exempting the rentals for the disconnected periods for this purpose the company is conducting special drives, conducting road shows, giving advertisements for awareness among the customers. So that the out going customer or the defaults can be given change to restore

the connection and retain the customer. The company should reduce defaulters payers by motivate and encourage them to pay the bills in time.

14. Waiting time of the respondents is one to two minutes and the response time through interactive voice response system (IVRS) is one to two minutes. The registration of the complaints by the customer is taken in one day.
15. IVRS numbers provided by BSNL should work effectively with out any disturbance like1500, 1503, 1504 etc.
16. BSNL is sending SMS messages to its customers relating to its new products and services.

Conclusion

Every organisation that aims for building and maintaining a relation ship may have to develop an excellent total customer care programme to suit to the specific requirements of its target customers. The total customer care programme evolved by an organisation after incorporating the said guide lines would certainly attract customers towards building everlasting relationship with the organisation. The words of Mahatma Gandhi on the significance of customer are the most appropriate in this context. Under the present context competitive environment, the focus of the organisation is more on customer retention than simply on customer acquisition. Customer retention is the process of keeping customers in the customer inventory foe an unending period by meeting the needs and exceeding the expectations of those customers. It is the approach of converting a casual customer into a committed loyal customer. Hence , using the data mining and data ware house the companies has to send the latest inventions and information to the target customers and build the relation ship with the customers for the survival in the competitive market.

References

Anand Byram (2008), *"Customer Services in Telecommunications–A Comparative Study"*, Unpublished Ph.D Thesis, Kakatiya University, Warangal-A.P, India.

Bhavani Prasad G.V.Prof, Varalaxmi.P.Dr and Anand.B (2008), "*Customer Perceptions on CRM Practices by BSNL*" Prakalpa"-The journal of commerce & Management, Vol.1. No.1 pg. 11-35.

----(2008), "*Emerging Trends in Service Sector-With Reference to Telecom Industry*" Business Analyst -The journal of Management studies, Vol.2 Warangal, Andhra Pradesh, Vol 2. No.1. pg. 191-202.

----(2005) ,"*Emerging Trends in Service Sector-With Reference to Telecom Industry*" paper presented at All India commerce conference , Varanasi, India, 27th -29th December.

----(2007),"*Emerging Trends in Service Sector With Reference to Telecom Industry*" paper presented at All India commerce conference, Osmania University , Hyderabad, A.P, India, 28th -30th December.

----(2006) ,"*Customer Perceptions on CRM Practices by BSNL*" paper presented at National conference , CKM Arts & Science College , Warangal, A.P, 27th -28th , November.

----(2008), "*Foreign Direct Investment in Indian Telecommunication Industry*" paper presented at International conference , Vinayaka Business School, Vinayaka Mission University, Chennai, 7-8th , November.

Harsh V.Verma (2008), "*Services Marketing Text and Cases*" Pearson Education New Delhi.

Jha SM (2003), "*Services Marketing*" Himalaya Publishing House, Mumbai.

Paul Greenbery (2004), "*CRM* ",TMH Edition New Delhi.

Peeru Mohamed .H. and Sagadevan. A. (2009), "*Customer Relation ship Management - A Step by Step Approach*" Vikas Publishing House Pvt. Ltd. Noida, New Delhi.

Philip Kotler (2003), "*Marketing Management*" 11th Edition, Pearson Education, New Delhi.

Ramphal M.K. and. Gupta S.L. (2005), "*Services Marketing Concepts Application and Cases*" Golgotia Publishing House, New Delhi.

Shajahan(2007), "*Services Marketing Application and Cases*" Himalaya Publishing House, Mumbai.

Venkata Janardhan Rao. K. Dr, Varalaxmi.P. Dr and Anand. B. (2007), "*Infrastructure Development in India Vis –a- vis Emerging Dimensions in Indian Telecom Sector -A Study*" paper presented at National Conference , Vignana Jyothi Institute of Management, Hyderabad, A.P .20-21,Novenmber.

Venkata Janardhan Rao. K. Prof., Anand.B and Varalaxmi.P.Dr (2008), " *Emerging Dimensions in Indian Telecom Industry-A Study*" Satavahana Journal,Vol.1. No.1 pg. 01-21.

Vasanti Venu Gopal and Raghu V.N. (2002), "*Services Marketing*", Himalaya Publishing House, Mumbai.

Venkata ramana.V and Somayajulu. G. (2003), "*Customer Relationship Management*" Excel Books New Delhi.

Reference for Table Figures

Table Figures1. Theodore Levitt; The *Marketing Imagination*, Free Press, New York, p.116.

Table-2: Philip Kotler, Marketing Management, p.50

Table-3:Source: CRM H.Peeru Mohamed & Asagadevan

Website

www.bsnl.co.in ,products & services accessed on 12-12-2008.

www.ap.bsnl.co.in, product & services accessed on 12-12-2008

www.crm2day.com ,customer relation ship management, accessed on 02-04-2010

www.outsource2india.com, customer relation ship management accessed on 02-04-2010

14

Customer Services in the Life Insurance Industry in India

G. Karunanithi, S. Banumathy

Introduction

The purpose of business is to create new customers and retain old customers. Customer orientation is the ultimate key to success of any business. Customer Relationship Management (CRM) is an intelligent blend of marketing and information technology for serving the customer with greater care and value. Computerisation of records, maintenance of customer data base, online customer service will entrance the customer loyalty in addition to exploring new opportunities for cross selling/sell ups. Today, marketing managers realised the fact that instead of adding some more new customers, it is always profitable and easier to concentrate on the known market with old customers with new options, opportunities for business with implementation of CRM, business concerns do a better job at a better price to retain old customers.

Continuous changes in the economic scenario and intense global competition are causing business of today to undergo radical changes in the approach to business.

To win the hearts of the customers, companies should analyse the customer needs, introduce technological aspects in services, improve communication, set and attain service delivery standards, handle customer complaints and grievances, introduce new services and measure customer satisfaction. Delivering high quality service and achieving high customer satisfaction has been closely linked to profits, cost savings and market share. The customers are becoming more affluent, increasingly comfortable with technology, demanding new financial services and are willing to go anywhere to get the products and services they need.

Life Insurance Corporation of India

Life Insurance Corporation of India (LIC) is a pioneering institution which ensures absolute security to the prospective policy holders. The corporation helps to boost the industrial growth in the country, life insurance provides against premature death and fixed sum at the maturity of policy. The two elements of protection and investment exist in various degrees is different types of policies. LIC of India has built up an efficient interface between various departments and segments which would reduce the paper work, improve efficiency of service delivery and provide competitive advantage.

The process of globalization and liberalization has exerted its huge influence in the Insurance sector. Life Insurance Corporation, a service sector, customer service is not considered as a junction, but a way of life also. The success of LIC depends on how much it fulfills customer needs. Therefore, LIC should be customer oriented to meet challenges of today's competitive environment.

CRM Basics for Insurance

In order to successfully plan and execute a CRM strategy, Insurance organizations need to understand four CRM essentials.

The CRM Drivers–Why Insurance Companies Need CRM?

Several drivers make CRM a necessity for insurance organizations to operate in the digital economy. These drivers can be generalized into main categories.

Empowered Consumer: In the digital economy, consumers are being transformed by more available information, the adoption of new technologies, more choice, globalization and deregulation. This transformation is adding complexity to managing customer relationships for insurance organizations.

Increased Competition: Globalization, insurance organization consolidation, new entrants and deregulation in the financial services sector are creating new competitive threats to traditional insurers. On the deregulation front, non insurance financial services firms can enter the commodity insurance markets through partnerships with relatively low entry barriers. Because financial institutions can offer consumers a broader spectrum of financial services and products, most insurers are looking to adopt new business strategies to compete.

Internet and E-business: The Internet has brought about convenience, control and personalization. This technology has enabled new distribution channels to emerge and compete with traditional channels and helps organizations be more effective and efficient in their sales, marketing and service efforts and hence has a great impact on insurance.

Insurance companies need to give their products high visibility on websites where particular customer segments spend most of their time. By providing best possible customer experience at a variety of touch point, insurers can ensure success on the internet.

Organizing for CRM

Customer Centric

To successfully implement a CRM solution, insurers must move from a product mind-set toward a customer-focused mind-set. Customer experience will be the key differentiator for insurers wanting to retain profitable customers. Insurers need to deliver consistent, personalized products, services and image regardless of the channel. They will need to strengthen communications, training and collaboration with these channels–both traditional and emerging–to emphasize a service focus. Communication across lines of business and partners is essential. Companies need to establish customer-centric performance metrics and ownership of the customer.

CRM Technology Needs–Adopting New Technologies

Insurance providers can enhance the sales process by providing agents, brokers, partners and sales representatives with sales automation and workflow management tools. Service automation solutions help insurers manage and synchronize customer interactions across multiple channels, route interactions to appropriate universal agents, enforce quality assurance, provide workflow management, enhance interaction and enable customer self-help knowledge centers.

By web-enabling legacy insurance systems, insurers can support new e-business initiatives, as well as integrate them into other front office channels.

Alliances and Partnerships–Sustaining Competitive Advantage

To tackle increased competition in the insurance industry, insurers are seeking out potential alliances and partnerships in the market place with leading CRM strategists, CRM technologists, business process outsources and channel partners to sustain competitive advantage and spread the risks.

CRM in LIC of India

In a vast organization like LIC, catering to the various needs and aspirations of millions of policyholders, grievances of customers do arise occasionally. In order to redress these grievance LIC has established an elaborate Grievance Redressal Machinery , various committees and other boards for rendering services to the policyholders. The details are under

Grievance Redressal Machinery

Grievance Redressal Officers have been designated at all levels of the organization

At the Branch Level: The Sr/Branch Manager

At the Divisional Level: Manager, CRM

At the Zonal Level: The Regional Manager CRM

At the Central Level: The Executive Director CRM/Chief(CRM)

The respective Grievance Redressal Officers are available at their Offices for personal interviews with the customers on all Mondays between 2.30 p.m. to 4.30 p.m., except on holidays without prior appointment. Customers can meet the Grievance Redressal officers on other days also with prior appointment.

The names of the Grievance Redressal Officers are displayed in the respective Offices and are periodically published in the local newspapers.

Claims Review Committee

The Corporation settles a large number of death claims every year. Only in case of fraudulent suppression of material information is the liability repudiated. This is to ensure that claims are not paid to fraudulent persons of the cost of honest policyholders. The number of death claims repudiated is, however, very small. Even in these cases, an opportunity is given to the claimant to make a representation for consideration by the Review Committees of the Zonal office and the Central Office. As a result of review, depending on the merits of each case, appropriate decisions are taken. The Claims Review Committees of the Central and Zonal Offices have among their Members, a retired High Court/District Court Judge. This has helped providing transparency and confidence in our operations and has resulted in greater satisfaction among claimants, policyholders and public.

Policyholder Councils and Zonal Advisory Boards

In all the 109 Divisional Centres, Policyholders' Councils have been established. Three policyholders of the area represent the interest of the policyholders and interact with the Divisional Management on consumer concerns. Similarly, at all the seven Zonal Centres, Zonal Advisory Boards are functioning.

Consumer Affairs Committee

A Consumer Affairs Committee has been constituted at the Central Office with many eminent consumer activists and members of public joining as members along with the Chairman and the Managing Directors of the Corporation. This Committee looks into various areas of consumer interests and advises the Corporation.

Citizens' Charter

LIC has adopted a Citizen Charter through which it reiterates its commitments to the customers and the standards for general procedures, the standards for policy servicing, the standards for easy access to information for customers and the standards for fairness in dealing with the customers have been laid down.

Settlement of Claims

The settlement of claims is the most important aspect of service to the policyholders. Hence, the corporation has laid great emphasis on expeditious settlement of the maturity as well as death claims. During the year 2008-09, the corporation has settled 1.54 crores (15.4 million) claims for Rs.40085.12 crores (Rs.400.85 billion Including Micro Insurance and Pension & Group Schemes) compared to 1.44 crores (14.4 million) claims for Rs.38864.01 crores (Rs. 388.64 billion) in the previous year. The percentage of claims outstanding(remaining unpaid) at the end of the year to the claims payable during the year is 0.33% by number and 0.97% by amount as on 31st March, 2009 compared to 0.28% by number and 0.94% by amount as on 31st March, 2008. During 2008-09, 97% of Maturity claims were settled on or before the date of maturity.

Conclusion

Today, the customer relations with management have come under sharp focus at the customer's ends. The success and failure of any business depends upon how for they satisfy the expectation of their customers. In the competition era, insurance industry can obtain the victory only by satisfying the desires of the customers through CRM.

The insurance companies are utilizing the Information Technology applications for better customer service, cost reduction, new product design and development and many more. In a vast organization like LIC, catering to the various needs and aspirations of millions of policyholders, grievances of customers do arise occasionally. In order to redress these grievances LIC has established an elaborate Grievance Rederessal Machinery. The settlement of claims is the most important aspect of service to the policyholders. Customer premium can be paid through various Banks. Premium can be paid through Credit Card also availing this facility.

References

Badra, S.T., Marrying the Customer–C.R.M. Approach, Productivity, Vol. 42, April–June 2001, p. 42

Mohammed, P.E., Sagadevan, H. P., CRM - Step by Step Approach, p. 6

Shivpur, C.R., Customer Oriented Service, IBA Bulletin, March 2002.

LIC - Annual Report

www.licindia.com

15

Service Orientation as a Tool for CRM

A.S. Saranya, Geetha Sankar

Service orientation is defined as an organization- wide embracement of a basic set of relatively enduring organizational policies, practices and procedures intended to support and reward service giving behaviors that create and deliver service excellence. Mounting evidence suggests that an organization's service orientation is a defining factor in the creation of superior customer value. In fact, research indicates that important organizational outcomes such as profit, growth, customer satisfaction and loyalty result directly from organizational service orientation (OSO).

Previous research studies have explored service orientation (SO), under two dimensions. As a dimension of an organization's overall climate, service orientation has been described as the service events, practices and procedures within a work setting that expect and reward service excellence. Kelly(1992) , suggests that a climate for service is one in which a descriptive set of characteristics concerning service delivery and service quality differentiate an organization from others and result in service behavior of the individuals in the organization.

Additionally, service orientation has been studied as an individual personality variable, suggesting that service oriented individuals have a disposition to be helpful, thoughtful, considerate and co-operative. As such SO emerges from a set of attitudes within individual employees and is expressed in their behaviors. Since organizations can only be as effective as the people that comprise them, individual attitudes and behavior directly affect the nature and quality of service delivery and any interaction between an organization and its customers.

Thus, OSO is best understood and measured by soliciting employee's perceptions of the events, practices, and procedures as well as their perceptions of the behavior that are rewarded, supported and expected which constitute the climate of the work setting in an organization (Schneider, Wheeler and Cox, 1992). In other words, service orientation (SO) of an organization is what the employees perceive it to be.

Empirical findings suggest that when employees perceive their organization as having a strong service orientation, customers report more positive service experiences (Schneider and Bowen, 1993). Thus OSO includes an understanding of the very nature of services. First, to be of service literally means to attend to someone's needs. Second, service is always rendered ultimately to people and / or their property either (1) directly via person to person service encounters(education surgery etc), (2) directly via person to property service encounters(car repair etc) ,(3) indirectly via high-tech service devices(ATM, internet etc) , or (4) some combination of these. Third, from an organization's standpoint , service can only be rendered if organizational servants exist at appropriate points in the service creation and delivery chain and are capable of attending to customer needs(Berry, Parasuraman and Zeithmal, 1994,).Thus, SO organizations engage in service giving practices that reflect the belief that service excellence is a strategic priority that impacts the creation of superior value, customer satisfaction, competitive advantage, growth and profitability. Against this background the researchers have attempted to study the service orientation of employees in the food service industry, by considering a sample of 84 respondents in the managerial and supervisory cadre belonging to various restaurants in the city of Chennai.

The food service industry is currently under great pressure to meet the fast changing needs of customers and the market as its operational environment has undergone enormous changes in the recent past, especially due to rising consumerism.

All of these changes send an important signal to the food industry as a whole, of the necessity to explore ways in which it can improve customer-driven competitiveness. One of the ways to achieve such a goal is, to create market-oriented organizations managed by service-oriented employees.

Do people go out to "eat" or to "dine?" The answer may depend on a number of factors including, but not limited to goals of the customer and type of restaurant chosen (fast food, family style, fast dining, etc.). Nevertheless, the success of restaurant managers/owners depends on their understanding of their customers' needs, expectations, and meeting these needs better than their competitors.

A standardized questionnaire on service orientation (serv*or) developed by Richard. S. Lytle, Peter. W. Hom and Michael. P. Mokwa (1998) has been adapted to measure employee perceptions of service.

The main objectives of the study are,

- To analyze the various dimensions of service orientation with respect to employees of the food service industry in the city of Chennai.
- To examine service orientation as ' a dimension of an organization's overall climate' and also as 'a dimension of being an individual personality variable' with respect to employees of the food service industry in the city of Chennai.

Lytle et al (1998) classified the integral ingredients of SO required to create and produce service excellence into four dimensions are depicted in Fig. 1 below.

Figure 1
Serv* or Dimensions

Service Leadership Practices	*Service Encounter Practices*
1. Servant leadership	1. Customer treatment
2. Service vision	2. Employee empowerment
Human Resource Management Practices	***Service systems practices***
1. Service training	1. Service failure prevention
2. Service rewards	2. Service failure recovery
	3. Service technology
	4. Service stds communication

Service Leadership

Leadership is the critical and integral ingredient necessary for creating and maintaining an effective and positive service orientation (Heskett, Sasser and Schlesinger, 1997). 'Servant leadership' and 'service vision' are the two fundamental elements within the service orientation model.

Service Leadership- Servant leaders set service standards by their own behavior and management styles. They lead by doing. They are actively engaged in helping, assisting and meeting the needs of employees through example rather than by simply dictating service policy for the organization. If employees receive excellent service from their own managers, they are more likely to provide excellent service to customers (Heskett, Sasser and Hart, 1990; Hallowell, Schlesinger and Zornitsky, 1996; Church, 1995).

*Service Visioni–*Service leaders who consistently communicate a service vision for the organization reinforce the importance of service quality and customer satisfaction in creating superior value for the organization. Service vision underscores important elements of service that must be provided and communicated in terms of results to be produced for customers.

Service Encounter

Service encounters are employee's interactions with customers which are important because often brief encounters with customers form the basis of important service quality evaluations. The two important dimensions within the service orientation (SO) model are "customer treatment" and "employee empowerment".

Customer Treatment- How customers are treated directly impacts their perception of service performance. Highly satisfied customers are believed to display sustained loyalty, lower price sensitivity, persuade new customers to switch from competitors, facilitate lowering of future transaction costs, and contribute to enhancement of a firm's reputation. Thus positive customer perceptions of service quality assures a firm of stable future cash flows yielding higher than average profits.

Employee Empowerment-Empowerment refers to a situation in which the manager gives employees the discretion to make day-to-day decisions about job related activities. This responsiveness is significantly and positively correlated with customer's perceptions of service quality and satisfaction. Advocates of empowerment claim that employees will be more responsive as service providers, have higher levels of productivity, deal with customer complaints more quickly, be better motivated and provide higher levels of service quality.

Service Systems

Systems, not smiles, deliver continuous and reliable service quality. (Sewell and Brown, 1992).When firms continue to make re-occurring and regular mistakes in delivery and when they do not keep promises, customers lose confidence in the firms ability to do what is promised dependably and accurately. Sincere apologies and friendly staff members do not compensate for unreliable service (Berry, Parasuraman, Zeithmal, 1994). Thus, an OSO requires service systems that include service failure prevention and recovery practices, service standards communication practices and high levels of service technology adaptation.

Service Failure Prevention and Recovery-If an organization fails to prevent and/or resolve customer problems, they have in fact disappointed the customer twice: once for initial failure and twice for failing to correct what had gone wrong in the first place. When immediate and planned responsiveness to service failure occurs, organizations are able to retain up to 95% of their dissatisfied customers (Albrecht and Zemke, 1985).

Service Technology-The utilization of "cutting-edge" technology is critical to creating a service system for the delivery of outstanding service quality. For e.g., customers desire for low prices are most of the times met by sophisticated purchasing and inventory control systems.

Service Standards Communication-Conformance to a set of standards is more likely to be met if those standards are understood by every employee in the organization. This in turn maximizes internal benchmark achievement and minimizes service failures. They also strengthen the firm's ability to recover from such failures.

Human Resource Management

Most research purports that an organizations ability to produce external service quality is directly related to issues of internal service quality. These issues are studied in terms of employee attitudes, personalities, beliefs and behaviors. Therefore a model of service orientation includes measures of service training and service rewards practices.

Service Training- Factors such as rendering service with a smile, thanking a customer and being courteous are examples of basic contact skills which influence customer satisfaction. Cutting-edge service providers are allocating substantial resources to improve service employee skills. Through advanced quality based team training, problem solving training, interpersonal skills training and other advanced training, employees are being trained and empowered to deliver excellent service to customers. Schlesinger and Heskett (1991) suggest that leading service organizations value investment in people and specifically invest in service skills training so that ability of the employees to meet the complex service demands of customers may be enhanced.

Service Rewards-service related employee behavior is set to result from conspicuous and specific compensation reward practices and programs. Recent research reveals that employee rewards, recognition and compensation are significantly and strongly related to passion for service and levels of customer satisfaction.

Table 1 given below depicts the weighted average mean of the above mentioned SO dimensions and sub-dimensions along with their ranks.

Table 1
Service Orientation Dimensions

Service Orientation Dimensions	*Wt mean of sub-dimensions*	*Rank*	*Wt mean of dimensions*
Service leadership			
Servant leadership	4.113	6	
Service vision	3.762	8	
Total			3.937
Service encounter			
Customer treatment	4.143	5	
Employee empowerment	4.286	2	
Total			4.191
Human resource management			
Service training	4.179	4	
Service rewards	3.452	9	
Total			3.936
Service systems			
Service failure prevention	4.405	1	
Service failure recovery	3.369	10	
Service technology	4.214	3	
Service standards communication	4.060	7	
Total			4.012

The above table clearly depicts that all the sub-dimensions have scored more than the average mean score of 2.5 indicating exceptional service orientation of employees in the present day competitive food service industry. The highest weighted average mean of 4.405 is for ' Service failure prevention ' and the lowest of 3.369 is for ' Service failure recovery' indicating that especially in the food service industry the most important attribute is service failure prevention, since a dissatisfied customer is likely to tell an average of 9 to 10 people about the bad experience he had undergone. Thus, through word of mouth publicity, happy customers will inform others that they are happy and unhappy customers may inform others that the service is not good. The urgency with which an organization views service failure is related to the future value of the customer and the organization's future health and vitality.

Employee empowerment has scored the second highest rank with weighed mean of 4.286, indicating that a successful service-oriented firm has to assign its highest priority to satisfaction of customer's needs through prompt redressal of their complaints by empowered customer contact employees. The more service- oriented the advanced economies become, the more decentralized decision making authority should be spread. The key is thus through employee empowerment, since speed of resolution of service complaints is critical for front line employees.

Today many customer expectations can only hope to be met, much less exceeded, with the assistance of sophisticated and integrated technologies as reflected in the above table with 'service technology' in the third position.

Human resource professionals have long recognized the importance of HR skills in front line employees through enhancement of service orientation training programs (fourth rank) which have been found to be more effective among those employees who already have a strong individual service orientation. Also it is learned from previous studies that the service orientation of an organization is dictated by how its CEO perceives service and therefore acts, which is the basis of the organization's service training programs. .

Enlightened companies realize that nothing can be gained by ignoring customers and their complaints. They realize that retaining customers is very important because of the life time value of their customers and render royal treatment to customers (fifth rank).

'Servant leadership' and 'Service vision' are found to be the fundamental relationship elements necessary to install widespread aspirations which become the driving force that enables organizations to deliver quality service in the market place.

Service standards (seventh rank) or bench marks must be understood by all employees since they are important antecedents to customer satisfaction. Similarly service rewards (ninth rank) is the link between employee behavior and service performance.

On the whole, the most important dimension is 'Service encounter' followed by 'Service systems', 'Service leadership' and 'Human resource management' as depicted in the above table.

To examine service orientation as a 'dimension of an organization's overall climate' and also as a 'dimension of being an individual personality variable', a null hypothesis has been framed as stated below.

Null Hypothesis: The sample means of 'service orientation as a dimension of an organization's overall climate' and 'service orientation being an individual personality variable' do not differ significantly.

Table 2 below depicts the 19 serv*or statements which have been classified under the two dimensions as specified above and T- test has been applied to study the association between them, the results of which are shown below.

The mean score of 'SO as a dimension of being an individual personality variable' (4.030) is more than that of 'SO as a dimension of organizational climate' (3.983) indicating the criticality of excellent behavior of front-line service staff for an organization's health, vitality and competitiveness. The calculated 't' value is 1.0323 and table value is 2.898 (1% level of significance). Since calculated t value is less than the table value, the null hypothesis has been accepted, indicating that both the above mentioned dimensions are closely associated.

In serious marketing, the behavior of employees plays a central role with regard to a customer's perception of satisfaction and service quality (Bowen & Schneider, 1985). This is especially true for boundary-spanning personnel, i.e., employees who interact personally with the customer as part of the service encounter. As a consequence, the customer orientation of service employees can be expected to strongly influence a service firm's business performance via the development of lasting customer-employee relationship.

Table 2
't' Value of Service Orientation Dimensions

Service Orientation Dimensions	*Wt. Mean*	*'t'value*
SO as a dimension of organizational climate	3.983	
We have freedom & authority to act independently to make important decisions in order to provide excellent service.		
We have customer complaint handling system for service follow-up.		
Service performance measures are communicated openly with all employees regardless of position or function.		
We understand all the service standards that have been followed by all departments.		
Management constantly communicates the importance of service.		
Management regularly spends time with customers and front-line service staff.		
Managers give personal input and leadership into creating quality service.		
Management is constantly measuring service quality.		
Management provides incentives and rewards for service quality & not just productivity.		
Service staff receive personal skills training that enhance ability to deliver high quality service.		
Service staff receive simulated training activities that help to provide higher levels of service.		1.0323
SO as a dimension of being an individual personality variable	4.030	
We care for customer as they would like to be cared for.		
We go out of way to reduce inconvenience to customers.		
We go out of way to prevent customer problems.		
We actively listen to customers.		
We do follow-up service calls to confirm proper delivery of services.		
We believe that organization exists to serve needs of customers.		
Customers are viewed as opportunities to serve rather than as sources of revenue.		
We improve service through the use of latest technology		

Employees can basically be divided into back-office employees and front-office employees (i.e., boundary-spanning personnel, or customer-contact employees, (Hartline & Ferrell, 1996). The former group has an indirect impact on customer's quality perceptions while the latter have a direct, non-mediated impact. Thus the behavior of service employees with inherent service orientation attitude and their behavior as a result of the organizations service climate are often stressed as being crucial for customer satisfaction and a high service quality.

Suggestions

- A *wireless reporting system* among branches helps in immediate sharing of crucial information thereby facilitating prompt *service failure recovery*. The urgency with which an organization views service failure and its recovery is related to the future value of the customer & the organisation's future health & vitality. A wireless reporting system also facilitates internal matching of demand & supply of raw materials, finished product and employees in times of emergencies.
- *Immediate rewards* to be announced every month for exemplary service oriented performance by the employees will motivate them to work harder towards reinforcement of their service oriented behavior. 'Awards/display boards of appreciation' of excellent performers for the month to be displayed in prominent places in each branch. According to George & Gronroos (1991), internal marketing ie. satisfaction of employees is the best means to motivate their service oriented behavior leading to customer satisfaction & loyalty.
- There should be *matching of "service vision and / or service standards communication" with " service delivery"*. Service vision should become an organizational manisfesto, ie., a clear pronouncement of service goals & objectives of the organization communicated in terms of results to be produced for customers.
- *Recruitment of only professionally qualified people as service leaders* should be strictly adhered to since they demonstrate

a higher passion for service excellence thereby inspiring , motivating, and enabling employees to achieve service excellence.

- Organisations must consistently engage in practices/ *training sessions enacting the 'golden rule as regards customer treatment'* during service encounters to create positive customer perceptions of service performance.

Conclusion

Dimensions of service orientation helps to set and monitor levels of benchmark performance for any organization to guide progress towards specific service goals. Managerial and employee rewards can be based on levels of SO existing within the organization. Moreover, trained and developed human resources can be deployed specifically where service problem areas exists. Thus an organization may be able to improve its service climate. Changing the service climate of an organization results from changing what organisational members believe and what they believe their organization values. Communication of new service values and beliefs, requires changing of everyday service practices and procedures thereby imparting new beliefs and values to guide employee activities. This in particular, is important because recent research indicates that employee perception of service practices are linked to customer satisfaction (Johnson, 1996).

References

Berry, Leonard L., A. Parasuraman and Valerie. A. Zeithmal (1994), "Improving Service Quality in America: Lessons Learned", Academy of Management Executives, 8 (2): 32-52.

Bowen, D.E., C. Siehl, and Benjamin Schneider, (1989), "A Framework for Analyzing Customer Service Organizations in Manufacturing," Academy of Management Review, 14th Jan; 75-95.

Hartline, Michael D. and O.C. Ferrell (1996), "The Management of Customer-Contact Service Employees: An Empirical Investigation," *The Journal of Marketing*, 60 (October):52-70.

Heskett,J.,Sasser,E. and Schlesinger, L. (1997), "The service Profit Chain: How Leading Companies Link Profit and Growth to Loyalty, Satisfaction and Value", New York: The Free Press.

Hogan, J., R.Hogan, and C.M. Busch (1984), "How to Measure Service Orientation," *Journal of Applied Psychology*, 69 (1): 167-173.

Johnson, J. (1996), "Linking Employee Perceptions of Service Climate to Customer Satisfaction", Personnel Psychology, 49 (4), pp. 831-51.

Kelly, Scott W. (1992), "Developing Customer Orientation Among Service Employees." Journal of the Academy of Marketing Science, 20 (1): 27-36.

Lytle, R.S., Hom, P.W. and Mokwa, M.P. (1998), "Serv*or: A Managerial Measure of Organizational Service Orientation, Journal of Retaining, 74 (4), pp. 455-89.

16

Customer Relationship Management and Hospital Services

T.J. Arun, J. Ashok

CRM defined and Questioned

Customer Relationship Management (CRM) is defined to be a "comprehensive strategy and process of acquiring, retaining and partnering with selective customers to create superior value for the company and the customer". The definition implies that creating superior value for the company and the customer starts from the point of acquiring and retaining the customer. However given the fact that the superior quality and value product creation and delivery" is a combination of quality inputs and quality processes, any CRM effort should logically begin from the supplier of inputs for the product, move on to operations and production personnel, then to the distributors and finally end with the customer. Any CRM effort solely directed at the customer, ignoring the other members in the value creation process will be falling into a trap of shortsightedness. Successful CRM programs extend beyond the acquisition, retention and partnering with selective customers; it should be a sustained effort at acquiring, retaining and partnering with selective suppliers, manufacturing personnel and also the distribution network. Unless the suppliers give qualitative inputs at the right time and place, no matter what CRM program is implemented, it will be a failure. Similarly, unless the production and operations personnel work in close coordination with the CRM implementers, no CRM program can be a success. Hence, CRM efforts should be a combination of Supplier Relationship Management (SRM) efforts plus Process Relationship Management (PRM) efforts.

Hospital Services and CRM

The current state of CRM programs and implementation in the service sector in Indian is very rudimentary. In fact "customer - focus" is very limited. With respect to Hospital service providers, CRM seldom goes beyond a one-sheet patient feedback form. It is again doubtful whether any of the feedback will be incorporated for rectifying current practices, thereby enhancing patient loyalty. Usually, such hospitals have a marketing wing, which is responsible for closely monitoring the feedback. However, the analysis subsequently carried out by them and the remedial measures implemented are not a stream lined effort or worst still are non-existent. They are also in the nature of "hospital acceptable" measures of patient satisfaction and no "patient driven" measures of satisfaction. The remedial measures are more in the nature of "damage control". They neither seek to delve into reasons for dissatisfaction nor origins of dissatisfaction.

There is a need to focus on additional ways of maximizing patient satisfaction with the care received: staff training, in how to maintain good customer relation; changes in organization and scheduling to minimize patient discomfort and waiting times; adoption of architectural and design styles that provide warm and appealing as well as functional environments; market research and so on. There is need to further appreciate that the above activities represent only one side of the coin. The providers need to go outside their walls to cultivate those who act as the distributors of health care.

In health-care provision, someone other than the end user (patient or client) typically decides which provider will supply needed health care services. A large percentage of hospital volume is tied to physician and corporate employers. Under such circumstances, there are special requirements for successfully developing enduring relationships with those who distribute health care services-the physicians and employers.

In today's environment customer cannot be taken for granted. There is an increasing trend towards corporatisation and privatization of hospital services. Gone will be the days when the loss of a patient can be shrugged of. More and more people have incomes and the desire for quality services. The smartest of hospital service providers need to spend time and resources looking closely at the reasons for patient loss and take steps to eliminate them. They must make sure that they understand the reasons why patients may take their business elsewhere. This could be due to quite a few reasons such as:

- Lack of proper procedures
- Unsatisfactory service
- Uncompetitive price charged for the service

The best way of retaining customers is to deliver a level of high customer (Patient) satisfaction through price, people, processes, physical evidence, place and promotion (product, yet another 'p' of the marketing mix is not mentioned because, in a constituent of all the other P's). This will result in strong loyalty and ultimately will show up on the bottom line as positive customer feedback and increased revenue; and the starting point is the development and implementation of an efficient CRM program, which is inclusive of SRM program and PRM program.

Customer Expectations from Hospital Services

In order to better understand how building relationships with suppliers and operations personnel within the hospital services would result in better CRM, it would be useful to list some of the expectations that the customers (patients) have from hospital service providers and also to list, the suppliers, who ultimately are responsible for fulfilling these expectations. Listed below are some of the typical expectations that patients would have:

Patient (customer) Expectations from a Hospital

- Proximity, central location
- Clean environment
- Adequate space to move about
- Comfortable lobby seating
- Adequate space in patient rooms
- Attached toilets in the patient rooms with a geyser facility
- Pure filtered water availability
- Timings to suit their requirements
- Diagnostic services, pharmacy and dietary services within the compound of the hospital
- Lift services
- Laundry services

Patient Expectations from Hospital Personnel

Some of the visible hospital personnel include doctors, nurses, attendants, reception personnel, billing personnel, ambulance personnel, and diagnostic report division personnel. These are the people with whom the customer has an immediate bearing.

From Doctors

- To be an expert in the field
- To be gentle, a querier, a confidence booster and wordy
- To be one how can explain the problem in common terminology and put the patient at ease
- To be tidy and smart
- To be able to justify the need for running umpteen diagnostic tests

From Nurses

- To be gentle, cheerful, helpful and friendly
- To be tidy
- To be able to answer simple queries pertaining to the disease

- To appreciate the need for privacy by the patient

From Attendants

- To be tidy
- To be cheerful

From Reception Personnel

- To be able to guide patients to respective divisions
- To be well groomed and courteous
- To be able to handle rush hour situations

Billing and Registration Personnel

- To be able to give a user friendly bill
- To enter registration details correctly
- To have technology and procedures which are customer focused

Patient Expectations, Expectation Fulfillers (suppliers) and Supplier Relationship

Tangibles (suppliers) that patient seeks in hospitals	*Suppliers of those tangibles*
Pure drinking water	Mineral water suppliers
Comfortable medical furniture	Furniture manufacturers
Geysers	Electric equipment manufacturers
Cleaning agents	Detergent manufacturers
Accurate diagnostic equipment	Diagnostic equipment providers
Good canteen food	Caterers
Wide range of drugs	Pharmacists
Clean linen	Laundry personnel
Specialized and expert doctors	Medical colleges
Cheerful and dedicated nurses	Nursing training institutes
Pleasant reception personnel	Management training institutes
Tidy attendants	HRD of the hospital

As already mentioned earlier, patients have expectations of hospitals and hospital personnel performance. If the performance of the two is to be in accordance with the expectations of the patients, it is obvious that the suppliers of those services be the best in the field. It is also essential that hospital service providers' develop a strong and positive relationship with the suppliers of these inputs even if they have to pay a premium for it. It is therefore essential that any CRM effort should first ensure a proper SRM followed by a PRM. This will automatically result in customer loyalty and retention.

Conclusion

Relationship is a natural prospect to any interaction. Hospital has to carefully allocate its energy towards patients and give them appropriate treatment so that they can be satisfied with the hospital. Any Customer Relationship Management effort should be a combination of Supplier Relationship Management and Process Relationship Management efforts. It is necessary that CRM developers and Implementers develop CRM programs and packages for customers only after they have developed close links and coordination with Supplier Relationship Managers. It is only such an integrated approach that will yield superior value for the hospital and the patient. From patients' viewpoint, they want to be actively listened to and their needs are to be fulfilled effectively at minimum cost, time and other resources from their end. So, it is very essential for the hospitals to maintain customer relationship management effectively.

References

Bergeron Bryan (2002), Essentials of CRM, Wiley Publishing .

David A. (2001), Client Relationship Management, Human Resource Press.

John Hallick (2010), "CRM Saves Lives", Destination CRM.Com, January.

John K. Higgins (2009), "RX for Hospitals: A Big Dose of CRM", CRM Buyer, November.

Lauren Mackay (2008), "Why Customers are Sick of Healthcare", Destination CRM.Com, December.

Madavilatha K. (2004), Analytical CRM- ICFAI Press, January.

Marshall Lager (2007), "Market Focus: Health care: The Great Divide", Destination CRM.Com, July.

Michalis Georgakas (2009), "CRM Model for Greek Public Hospital", 7th ICICTH Samos, National and Kapodistrian University of Athens.

Websites

www.iiml.ac.in

www.crmguru.com

www.bus.emory.edu

www.CRMCommunity.com

17

The New Management Tool: Customer Relationship Management

Chirag V. Raval

Introduction

In the implementation of CRM, management plays a vital role. It cannot be implemented without their cooperation. This is because CRM includes changes long term aspects and the revision of long tem goals. These organizational objectives need extra scrutiny. It is insufficient if employees involved in the CRM process alone pay due attention to it. Management needs to have a clear cut idea of CRM goals before it actually implements it. It is important to note that short term achievements should not be regarded by management as indicative of long term gains. These changes can have varied impacts and it is but Managements responsibility to carefully weigh the pros and cons of such steps before its actual implementation.

Why Choose CRM?

CRM (Customer Relationship Management) aids in increasing efficiency, serves to aid the sales department in all of its efforts, manages to boost sales, and fundamentally contributes to the overall development of the company. It also manages to work towards organizational goals. This is achieved through a concise study of potential customers.

Their preferences are taken into consideration and used to coordinate and implement a customer centric business strategy that focuses primarily on the customer, yields to recording the importance of his ideas and suggestions and results in increased customer retention.

CRM facilitates growth in that it aids the reduction of costs and the increased availability of information to the organization-that can be used according to customer information requirements. This information is increasingly important to an organization and can prove to make the difference between success and failure.

CRM is Rewarding

The benefits of CRM are enormous. The marketing department is yet another department that stands to gain enormously as CRM aids in marketing functions. The customer centered strategy that provides information on potential customers, boosts the marketing function by providing the marketing department with a clear idea of what the customer needs are and enables them to work accordingly.

Why CRM is Crucial to Your Organization?

CRM is a business process that enables the organization to adopt a methodical manner of dealing with customers and their relationships on a bigger scale.

CRM Boosts Overall Development

CRM on account of its acute involvement in marketing, sales and service manages to sustain and increase customer retention.

Why use CRM? This undying philosophy has proven to be beneficial in overall cost reduction, better management strategies and enhancement of sales. Mass marketing is made possible on account of the increased focus placed on marketing functions.

Customer relationship management tools enable an organization to work in a competitive environment and manage to supersede competitor efforts with its customer centric approach. It carefully studies customer attitudes and ingrains customized approaches in the business activities.

From Strategy to Results- CRM Vital

The primary step in CRM implementation involves a sound business philosophy with customer satisfaction and learning at the focal point. After this comes the actual implementation itself whereby technological processes are used to convert this philosophy into results. CRM is the bed for this launch. It enables this act and facilitates a better understanding between the customer and the organization.

It manages to cultivate a one on one relationship with its end users. Strengthening a relationship with long standing customers is more than beneficial because almost 80% of profits are actually generated from loyal customers. CRM ensures that the organization pays adequate attention to customer ideas. It instills the idea that these end users- customers are highly essential to success and focuses on the organizations need to study their behavioral patterns.

Why use CRM? CRM basics studies customer responses and use it to identify the market trends and then use this information to advocate marketing plans. CRM with its use of software analyzes and assimilates customer data so as to study purchasing patterns. This clearly indicates to the organization what means of communication to the customer is most effective. Irrespective of what is used CRM does reward.

CRM Facilitates Customer Loyalty

Since CRM constantly serves to keep a tag on what a customer is buying, these opportunities can be utilized to encourage sales leads. Slipping in at the time of purchase with an offer of discount on another purchase induces him to purchase further. CRM is basically a highly developed marketing strategy that uses the organizations resources by delivering personal messages to a target audience.

This target audience is generally the most profitable customers.

CRM also serves to measure the effectiveness of marketing campaigns. Customer relationships are the back bone of an organization and are essential to almost all departments. CRM manages to turn an organization image into one of warmth and portrays a customer friendly attitude to its users. CRM enables organizations to deal out better customer care, one that is more personalized. Customer relationship management seeks to encourage better marketing effectiveness and helps in identifying potential customers.

CRM's impact on the world has been phenomenal. Customer service sectors are proof of this growth. As companies opt for CRM strategies, the ones who haven't will lose the competitive edge. Why use CRM? CRM tends to get hold of peoples potential and uses this to make the customer service experience of its customers much better. Statistics state that CRM is implemented in almost 30 % of American companies. The estimated amount that is likely to be poured into the CRM industry is $90 million. With such staggering statistics it is but right for those who haven't opted for it to do so.

Steps for Involvement in CRM Implementation

Endeavoring to make sure that appropriate vendor selection takes place should also be one of Management's efforts. Placing the right person in control of the entire CRM process or placing a separate department to deal with the CRM efforts right upto the results is mandatory and of supreme importance to managerial functions.

- Customer contact is also essential for top management. Knowing the ins and outs of the customer process as well as maintaining personal contact is essential. In some areas this may not be possible to achieve. In this instant Management can opt to study the customer data made available to them through the CRM software and use it to identify customer preferences and act accordingly.

- For CRM, Management should also provide sufficient motivation to employees before focusing on a customer oriented strategy. Sufficient time gap should be allotted for the required ROI as well as the expected affect on customer retention.
- Ensuring that the employees dealing with the CRM process have sufficient knowledge about it and identifying areas of training and making sure that these areas are covered with adequate training methods is the work of Management. CRM managing software can also be beneficial to Management seeking to help employees engaged in the CRM process.
- It is essential that managers find out what the main issues of concern are where customers are concerned, pay adequate attention to the collation of customer data and study that data in an effort to find out more about the customer.
- CRM managing software gives adequate support to people involved in the CRM process. Establishing the right authority and responsibility to carry out the CRM process, ensuring that they have adequate resources at their disposal and making sure a separate CRM budget is implemented is mandatory. It is imperative that top Management get directly involved in the CRM process.
- Periodical monitoring of achievements, failures, cost adherence etc is essential as managerial functions to ensure CRM success. It is vital to management functions as it ensures that the CRM process is going as planned. Any deviation should be immediately identified and corrected.
- An established CRM grievance cell should be administered with the option of bringing in outside resources if required and CRM fails. This should be made ample use of for the identification of any CRM problems and the offering of solutions for CRM problems.

It is the responsibility of management to identify organization objectives, communicate these objectives to the necessary employees, employ CRM managing software and basically serve to ensure that employees dealing with the CRM implementation are adequately educated.

The Secrets Out- CRM is the Best Customer Strategy to Implement

The basics of CRM include a business strategy that focuses on developing and retaining the relationships existing between customer and organization. The general perception is that CRM is but a hype and the chance of CRM failure is high. Despite this, experts have speculated that billions of dollars are going to be poured into the CRM industry making it one of the fastest growing sectors in the market.

CRM Basics

CRM systems basics focus on the idea that customers hold the key to success and this is easily evident from their phenomenal impact on sales, marketing, and market trends .While choosing a solution it is important to scrutinize each vendor and make sure that the chosen solution contributes to organization goals.

Technology Vs. Customer Strategy

Merely focusing on the implementation of varied technology would not suffice. It is evident that personal contact, employee knowledge of customers, establishing an excellent rapport with the customer himself all contributes to the success of the organization. With the installation and use of technology alone customer pitfalls cannot be overcome.

CRM Rewards

CRM also provides the customer with a much needed avenue to vent his problems, ideas and suggestions. Hundreds of sales leads are lost yearly as disinterested employees pay slack attention to customer suggestions. A venue is required for these suggestions. This is supplied by CRM implementation.

What CRM Offers

CRM has a lot to offer most industries but it is the mode in which it is actually implemented that holds the key to actual CRM success. It is the common misconception that technology comes before customer strategies but in reality it is the other way around. Customer strategies are the keystone to business activities and technology is the latter half. There can be such a thing as CRM collapse if the organization fails to do what it needs to in order to ensure success and use adequate management and other resources required .

The basics of CRM require a comprehensive study of the customer, collation of his data and provision of this data to the organization. It is imperative that organization employees gain access to this data especially those that are engaged in direct dealings with the customer himself. This collated data proves rewarding in that it is an insight into the customer and thereby provides the person / persons using it to find solutions to customer problems.

What Makes CRM Withstand the Ravages of Time Despite the Fact that Erp has Failed?

CRM services include a concentrated focus on the customer, adhering to his likes and dislikes, endeavoring to create and sustain a relationship with him-all this serves to increase CRM s salability and to boost its status to that of one of the most rewarding customer centric strategies of the decade.

Why CRM is Your Organizations Biggest Asset

Why CRM? When we look around us we see that the hand of business touches us in every walk of life. We're faced with products and services at every single turn. How many of those products and service providers actually know the person who uses them?

Major corporations fail to realize that it is the customer who is their biggest ally.

Their employees prefer to treat them at times with indifference, at times with arrogance and sometimes even with anger. The customer is in reality the king, the one who makes the difference between a company's success and failure and yet from the corporate giant to the small entrepreneur struggling to keep his business alive, they are all prone to making the same mistake at some point of time.

What is this grave mistake, so often overlooked yet so profound in its impact, making the difference between the success and failure of million dollar enterprises? The answer lies in a companies "attitude" towards its customers. This approach is by far the most vital in any organization.

Know Your Biggest Asset

Several million dollars are lost yearly as corporations scramble to make profits, beat competitors, and stay ahead in the rat race. Huge amounts of money are spent on marketing, endeavoring to gain customers, often in vain. What is it that the "lucky few" or shall we say "successful few" organ inactions have, that actually give them that edge over the others? Why is it that organizations very often find their best customers drawn to competitors?

Most organizations have an extremely faulty customer centered system being adopted. They are not open to customer suggestions and more often than not they do not provide the customer with a proper avenue to vent his ideas. This often leads to unhappy customers and eventually their loss.

Conclusion

We conclude by saying that CRM is best tool of to build a powerful customer experience as the most competitive weapon around our businesses. CRM invert the pyramid for achieving success in businesses in the 21st century and CRM as the prime focal weapon to win over your customer and competition.

If you want to drive the competition crazy, ignore your competitors and concentrate on your customer's one on one.

References

Philip Kotler, Marketing Management, Pearson Education, Eleventh Edition.

B.S.Bose, Marketing Management, Himalaya Publishing House, First Edition, New Delhi.

Synergy Journal

Articles on CRM and beyond by Manoj Malhotra

www.google.com

18

Customer Relationship Management in Organisations

P. Abirami

Introduction

Customer relationship management is a broadly recognized, widely-implemented strategy for managing and nurturing a company's interactions with customers and sales prospects. Customer Relationship Management (CRM) is developing into a major element of corporate strategy for many organisations. CRM, also known by other terms such as relationship marketing and customer management, is concerned with the creation, development and enhancement of individualised customer relationships with carefully targeted customers and customer groups resulting in maximizing their total customer life-time value. It involves using technology to organize, automate, and synchronize business processes—principally sales related activities, but also those for marketing, customer service, and technical support. The overall goals are to find, attract, and win new customers, nurture and retain those the company already has, entire former customers back into the fold, and reduce the costs of marketing and customer service. Customer Relationship Management, is an essential part of modern business management. Customer Relationship

Management concerns the relationship between the organization and its customers. Customers are the lifeblood of any organization, be it a global corporation with thousands of employees and a multi-billion turnover, or a sole trader with a handful of regular customers. Customer Relationship Management is the same in principle for these two examples - it is the scope of CRM which can vary drastically.

Company Goals

Corporate goals are generally spelled out as sales, market share, profit and return on investment. Each of these goals has a different implication marketing strategy. For example: If the company's priority is sales maximization then the strategy revolves around aggressive selling. It is presumed that the route to customer acquisition and retention is aggressive salesmanship, low prices, attractive payment terms, advertising and sales promotion. The value drivers, as perceived by the company, are low price, incentives to customers and salesmen. But if the corporate priority is market share,then the strategy is that of competitive differentiation. Here the company allocates its resources to create this edge on an on going basis in R&D ,competitive advertising, pricing, distribution models and after sales service. In order to remain a leader or retain its position in the market place has to continuously differentiate its offer. The customer is believed to value this differentiation and is

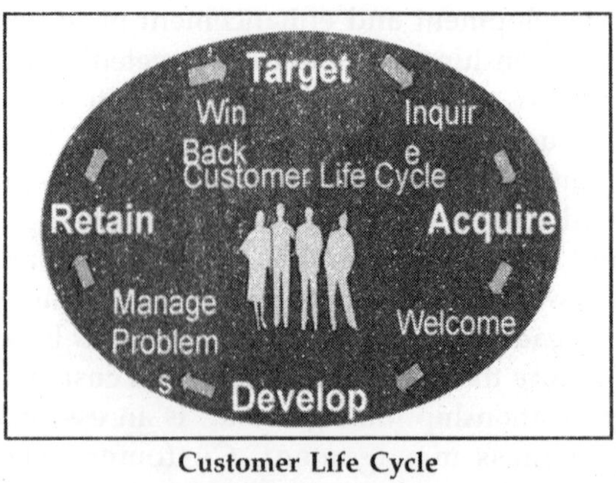

Customer Life Cycle

hence willing to pay a premium or higher price to such an enterprise. The entire value creation process is seen from the brand or company's perspective.

To avoid the above situations, market leaders focus on the following goals:

- Enhancing customer loyalty
- Maximising returns on customer segments or customer accounts
- Creating strong independence between the customer and the company.

CRM Focuses Steps to Build Customer Relationship

Successful organizations use three steps to build customer relationships:

- Determine mutually satisfying goals between organization and customers.
- Establish and maintain customer rapport .
- Produce positive feelings in the organization and the customers .

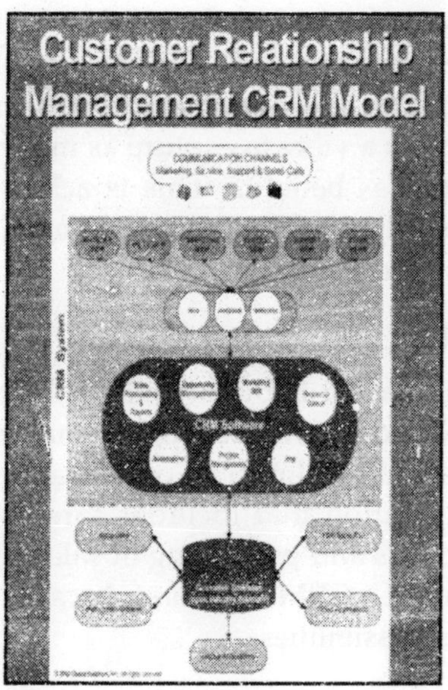

CRM and Its Components

CRM comprises several components absolutely essential to the organization. Each of them offers something different yet its importance cannot be undermined. Recent trends have enabled users to combine two or more components for better success. The Components of CRM are:

People Management

People Management is nothing but the effective use of people in the right place at the right time. It is imperative to adopt the right measures to ensure that the people skills match their job profiles. This is every large corporates requirement as well as small and medium industries. According to People Management an effective people strategy is first adopted, then the workforce is studied, skills and development analyzed and finally the required strategy needed for development and change is set down and implemented.

Lead Management

Lead Management basically involves the tracking and distribution of sales leads. This benefits the sales, call centre and marketing industries as well. The work involves managing market campaigns, making customized forms, mailing lists etc. All this is done with a view to capture as many sales leads as possible to that sales benefits. This is achieved through a comprehensive study of customer purchase patterns and the identification of potential sales leads.

Sales Force Automation

Sales Force Automation is by far one of the most essential components of customer relationship management and also one of the first. Used by almost all organizations it is nothing but a software solution that includes forecasting, tracking potential interactions and processing of sales. The reason this is adopted as part of a CRM solution is because of the need to identify revenue possibilities.

Customer Service

The customer service component in CRM is essential. This is because CRM focuses on collation of customer data, gathering information about their purchase patterns and provides this information to every department that requires it. Therefore vital departments like sales, marketing and personnel stand to gain in their knowledge of the customer. This enables the organization to provide suitable solutions to every customer and thus enhances customer retention and loyalty.

Marketing

Marketing is nothing but the promotional activities that are involved in promoting a product either to a general public or to a specific group. Marketing is different from sales and advertising in that one refers to act of selling itself while the other refers to the strategy involved. Customer Relationship Management facilitates the marketing function in that it increases the effectiveness of marketing by studying the potential targeted customers.

Work Flow Automation

Work flow processes include cutting costs and streamlining processes. It basically saves several people from doing the same job again and again. It reduces work and relieves work force of unnecessary tasks. It also includes things like routing out paperwork and filling out of forms that are essential. It also includes the integration of people and processes so that they work together in harmony towards a common objective without any loss of time, money or effort.

Business Reporting

This is nothing but being able to identify the exact position of the company at any given point of time. CRM plays a pivotal role in that it provides reports on the business. The advantages of this component include the ability to have this information at your instant access at any time. Accurate reports are also ensured. While forecasting is yet another feature it is also possible to actually export these reports to other systems. Historical data can also be saved to use for comparisons later on.

Analytics

Analytics involve the study of data so that information can be used to study market trends. A complete trend study is made possible due to the ability to create charts, figures and diagrams using both historical and current data. For information like charts, tables, log INS etc dashboards can also be used for increased visibility. This is an essential and pivotal part of CRM as it enables a study of data that is needed to make an estimate of the business condition at any given point.

The latest trend involving CRM components is the use of web services which enables organizations to take various components from different industries and basically use them together in a manner that suits their business needs. CRM reviews and will give the required information pertaining to what solution provides which functional component .

CRM Conditions

The organization and the customers both have sets of conditions to consider when building the relationship, such as wants and needs of both parties;

- Organizations need to make a profit to survive and grow.
- Customers want good service, a quality product and an acceptable price.
- Good CRM can influence both sets of conditions.

CRM Impacts on the Organization

CRM can have a major impact on an organization through:

- Shifting the focus from product to customer
- Streamlining the offer to what the customer requires
- Highlighting competencies required for an effective CRM process .

Organization Need CRM

The ultimate purpose of CRM, like any organizational initiative, is to increase profit. In the case of CRM this is achieved mainly by providing a better service to the customers than your competitors. CRM not only improves the service to customers though; a good CRM capability will also reduce costs, wastage, and complaints. Effective CRM also reduces staff stress, because attrition - a major cause of stress - reduces as services and relationships improve. CRM enables instant market research as well: opening the lines of communications with the customers gives us direct constant market reaction to your products, services and performance, far better than any market survey. Good CRM also helps the organization to grow our business: customers stay with you longer; customer churn rates reduce; referrals to new customers increase from increasing numbers of satisfied customers; demand reduces on fire-fighting and trouble-shooting staff, and overall the organization's service flows and teams work more efficiently and more happily.

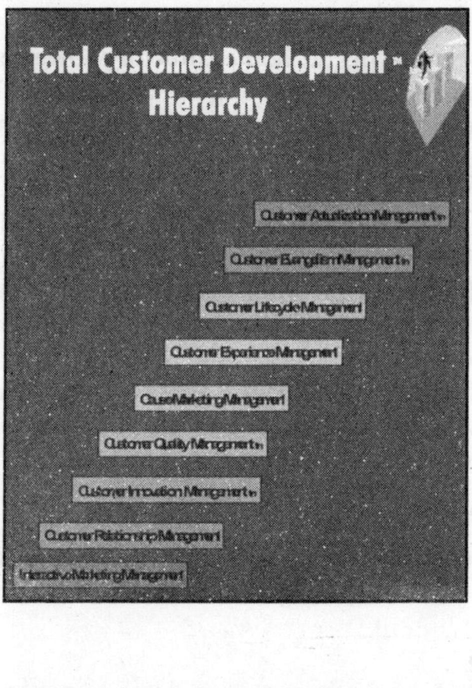

Costs Involved in CRM

A company needs to consider the costs that are going to be involved in it.Generally these costs are :

Exorbitant Costs

One of the problems with CRM is the huge investment needed to maintain a customer database. The additional expense comes because of the money needed for computer hardware, software, personnel etc. The costs involved are enormous and most often than not the resultant ROI from the CRM implementation fail to cover the costs involved.

Inadequate Focus on Objectives

Secondly when starting off on a CRM strategy the objectives are clearly established and followed. Management and employees know fully well what is needed to work towards organizational goals. The goals themselves are clearly laid out after meticulous planning. However midway during the CRM implementation, when hard times hit, the organization loses sight of its goals and ultimately steers away from it. At times goals get interchanged and lose their importance. Companies find themselves work at home directory towards goals that are less important and forgetting the ones that really are. This is one of the fundamental and mostly felt problems in CRM.

Insufficient Resources

Sometimes in phased implementation of CRM, if conditions worsen within the company or without, organizations start lessening their budgets for the current phase. When funds are less, budgets strained, the necessary costs required for CRM success are not employed. As a result CRM starts failing midway. The most important aspect- that of maintaining consistency is lost. Organizations fail to utilize the necessary resources for success and thus result in failure.

Inappropriate Metrics

Organizations have basically failed to use the right metrics. Failure to choose the right method of measurement and implement it is one of the chief reasons why CRM fails. Different metrics have to be employed for the calculation of different goals. Companies seldom pause to analyze which metric is needed for which element and ultimately use the wrong one. This results in faulty measurement and CRM disappointments.

Complex Systems

Organizations who have employed CRM though have a different opinion. They are witness to the fact that CRM packages can be highly complex, with vast amounts of intricacies. If this is the case then how do simple employees cope. The answer lies in sufficient training being given in order that they are able to comprehend and deal with the difficulties easily.

Business Needs Most Important

One of the chief mistakes companies make is letting the technology drive their CRM functionality. What's happening is that companies are endeavoring to go to the industry leaders, gain the technology needed and then apply it to the business problems only to find that it isn't solving any of them. Instead they need to analyze their business problems first and then find the appropriate CRM solution for it. This backwards step is responsible for CRM failure.

No Customer Focus

It requires an effort on the part of the organization. It needs to motivate employees to be absolutely customer centric. This involves tremendous effort on the part of the company but is highly essential. CRM problems arise because of employee reluctance to be more customer focused. The result is a highly expensive customer strategy being adopted by the company in an effort to retain customers, with reluctant, unfocussed employees implementing it.

Slow Returns

Another failure of CRM is its inability to provide quick returns on investment. Organizations find themselves waiting for years before they are able to see actual returns on their investment. Most experts view the low ROI as a major problem with CRM but fail to see that the long wait is just as difficult. Waiting for years to see their investments show results, tests patience and leads to both employees and management slackening their efforts in the implementation.

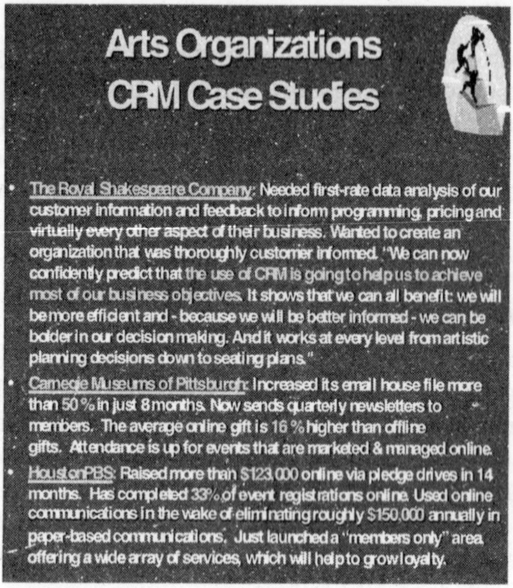

Features of Good CRM

The new viewpoint in industry is:

- What exactly do our customers want and need? and
- What do we need to do to be able to produce and deliver it to our customers?

This is a significant change of paradigm and a quantum leap in terms of how the organisation look at our business activity.

Modern CRM theory refers to the idea of 'integrating the customer'. This new way of looking at the business involves integrating the customer (more precisely the customer's relevant people and processes) into all aspects of the supplier's business, and vice versa. This implies a relationship that is deeper and wider than the traditional 'arms-length' supplier-customer relationship.

The traditional approach to customer relationships was based on a simple transaction or trade, and little more. Perhaps there would be only a single point of contact between one person on each side. All communication and dealings would be between these two people, even if the customers' organization contained many staff, departments, and functional requirements (distribution, sales, quality, finance, etc).

The modern approach to customer relationship management is based on satisfying all of the needs-people, systems, processes, etc-across the customer's organization, such as might be affected and benefited by the particular supply.

Generating a Customer Focused CRM Solution

A new way of thinking:

Change in paradigm ,Change in the messages sent and received ,Change in the overall culture .

And a new way of doing things:

Processes that are capable and effective,Structures and systems that support a business centred on its customers,Connectivity (end-to-end processes) both internally and externally (eg., with suppliers).

Customers' Expectations

If an organization cannot at least meet its customers' expectations it will struggle. Ideally a business organization should exceed its customers' expectations, thereby maximising the satisfaction of its customers, and also the credibility of its goods and services in the eyes of its customers. Customers normally become delighted when a supplier under-promises and over-delivers.To over-promise and under-deliver is a recipe for customers to become very dissatisfied.

Rule No 1: The organisation cannot assume what a customer's expectations are.

Rule No 2: Customer expectations will constantly change so they must be determined on an on-going basis.

The expectations of different customers for the same product or service will vary according to:

- Social and demographic factors
- Economic situation
- Educational standards
- Competitor products
- Experience.

Therefore, given all these variable factors, it is no surprise that one size certainly does not fit all. The organization should ask their customers what is important to them. There are a wide variety of relationship drivers.

For example:

- Quality
- Price
- Product
- Location
- Customer service

For example:

- Health and safety support
- Systems compatibility
- Contract structure
- Distribution flexibility
- Technical support
- Troubleshooting and problem-solving, to name just a few.

CRM as a Process

CRM can be regarded as a process, which has:

- Identifiable inputs
- Identifiable components

- Identifiable characteristics, which define CRM for your organization and customer base
- Capacity for improvement and evolution over time.

Manage Customers

Organizations who have many transitory relationships with customers consequently have to spend a lot of money on finding new customers. The cost of keeping existing customers is a tiny fraction of the cost of acquiring new customers. Customers are the usual source of income for an organization. (If not then they will certainly leverage your income, as in the case of readers of a free publication which is funded by advertising. As such there are two types of customers: the readers and the advertisers).Customers are also an exceptional source of information-information which is vital to enable a business to succeed; ie., giving customers what they want.

Managing Customers Entails

- Knowing what customers want and need - which enables the organisation to focus the production and service efforts.
- Knowing which products or customers have most growth potential-which enables to focus on developing highest potential.
- Knowing which products or customers are most or least profitable-which enables to focus on maximising profit.
- Knowing which customers will be advocates and supporters-which enables to provide references, case studies, and to safely test new products and services.

Achieving Good CRM

Achieving effective Customer Relationship Management requires many organizations to adopt a new perspective. Consider the following:

- Traditional *Customer service* is something *'do to'* the customer
- Modern *Customer Relationship Management* is *'done with'* the customer

The second statement is emphasises the big differences between conventional traditional customer service, and the modern progressive CRM approach.

The relationships with customers should be ongoing, cooperative, and built for the long term.

Implementation Issues

Many enterprises have derived great benefit from customer relationship management. Dramatic increases in revenue, higher rates of customer satisfaction, and significant savings in operating costs. For others, however, the benefits have been limited and disappointing .Under-performing deployments peaked in the early 2000's, when a number of companies spent large sums on solutions only to have it fail to deliver the hoped-for results.

Proponents emphasize that technology should be implemented only in the context of careful strategic and operational planning. Implementations almost invariably fall short when one or more facets of this prescription are ignored:

- Poor planning: Initiatives can easily fail when efforts are limited to choosing and deploying software, without an accompanying rationale, context, and support for the workforce. In other instances, enterprises simply automate flawed customer-facing processes rather than redesign them according to best practices.
- Poor adoption: In an early-2000's survey of more than 600 enterprises, Gartner reported that 42% of all purchased licenses had become "shelf-ware" – software paid for but never installed. This often stems from a poor technology fit: A company compromises on capabilities or else tries to achieve too much in a single stroke, ending up with an overly complex and costly deployment that yields scant ROI.
- Poor integration: For many companies, customer relationship management manifests in the form of piecemeal initiatives that address a glaring need: improving a particular customer-facing process or two

(via simple contact management or sales planning), or automating a favored sales or customer support channel. Such "point solutions" offer little or no integration or alignment with a company's overall strategy. They offer a less than complete customer view and often lead to unsatisfactory user experiences.

- Toward a solution: Experts advise organizations to recognize the immense value of integrating their customer-facing operations. In this view, internally-focused, department-centric views should be discarded in favor of reorienting processes toward information-sharing across marketing, sales, and service. For example, sales representatives need to know about current service issues and relevant marketing promotions before attempting to cross-sell to a specific customer. Marketing managers should be able to leverage customer information from sales and service to better target campaigns and offers. And support agents require quick and complete access to a customer's sales and service history.

Pareto's Law ('The Pareto Principle')

Pareto's Law is commonly known as the 80:20 rule. Typically in any organization:

- 20% of customers account for 80% of the turnover
- 20% of customers account for 80% of the profits
- 20% of customers account for 80% of the service and supply problems

It is important to know is which customers fit into which category and then to manage them accordingly.Highly satisfied customers who perceive a high value in your products and services commonly make excellent advocates for your organization-nurture these customers and give the special treatment. Dissatisfied customers who perceive a low value in your products and services are potential saboteurs. These customers could have little or no loyalty and may actively 'engage' against your organization. Therefore the organization should seek to rebuild relationships and trust, and a new basis for a future relationship, or manage the separation with dignity, professionalism and integrity.

Focus on Building Relationships

The essential CRM focus of any organization should be on developing core competencies, and an overall strategy of building customer relationships. In this way, all efforts in the organization can be aligned to:

- Customers and the culture of exceeding of customer expectation
- Understanding and managing the people impact on the culture of the organization
- Customers being recognised and treated as partners
- The value of relationship-building being valued
- Service being seen as a value-adding activity
- Reward and recognition being based on customer focus ie., 'going the extra mile'
- Evidence of corporate support for service activity

Characteristics of Excellent CRM

The following characteristics are associated with delivery of excellent CRM:

- Reliability
- Responsiveness
- Accessibility
- Safety
- Courtesy
- Consideration
- Communication
- Recognising the customer
- Competence

CRM and Communications

Communication is central to any successful relationship. In terms of Customer Relationship Management, communication needs to be consistent and high quality; as determined by:

- On time
- Focused
- Relevant
- Reliable
- Coherent

Importantly also, for effective communications it's the message and meaning that is received that counts, irrespective of what the communicator thinks they've said, or written. Communications must be judged most vitally by the reaction of the receiver. If the reaction is not good then the communication is poor. The information contained in a CRM system allows communication to be directed at the correct audience, in the correct way. The communication system must also encourage and facilitate honest and actionable feedback. Feedback from customers-especially complaints - are essential for good organizational performance and ongoing development. Most organizations avoid, discourage and hide from complaints. Don't. Complaints are free guidance for improving your quality, and free opportunities to increase customer loyalty.

People and CRM

As with any other business process the people have a huge impact on the success of the CRM process.

Successful and effective Customer Relationship Management people tend to display the following key characteristics:

- Positive attitude
- People orientation
- Organizational skills
- Analytical skills
- Customer focus (natural empathy)

- Understanding of the link between CRM and profitability

On the subject of empathy: Empathy is about understanding, not necessarily agreeing. Effective customer focus enables the organization and its staff to see both sides, and to work with the customer to arrive at a mutually satisfactory and sustainable solution. Agreement alone amounts to capitulation, which is neither practicable nor sustainable.

Benefits of Effective CRM

There are significant business benefits which accrue from an effective, integrated Customer Relationship Management approach. These include:

- Reduced costs, because the right things are being done.
- Increased customer satisfaction, because they are getting exactly what they want
- Ensuring that the focus of the organization is external
- Growth in numbers of customers
- Maximisation of opportunities (eg., increased services, referrals, etc.)
- Increased access to a source of market and competitor information
- Highlighting poor operational processes
- Long term profitability and sustainability

Forward thinking organizations understand the vital need to maintain a strategic focus on CRM and to resource and manage it appropriately.

Conclusion

This toolset is designed not only to save you time, effort and resources, but to set your organization on the right CRM track. It includes items which will not only provide templates for successful CRM, but pro-actively explain the processes and objectives of different disciplines. Market leaders focus on the goals of enhancing customer loyalty, maximizing returns on customer segments or customer accounts and creating strong interdependence between the customer and the company. Customer relationship management is a process whose objective is to enhance customer loyalty. CRM for business success provides a best practice template for building an adaptive and dynamic that supports organization's business goals. CRM has a powerful impact on bottom-line performance and shows that possessing strong is not in itself a guarantee of success. Rather, CRM must be adaptive to changing marketplace and customer demands. Understanding and leveraging the power of corporate is pivotal to long-term change success. Overall we conclude that, a Strong and Adaptive CRM definitely has a positive impact on the business strategy and overall performance of the organization.

In this new millennium, Customer Relationship Management will need to advance considerably and we will reach much more sophisticated levels of one-to-one marketing and data mining. There is now an enormous opportunity for organisations to improve their 'customer ownership' by building a co-ordinated and integrated set of activities which address all the key strategic elements of CRM. Ultimately, however, organisations' success in CRM will involve creating an appropriate strategic vision for the future, making the appropriate choice of applications, creatively using appropriate analytical techniques to exploit the data, and choosing the right vendor for supply of the technology solution.

References

website: www.theleaningpath.co.uk

http://www.artsalliance.org/docs/conf/IAA.

http://www.ecustomerserviceworld.com/earticlesstore_articles.asp

19

Customer Relationship Management in Banking Industry

R. Sivakami, B. Maragatham

Customer Relationship Management entails all aspects of interaction a company has with its customer, whether it is sales or service related; it starts with the foundation of relationship marketing. CRM is a systematic approach towards using information and on going dialogue to built long lasting mutually beneficial customer relationship. The use of CRM technology forms the crucial front-end of any e-business strategy, essentially CRM has emerged as a convivial weapon in the hands of the industry laggards as well as leaders to cascade the business suites; the only touch point which is formulating this base is the awareness amongst the corporatists to suffice the customers already available to the companies to large extent.

Customer Relationship Management is a process whose objective is to enhance customer loyalty. Customer Relationship Management is an organizational process which includes people, infrastructure, performance measure and controls, organizational alignment to the environment and the new strategic patterns.

The aim of customer relationship management is to produce high customer equity. Customer equity is the total of the discounted life time values of all the firm's customers. This process consists of the following:

- Creation and management of data mines and warehouses
- Development of appropriate organizational structures
- Investment in Technology
- People development

Today customer relationship management has a significant role in creating strong customer bondage. Close and long term relationships with customers imply continuing exchange opportunities with existing customers at a lower marketing cost per customer. Strong customer relationships with a high degree of familiarity and communications on both sides can generate more practical new product ideas from customers and contact personnel.

Good relationships with customers can result in good work for publicity from successful exchanges and minimal bad word of mouth in the event of unsuccessful exchanges. Service quality cracks can often be papered over where good relationships have existed previously.

In the words of Smith, " we may think that something will be great to do for our customers, but before we take actions we need to really step into their shoes". Companies often focus on customer relationship management functionality and integration. But they forget about some of the most basic touch points.

Customer relationship management enables companies to provide excellent real time customer service through the effective use of individual account information. Based on what they know about each valued customer, companies can customize market offerings, services, programs, messages and media. Customer relationship management is important because a major driver of company profitability is the aggregate value of the company's customer base.

Customer Relationship Management–Meaning

Customer Relationship Management is the process of bringing the customer and the company closer together. There are many different areas in which Customer Relationship Management can be implemented.

Customer Relationship Management is a process whose objective is to enhance customer loyalty. Customer Relationship Management is an organizational process which includes people, infrastructure, performance measure and controls, organizational alignment to the environment and the new strategic patterns.

The goal of Customer Relationship Management is to help a company maintain current customers, as well as gain new customers. Knowing the customer is the key to a successful business. Customer Relationship Management is the process through which a business analyzes their customers and makes changes accordingly. Customer Relationship Management vendors provide applications and advice on the best Customer Relationship Management methods. Most observers believe that Customer Relationship Management practices will continue to flourish as new Customer Relationship Management strategies and technologies are developed.

Customer Relationship Management is the establishment, development, maintenance and optimization of long-term mutually valuable relationships between consumers and the organizations. Successful customer relationship management focuses on understanding the needs and desires of the customers and is achieved by placing these needs at the heart of the business by integrating them with the organization's strategy, people, technology and business processes.

At the heart of a perfect CRM strategy is the creation of mutual value for all the parties involved in the business process. It is about creating a sustainable competitive advantage by being the best at understanding, communicating, and delivering, and developing existing customer relationships in addition to creating and keeping new customers. So the concept of product life cycle is giving way to the concept of customer life cycle focusing on the development of products and services that anticipate the future need of the existing customers and creating additional services that extend existing customer relationships beyond transactions.

A Relationship-based Marketing approach has the following benefits: -

- Over time, retail bank customers tend to increase their holding of the other products from across the range of financial products / services available.
- Long-term customers are more likely to become a referral source.
- The longer a relationship continues, the better a bank can understand the customer and his/her needs & preferences, and so greater the opportunity to tailor products and services and cross-sell the product / service range.
- Customers in long-term relationships are more comfortable with the service, the organization, methods and procedures. This helps reduce operating cost and costs arising out of customer error.

Consumers largely selected their banks based on how convenient the location of bank's branches was to their homes or offices. With the advent of new technologies in the business of bank, such as Internet Banking and ATMs, now customers can freely chose any bank for their transactions. The pressures of competitive and dynamic markets have contributed to the growth of CRM in the Financial Services Sector.

Private Banks have traditionally viewed themselves as exceedingly 'Customer Centric' offering what they believe to be highly personalized services to the High Net Worth Customers. However, changes in the customer behavior and accumulation of wealth are resulting in the needs of HNW customers becoming more diverse and complex in terms of the sorts of products they want, the channels through which they want to access them and the associated range of advice.

The wealthier the customers, the more demanding they are-and the clients expect more and more from their banks. Competition for "Supremely elite" is increasing.

Benefits

Customer relationship management tools have been shown to help companies attain these objectives:

- Streamlined sales and marketing processes
- Higher sales productivity
- Added cross-selling and up-selling opportunities
- Improved customer service, loyalty, and retention
- Increased call center efficiency
- Higher close rates
- Better customer profiling and targeting
- Reduced expenses
- Increased market share
- Higher overall profitability
- Marginal costing

Challenges

Tools and work flows can be complex to implement, especially for large enterprises. While some companies report great success, initiatives have also been known to fail—mainly owing to poor planning, a mismatch between software tools and company needs, roadblocks to collaboration between departments, and a lack of workforce buy-in and adoption.

Previously these tools were generally limited to contact management: monitoring and recording interactions and communications with customers. Software solutions then expanded to embrace deal tracking and the management of accounts, territories, opportunities, and—at the managerial level—the sales pipeline itself. Next came the advent of tools for other customer-facing business functions, as described below.

Customer relationship management technology has been, and still is, offered as on premises software that companies purchase and run on their own IT infrastructure. Vendors include: Oracle Corporation, SAP AG, and Amdocs. Perhaps the most notable trend has been the growth of tools delivered via the Web, also known as cloud computing and software as a service (SaaS). In contrast with conventional on-premises software, cloud-computing applications are sold by subscription, accessed via a secure Internet connection, and displayed on a Web browser. Companies don't incur the initial capital expense of purchasing software; neither must they buy and maintain IT hardware to run it on. In 2009, SaaS represented approximately 20% of all customer relationship management spending, and continues its trajectory of outselling on-premises software by a ratio of 3-to-1. Vendors include: Salesforce.com, RightNow, and SugarCRM

CRM Lends a Hand to the Banking Industry

Despite the fact that in most banks profits sometimes fail, they seldom pay attention to or adopt any customer strategy. It has long been the misconception that banks need not pay much attention to customer focus just because they had customers. Some banks even if they possess good customer relationships are unable to cross sell as they have not figured out who to target with what product/service. What happens is that customers are often approached for the wrong products.

However the new millennium has resulted in banks and financial agencies rethinking their strategies and goals. They have come to understand the importance of hanging onto the customer and keeping him happy. The rules that once governed the banking industry have changed. They have realized that adopting a customer centric strategy is essential and needs to be compulsorily undertaken. The vast majority of banks now realize they need a customer strategy and are opting for CRM- Customer RelationshiManagement.

Banking CRM software serves to increase the market share and boost growth in the banking industry. What happens in CRM banking solutions is that they change the way the employees think and mould them into customer conscious people. CRM induces bankers to know that they are required to maintain good relationships with their customersand should strive to retain them.

They are made to realize that the business process should consist of efforts to discover and satisfy customer requirements. Since the banking field now boasts of so much of technological innovations there has been a wide variety cf innovations in

CRM banking as well. Statistics show that bankers will spend $7 billion on CRM. The sector will also evidence an increase in expenditure of 14 percent each year. With such phenomenal statistics it is but a surety that CRM banking solutions sales will soar in the coming years.

What Does CRM Have to Offer Banks?

- Customer Information Assimilation and Storage
- Analyzing Profitability
- Aiding Marketing Efforts
- Gaining New Customers
- Relationship Management
- Assisting Customer retention
- Cross-Selling

CRM Banking Benefits

CRM Banking Focuses on the Customer

CRM manages to places the customer at the focal point of the organization in order to cater to his needs, satisfy him and thus maximize the profits of the organization. Banking CRM understands the needs of the customer and integrates it with people, technology, resources and business processes. It focuses on the existing data available in the organization and uses it to improve its relationship with customers. Banking CRM uses information and analytical tools to secure customer focus. Thus it is completely essential that banks implement CRM in order to secure this.

Overall Profitability

CRM enables banks to give employee's better training that helps them face customers easily. It achieves better infrastructure and ultimately contributes to better overall performance. The byproducts of CRM banking solutions are customer acquisition, retention and profitability. Banks that don't implement CRM will undoubtedly find themselves with lesser profitability coupled with a sharp decline in the number of customers.

Satisfied Customers

It is important to make a customer feel as if he / she is the only one - this will go a long way in satisfying and retaining them. Bankers need a return on investment and it has been proved that increase in customer satisfaction more than contributes a fair share to ROI. The main value of CRM banking lies in satisfaction and increased retention of customers.

Centralized Information

CRM banking solutions manage to clearly integrate people, processes and technology. CRM banking provides banks with a holistic view of all bank transactions and customer information as well and stores it in a single data warehouse where it can be studied later.

CRM Banking Boosts Small Banks

Banking CRM software meets the needs of banks of all sizes in terms of attaining the required accuracy and understanding of customers. Merely assuming that banks that are considerably smaller in size have a better customer approach and are able to deal with their customers in a better manner is wrong. They are just as much in need of CRM aid as the others. Small banks on account of a limited amount of money have had to realize that a large contribution to profits is directly the result of good customer service. CRM makes sure that the bank delivers exactly what the customer expects.

Customer Segregation

CRM enables a bank to see which customers are costing them and which are bringing benefits. CRM provides them with the required analytical tools that will help them focus on the importance of segregating these two and doing what is required to avail of the maximum returns. After this segregation is done CRM easily enables banks to increase their communication and cross-selling to their customers effectively and efficiently.

How to Get the Most Out of CRM Banking Systems

- The main problem the CRM industry now faces is reluctant, hesitant bankers who seldom opt for CRM implementation. This is because banks feel that the transition to being customer centric involves a lot of problems and costly. They are of the opinion that returns hardly ever equal the expected profits and that the entire implementation is unnecessary and time consuming. In addition to this the number of failed CRM implementations has also resulted in invoking a feeling of reluctance in banks, making them hesitate. This needs to be obliterated in order to succeed.
- It is imperative that business policies and processes are put early in place in order that the best can be got out of the CRM business solution. Doing this at a later stage will result in untoward complications.
- It is imperative that business policies and processes are put early in place in order that the best can be got out of the CRM business solution. Doing this at a later stage will result in untoward complications.
- Training of customer-facing staff is being given more importance now. This not only equips them to better deal with the customer but CRM learning also empowers the employee with sufficient knowledge to carry out his job confidently and to the best of his ability.
- The assimilation and storage of bank customer data is a tedious task. Since this sector mostly involves numerical data this is highly essential and needs to be undertaken. It involves a lot of added work and minute attention to detail. There are loads and loads of data that need to be evaluated. Minute attention to detail is essential so that discrepancies and errors don't take place. With technology getting more complicated banks need to attend to minute details to ensure success.
- It is important to test the CRM system before implementation. Aside from minimizing errors this will go a long way in alleviating problems and difficulties. The new trends in CRM have seen banks adopting methods like phased CRM

implementation - adopting incremental approaches and getting ample rewards.

- It is not sufficient to merely install CRM software. For CRM to be truly successful it is imperative that there is a well established strategy. For CRM to be truly effective, it requires a carefully planned strategy that makes proper use of people and business processes in order to secure the maximum CRM ROI.
- When adopting CRM it is essential that banks realize that incremental adoption is essential with a firm commitment to learn at every stage. A well developed CRM strategy catering to phased implementation should be established and implemented.

The gains are enormous. Banking CRM software endeavors to improve customer profitability and manages to keep banks way ahead of the others by helping banks to study customer activity and satisfy customer needs through the help of CRM banking solutions. It is definite that the future will see CRM being adopted by banks as a part of their everyday business.

Banker Customer Relationship

Debtor and Creditor

A fundamental relationship between a banker and a customer is that of a debtor and a creditor. Where the customer has a credit balance in his account, the customer is the creditor and banker is the debtor. Conversely, where the customer has a debit balance in his account, the customer is the debtor and banker is the creditor.

Trustee and Beneficiary

Where the banker maintains the deposit balances of customers and allows them to use those deposit money as per their wish he is said to be acting as a trustee of the customer. Similarly, where the banker accepts securities and other valuables for safe custody, he becomes the trustee and the customer becomes the beneficiary.

Agent and Principal

A banker essentially acts as an agent of a customer as he carries out the agency functions such as collection of cheques, bills of exchange, payment of insurance premium, etc.

Customer Relationship Management Software

Customer relationship management (CRM) comprises the processes by which a company can arrange and organise its information on current and future customers. By extension, CRM software helps to consolidate data about customers and their habits in order to improve both customer service and marketing campaigns.

An effective CRM package will not only collect the right data, but also organise and interpret it to provide relevant and up-to-date information about how a business can best serve and market to a particular client.

Particularly useful for companies with a varied product portfolio, a good package may be able to segment key customers by calculating their average value order or frequency of puchasing. Sales departments will also find CRM software valuable, with many reporting increased confidence and less time spent on paperwork after its implementation.

When buying a CRM software solution, it may be useful to consult the software dealer to find out which package suits a particular business. The dealer may also be able to offer expansions to the software that covers additional aspects, such as strategic planning and process management.

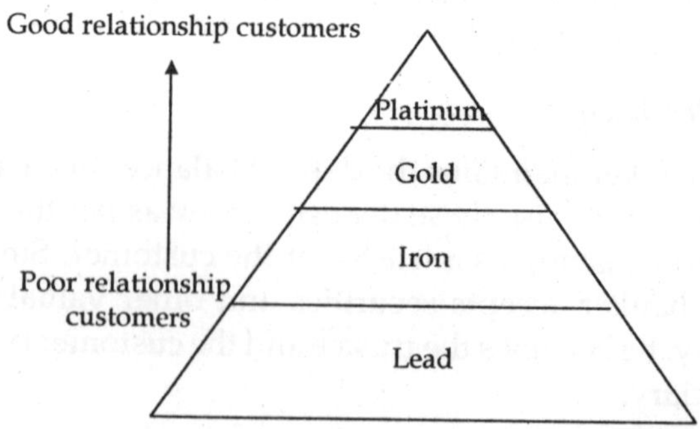

Tiering the Customer Base

Platinum: These customers, who constitute a very small percentage of a firm's customer base, are heavy users and contribute a large share of the profits generated.

Gold: The gold tier forms a larger percentage of customers than the platinum, but individual customers contribute less profit than do platinum customers.

Iron: These customers provide the bulk of customer base. Because their numbers give the firm economies of scale, they are often important so that a firm can build and maintain a certain capacity level and infrastructure, which is often needed for serving gold and platinum customers.

Lead: Lead-tier customers tend to generate low revenues for a firm but often still require the same level of service as iron customers, which turns them into a loss -making segment from a firm's perspective.

Improving Customer Relationship Management in Banking with Integrated Delivery Channels

The capability to integrate two or more delivery channels through shared technology has only recently been deployed in any significant way. Today, a handful of retail banks can boast of globally integrated delivery channels that are built on standard technology principles. These channels can, for example, deliver consistent balances regardless of the customer's location because of the consistent architecture. No institution, however, can claim to have all channels working on a common platform or claim even to share information or process across all channels.

IT managers within the bank, as well as business managers that rely on the delivery channels to service their products, know deep down that integrating the channels is the right thing to do because some benefits of channel integration are intuitive if not scientifically provable. The example of inconsistent account balance information is one that integrated delivery channels can solve and that most bankers agree is a source of frustration for the *customer*. Quantifying the effects of fixing this problem proves to be tricky, however.

Service and Sales Processes made More Predictable

Still, many banks have implemented, or are in the process of designing, integrated delivery channel architectures based on these soft benefits as well as on the goal of maintaining and deepening the *customer relationship* in the face of competitive pressures. The implementation of integrated delivery channels has to date focused on the service side of the *relationship* equation.

On the sales side, marketing and product line managers have benefited greatly from a relatively plentiful source of analytics systems in the market. Bankers are getting better at knowing how to calculate *customer* profitability, predict propensity to buy, and even recognize attrition behaviors thanks to the segmentation and focus of solution providers in the analytics markets.

Customer knowledge databases and analytics engines have made the selling process more predictable then ever before. But the actual use of the information from these systems has been limited to mail campaigns and outbound telemarketing, both of which traditionally have had low response rates. Although, these rates have improved somewhat with the improved *customer* knowledge in hand.

Thus, for banks, neither the chicken nor the egg came first. Both arrived at the same time. The opportunities to combine these powerful capabilities are built-in to the very systems that enable them individually. But the marriage of integrated delivery channels and *customer* knowledge is not a trivial arrangement. For once, perhaps, technology is not the problem.

Effective Use of Information Builds Key Customer Benefits

The issues surrounding the collaboration of knowledge and delivery have to do with the *management* of the data and processes involved as well as some very emotional aspects of the customer's *relationship* with the bank and the extent to which individual customers perceive the bank as a threat to their privacy. To build on the full strength of this collaboration, banks need to completely understand the issues surrounding the use of knowledge, and then tread lightly.

Data acquisition through *customer* interaction is determined by the delivery channels, themselves, or through some integrated channel *management* architecture. Institutions are already collecting most of the available information today such as *customer* identity, accounts, channels, transactions performed, time of day, and all the pieces of information that have some value to the institution. Such basic information is included in the transactions that are sent to the core *banking* system or to some external system such as a credit processor. For now, there seems to be no need to collect additional information that is not currently acquired. What is required is the use of the data in managing the *relationship* with the *customer* in a more fulfilling way.

The shift to the existing use of data comes in the form of the centralized acquisition (or processing) of this information *outside of the transactional sense.* Along with the use of transactional information by the systems that perform the basic units of work, specialized applications collect and analyze information about the *customer* interaction, itself, to give insight into *customer* behavior. Banks can also collect and store information about nontrivial transactions to provide continuity among *customer* contacts. So if a *customer* has an unresolved problem, that information is available at all appropriate channels (see Exhibit).

While many institutions are currently performing such analysis within a given channel (online *banking* navigation behavior, for example), the next step includes analysis of the customer's behavior across all delivery channels in the network. This enables gauging behavior in a broader context, analysis of all external providers of service, and analysis of how the *customer* uses these products.

The following list presents a few examples of this information *management* strategy:

- Using *channel analysis* to model and predict demand at the delivery channels after marketing campaigns or to gauge the impact of channel downtime on service or revenue, tying downtime to a quantified loss.

- Using *customer preference* to understand the individual customer's favorite channels for specific transactions.
- Keeping certain *transactions open-ended* to maintain continuity of service. This is done by having recent problem reports or unresolved account applications available at all delivery channels to present the agent with what may be peripheral yet important information about the current state of the *customer relationship*. This information can also be made available to the automated channels to keep the *customer* aware of the status of problems or account applications.

By itself, this *management* of information from the delivery channels offers many benefits to the institution and the *customer*. But the real value in the effective use of *customer* information at the point of interaction comes from the *customer* knowledge systems that are becoming pervasive in most retail banks.

Powerful Customer Knowledge Systems for the Future

The pace of implementation of integrated delivery channel architectures will quicken and eventually prevail at top banks. The deployment of powerful *customer* knowledge systems will also increase as more and more useful information can be distilled from the myriad of resources in the bank IT network.

As these two infrastructures evolve, the integration between them will also increase. Already, many institutions use information gleaned from *customer* knowledge systems to suggest new products to customers at the branch teller. Nonetheless, TowerGroup believes that much of the use of information between the knowledge systems and the delivery channels has yet to be fully realized. With most of the technology in place, banks must begin to form strategies around the use of information in the day-to-day contact with its customers.

As the capability to build on this flow of information grows, it has the potential to outpace the customer's acceptance of the bank's knowledge. Privacy is an emotional issue and, so, not entirely rational. Technology and policy can only go so far in ensuring that the use of information at the point of contact is not intrusive to the customer's comfortable level of privacy. *Relationship* training is more important than before as banks begin to learn more about their customers and use that information to bring financial value to them.

Ultimately, the *management* of *customer* information at the point of interaction is about service, about keeping the *customer* happy, and, simply put, about keeping the *customer*. It's about strengthening the *relationship* and showing the *customer* that the bank's knowledge can lead to real benefit. It's about increasing the bank's benefit as well, and doing it in a way that does not sacrifice the customer's long-term well-being. Finally, it's about trust as a result of knowing the *customer* and not as an excuse for misusing information.

References

Books

1. Philip Kotler (2002). Marketing Management.

2. Rajan Saxena(2002). Marketing Management.

Website

(http://www.addthis.com/bookmark,php"\t"_blank)

20

Marketing Prospects of Beach Tourism in Kerala

Shoby Das, G. Raju

Tourism Industry today is considered as the world's largest export industry. In the new millennium, the global economy is exploring all the possibilities of Tourism industry. It is emerged as an important contributor to the growth of an economy. It is a major social phenomenon of the modern society with enormous economic effects. Growth of tourism is a significant part of the global expression of the new service economy. It has carved a niche for itself as a very effective instrument for generating employment, earning foreign exchange and thereby facilitating overall development. With the weakening of many other aspects of the economy, tourism is a new opportunity.

According to WTTC Report "Progress and Priorities 2008/09" India will be the world's number one destination in terms of annual growth in travel & tourism demand between 2008 and 2018, averaging 9.4% per annum – ahead of China, Libya, Vietnam and Montenegro. Looking past the present cyclical downturn in the global economy, the prospects for travel & tourism over the coming decade also look bright, and forecast to sustain annual growth of more than 4% over the next ten years. Emerging economies are expected to continue growing rapidly, boosting both international and domestic travel. And globalization will be sustained, as these economies become increasingly integrated into the world economy, providing ongoing support for both business and personal travel. Countries expected to row their travel and tourism demand most rapidly between 2008 and 2018 0n a relative scale are as follows (Table 1).

Now tourism is a new sense of sound partnership between private sector and public authorities and it looks beyond short-term considerations. It focuses on a responsible approach i.e. benefits not only for the people who travel but also for people in the communities they visit and for their respective natural, social and cultural environments. With the public and private sectors working together at all levels, growth can be strategically planned to be sustainable and sensitive not only to develop the sectors potential but also to defend it against the severe disruption due to external events beyond its direct control.

Table 1
T& T Demand, 2008-18 (% annualized real growth)

Rank	*Countries*	*Growth Rate*
1.	India	9.4
2.	China	8.9
3.	Libya	8.1
4.	Vietnam	8.1
5.	Montenegro	7.4
6.	Romania	7.1
7.	Macau	7.1
8.	Namibia	6.9
9.	Croatia	6.9
10.	Czech Republic	6.8

Source: Progress and Priorities 2008/09, WTTC

India has been mainly conceived as a cultural tourist destination, but it has diverse tourist attractions. Of course, India is the only destination that offers a myriad experiences: beaches, Himalayas, backwaters, wildlife, etc. India is positioned as a high value destination for the tourists in terms of products.

It is possible during a single trip to India to experience each one of them, unlike in Spain which can only be a beach experience, or Maldives which can only be an island destination, or Costa Rica, an eco destination, or Morocco heritage destination, India combines all of this, and we have to market that aspect of high value experiences (Amitabh Kant).Among these Beach tourism is one of the oldest forms of tourism in India.

Beach Tourism

Originally it was only the elite who visited the seaside. But todays beach resorts, takes the form of a very high concentration of tourists staying at the same destination, chiefly during the summer (Romila Chawla). Geographically saying a beach is a temporary deposit which are deposited and removed by beach cycles (Shepard, F.P., 1967,). In simple terms a beach is a geological landform along the shoreline of a body of water. It usually consists of loose particles which are often composed of rock, such as sand, gravel, shingle, pebbles, or cobble. The particles of which the beach is composed can sometimes instead have biological origins, such as shell fragments or coralline algae fragments. Beaches often occur along coastal areas, where wave or current action deposits and reworks sediments. The seashore is most commonly associated with the word "beach", beaches are not only found by the sea or ocean: beaches also occur at the margin of the land along lakes and rivers where sediments are reworked or deposited.

The background the beach areas present a fantastic view of color contrasts with blue waters, golden sands and clear sky. Beach Tourism is a major segment of destination development and has ample scope for water borne recreation. The beach remains the main recreational focus with greater diversifications of holiday experiences like sun bath, surfing, boating, yachting, wind surfing, snorkeling, water scootering etc. The most famous Indian beaches those offers an unlimited beach holiday options in India are beaches of Goa, Orisaa, Tamilnadu, Kerala, Andaman and Lakshadweep. More than 7500 km long Indian Coastline provides hundreds of options for the beach lovers. For the families there are city beaches, which are good breaks and provide wholesome entertainment for the family members. Indian beaches offer amazing water sports facilities. The best choices of water sports facilities are available in Goa, Andaman Nicobar Islands and Lakshadweep islands.

Many of these beaches are developed as tourist destinations and many potential beaches are in need of attention and planning for future developments. The studies have showed that beach tourism has led to an overall development of tourism in many parts of the world. It has become main source of income in many coastal regions. Beach tourism utilizes the aesthetic and environmental values of the beach. It also combines the usage of water (water sports) and land by providing necessary infrastructure. The water usage comprise swimming, surfing, sailing wind-surfing, water scootering, motor boat skiing, para-sailing, snorkeling etc. The land use pattern is inclusive of basic infrastructure for touristic activities such as parking areas play grounds and other recreational facilities. Besides it enhances the opportunities of visits to tourist attractions in the vicinity of beach areas. As a multidimensional area the beach area needs special care for developing a particular beach for tourism. We can see that there are several issues occurring from the development and management of a beach destination. (Ravi Bhushan Kumar, 1995) .

Till very recent years, Kerala was considered as a peaceful destination, but after the terrorist attack of Mumbai there was a long period of disturbance. However the central and state governments are getting positive response from the Indian and international tourism markets. However Beach tourism in Kerala had not achieved its full potential despite the pioneering effort made in 1969 with the opening of the Kovalam beach resort. It is mainly because of the marketing thrust given to the backwaters. It cannot be denied that in recent years Kerala has been concentrating on marketing the backwaters as the unique selling proposition of its tourist appeal. If Kerala is a hot destination today, it is surely due to the astute selling of its backwaters. And, equally, it cannot be denied that this approach has won the State not only laurels but also substantial increase in tourist arrivals. In the process, beach tourism, commands an average stay of 10-14 days compared to the two-day average stay of backwater tourism, had lost out.

Vibrant Kerala

Kerala is one of those states in India that defines the belief that attractions cease to have an impact on visitors after a while. Kerala springs up new surprises every time to its guests. One of these significant attractions in Kerala is its beaches. Kerala was the first state in India to be accorded the status of World travel and tourism council (WTTC) in 2000. The WTTC report projects that by 2016 the total travel and tourism activity is expected to post a total demand of economic activity of US $ 12,118 billion. The world's travel & tourism is expected to contribute US $ 2,969.4 billion in nominal terms (3.6% of total) by 2016. The contribution of tourism economy is expected to reach US $ 8.971.6 billion (10.9%) in the year 2016. By 2016, travel & tourism is expected to create 9 per cent of total employment or one in every 11.1 jobs and is expected to get capital investment in both public & private sector by US $ 2,059.8 billion or 9.6% of the total global investment. The Government is expected to spend on travel & tourism US $ 480.9 billion or 4% of total government expenditure by 2016.

Geographically Kerala is located on the south western tip of India with the Arabian Sea on the west and the Western Ghats on the east. The state is divided into three regions-the coastal lowlands, the fertile midlands and highlands. The lowlands of Kerala are rich with endless backwaters and the deltas of forty four rivers. The midlands are abundant in cashew, coconut, arecanut, tapioca, banana, rice, ginger, pepper, sugarcane, and vegetable plantations. The forested highland is plentiful in tea, coffee, rubber and spice plantations and wild life reserves. Amidst their rich shades of blue and green shades, every region shares the natural splendor and charmness. Today the state has become one of the most sought-after tourist destinations in the world.

Kerala occupies a unique position in the tourism map of India and has been granted the "Super Brand Status", known as the 'Oscar' in the world of branding. At the same time it was the first state in India to be accorded the status of a partner state of the World travel and Tourism Council in the year 2000. According to the World Travel and Tourism Council (WTTC), tourism arrivals in Kerala are expected to grow by 11.6 per cent per annum over the next decade. This is the highest growth in the world, surpassing Turkey's 10.2 per cent and the all-India growth of 9.7 per cent. A record growth of 23.5 per cent is also expected in external account earnings from travel and tourism over the next 10 years (India's estimates for this period are 14.3 per cent, while the world average is only 6.5 per cent).These figures show high levels of consumption of the tourism product in the state by both domestic and international tourists.

It is evident that the aggressive marketing of the tourism products of the State have started yielding results. According to the statistics of tourist arrivals provided by the Department of Tourism, Government of Kerala, the share of International Tourist arrival to Kerala during the year 2008 is 5, 98,929. It shows an increase of 16.11 per cent over the year 2007. Domestic Tourist arrival to Kerala during the year 2008 is 75, 91,250 and it shows an increase of 14.28 per cent over the previous year. Earnings from tourism are also projected to grow at a record level of Rs.3, 066.52, which shows a growth rate of 16.11 per cent over the previous year. Total Revenue (including direct & indirect) from Tourism during 2008 is Rs.13, 130.00 Crores, showing an increase of 14.84 per cent over the last year's figure. Considering the district wise Foreign Tourist arrival, Wayanad district shows the highest variation of 37.75 per cent over 2007. Considering the district wise Domestic Tourist arrival, Alappuzha district shows the highest variation of 37.47 per cent over 2007.

Kerala is now emerging as a new age destination. The Kerala model of tourism development looks to provide unique experiences to the tourists. The Kerala government was successful in marketing Kerala a one of the most beautiful and safest tourist destinations all around the world (Saroop Roy B R 2006). The Kerala Tourism Department has initiated various projects for the development of basic infrastructure at tourist destinations, creation of new products and en-route facilities. Some of the finest beaches on earth can be seen on the famed Kerala coast and Kerala is a tropical paradise with the visual melody of green field, thatched huts and blue waters. It is commonly accepted fact that any tourism product of Kerala is sandwiched with the crystal blue waters of whether it is in the form of beaches or backwaters or waterfalls or rivers.

God's Own Beaches

Kerala enjoys extra ordinary wealth of finest beaches in India and have all the makings of a beach lover's paradise with their laid back old world charm and sparkling. These beaches offer sun, sea, sand and surf. Though extremely popular worldwide, the beaches remain strangely calm and bewitching. They are beautiful as the beaches of Goa, without the large crowds. The cool breeze that blows on the beaches will work like a balm to the tourists and are a real haven to find the supreme rejuvenation. The southern part of Kerala has been blessed with beautiful beaches like Kovalam, Chowra, Shanagumugham, Varkala, Papanasam, Bekal and Kollam. The unexplored beaches of the Malabar, such as Meenkunnu, Muzhupilangad and Kappil are selected for the new developmental projects. Based on the unique strength Govt. of Kerala has identified these beaches for development of new tourism circuits.

There are several beach resorts in Kerala. Many of them are centers of Ayurvedic health holidays. While Kovalam is the most famous of beaches, there are several less known ones with bliss of solitude. The beaches of Kerala are inseparably linked with the lands history that is the unmistakable footprints of ancient travelers and explorers on the sands of time. The Kappad beach, where the Vasco da Gama,the pioneering Portuguese traveler landed in 1948. Besides the historic Fort Kochi was the first European township in India. Cochin, the queen of the sea has the best natural harbor in the country. On the Malabar coastline, the Bekal Fort, this stands on 35 acres of headland that runs into the Arabian Sea. It is the largest and best preserved fort in the state.

Manoj Edward and Babu P George in their research paper "Destination attractiveness of Kerala as an Internatinal Tourist Destination: An importance-Performance Analysis" found that the destination development and marketing efforts need more attention and it is revealed that the beach attractions has more potential in improving the destination attractiveness of Kerala.In their opinion beach attraction of Kerala needs more attention in the development and marketing for enhancing the quality of beaches and its appeal.

Beaches in Kerala

The most famous beach destinations in Kerala are Kovalam, Varkala, Alappuzha and Kappad...a brief description about these prominent destinations are described below:

Kovalam

Kovalam, a tiny little town in the district of Thiruvanantpuram, is pretty well known for its beaches. Many passionate admirers of Kovalam eternally project it as the best beach destination of the country. The number of tourists flocking to spend some time on the beach has been increasing. There are actually three beaches that make Kovalam so popular - the Lighthouse beach, Eve's or Hawa beach and Ashok beach. The Lighthouse beach is the southernmost beach and perhaps the most popular amongst the tourists. A rocky promontory separates it from the second beach, Hawa, which in turn is again disjoint from the third beach, Ashok, by a rocky promontory. Apart from these crescent shaped beaches, there are a few other lesser known beaches that are equally beautiful and charming in their appeal.

The history of the Kovalam states that it was a small fishing village, spotlessly clean, till the time the hippies stepped on it. The pristine beauty of the beach and the sparkling views from the rocky promontory entranced them infinitely and the rest as they say is history. People soon began to pour in large numbers to catch a glimpse of the by now famous beach. Its proximity to the capital city of Thiruvanantpuram also ensured that accessing the beach was not a problem for the enthusiasts. Today, beaches of Kovalam are not as clean as earlier; nevertheless, the magnificent views still continue to enamor tourists beyond words.

The first sight in the Lighthouse beach is the dominating rocky promontory Vizhinjam Lighthouse. The lighthouse still glows in the darkness of night at regular intervals. The light emitted by it during this time creates a magical, lovely atmosphere on the beach. The visitors are not allowed inside this light house because of safety concerns. Quiet close by another monument dedicated to two 15th century poets from Kovalam, Ayyippilla and Ayyanappilla Asan, is worth a visit. The rocky promontory that divides the second and the third beach has yet another attraction in the form of the Halcyon Castle. The castle that presently remains vacant due to an ongoing political tussle. A small mosque by the name of Kovalam Jama Masjid stands on the Ashok beach and right across, on the other side of the road, is a Ganapati Temple.

Kovalam beach is ideal for swimming, kayaking, surfing and skiing. However, take care as though the water here may look very quiet, yet it has a history of quiet a few drowning cases. There are instructions in English, Hindi, and Malayalam and German that specifically point out that only the area marked by green flag is safe for tourists. The red flags indicate zones that can be precarious if ventured into. There are lifeguards as well, so pay attention to the instructions and can have fun on the beach. Angling is also an option. There is an opportunity for hiring boats from fishermen and involving in fishing activities.

The traditional catamaran ride, is a unique experience and it is advisable that to take the ride along the fisherman for the safety. Facilities for water sports, shopping, alternatively, a brilliant Kathakali performance, the classical dance drama of Kerala, are the other entertainments. Well, the rocky promontories still invite the guest to view some magnificent sights from the top, especially during sunset. Walk barefooted on the sands of the beach and admire the greenery around.

Varkala

The small town of Varkala, 46 km north of the capital city of Thiruvanantpuram is mostly known for the unblemished beauty of its beaches. It is actually a long stretch dominated by red cliff and green coconut palm trees. The two km long cliff extends from the south, Papanasham beach, to the north to the Thiruvambady beach. Providing a spectacular contrast is the blue hues of the water and sky. In brief, the scenic beauty of Varkala beach is almost thrilling. Varkala beach is more than just beach for it carries along a religious as well as medicinal significance. It is also one of the quietest beaches of Kerala and resembles Kovalam in its charm. However, the added attraction here is the lesser number of people which means more space with little dirt

Since Varkala is known as a Hindu pilgrimage destination, as it is a venue for the famous Janardhan Swami Temple. Like numerous other pilgrimage destinations in India, this temple too has a legend attached to it. Visit this 12th century temple (it is actually supposed to be much older) and listen to the pious story that also gives the Papanasham beach and even Varkala their name. The spring that originates from the cliff here is supposed to have curative properties. t is better not to visit the beach on the new moon day, because it is heavily thronged by devotees. A dip here is believed to carry away all the sins of soul and purify it. Varkala presents an opportunity to enjoy water sports like parasailing, scuba diving and windsurfing and even deep sea fishing.

Being one of the most tranquil beaches in Kerala, the Varkala beach offers an unlimited holiday. The Thiruvambady beach specially is preferred here for the simple reason that it is more silent and devoid of a lot of shops and restaurants. The Kappil Beach is practically the place where the beach and the backwater merge together. The place is also quiet and offers you an opportunity to set out for a boat ride in the backwaters. Beach bazaars are very common in Varkala.

Alappuzha

Alappuzha is a tiny place located on a thin strip of land between the Arabian Sea and the Punnamada Lake. The place is fondly referred to as the Venice of East because of its striking similarity between the two (Alappuzha and Venice) with regards to intricate maze of backwaters, canals and bridges. In the east the canals open to the Punnamada Lake while on the west they end close to the pier of Alappuzha beach. Alappuzha was once a thriving port and also a gateway to enter Kerala. The port was built by Raja Kesava Das, the Diwan of Travancore in the 18th century and facilitated the passage of goods to and from the region. Today, Alappuzha and its beach are a huge attraction for tourists who are in search of some different experience. The waters of the sea rush towards you as you approach it and seem more than willing to reveal the earthly story of this quaint little town. The Alappuzha beach, also known by the name of Alleppey is not popular amongst tourists without reason.

The 1000 feet pier at the Alappuzha beach that extends into the sea dates back to 1862. It was constructed by Captain Huge Crawford and served as a platform that provided access and protection to ships and boats. The lighthouse, that once showed way to boats and ferries in the midst of pervading darkness of night, today allows very restricted entry. Together, the pier and the lighthouse recreate the era when boats sailed in large number to the ports of Alappuzha. They actually lead the visitor back into time. Alappuzha beach beckons you to leave all inhibitions behind and indulge in a variety of water sports like surfing and parasailing. Alappuzha provides some of the best of aqua-sport equipment such as water-scooters and high-speed boats in the entire state so there is absolutely no stopping to fun. Alappuzha, with its scenic beauty, is a perfect place for the visitor to unwind and give a break.

Kappad

Located at a distance of 16 km from the Kozhikode town, the Kappad beach is wrapped in a sheet of history. Uncover it to know that this was the land where the famous Portuguese sailor, Vasco da Gama set his feet in the year 1498. This marked the beginning of a new era and new relationship between the Indians and the Portuguese which lasted for 4 to 5 centuries later. Today, Kappad attracts a whole lot of visitors desirous of knowing more about the Portuguese and the native Indians of that time. Also, the unblemished beauty and serenity of the beach is something that is intact despite increasing tourism.

With such a historic significance attached, it is quiet obvious that the past of the Kappad beach, known as the Kappadavu by the local inhabitants, is the prime attraction for any visitor. There is not much of monuments around to reveal the past before you apart from a stone pillar with an inscription "Vasco da Gama landed here, Kappakadavu, in the year 1498". You will come to know that it was the excellent quality of spices and abundant wealth of Kerala that caught the attention of early traders - brought the Arabs, the Phoenicians', the Greeks, the Romans, the Portuguese, the Dutch and finally the English. Kappad, specially has been witness to plenty of such attention. On the Kappad beach itself, there is a rock on the top of which there is a Devi temple believed to be around 800 years old. Kappad is a quiet place where it is pretty easy (and loved) to loose connection with the outside world and turn attention inwards.

The other beaches are

1. *Shanagumugham (Thiruvananthapuram):* Just 8 k.m. from the city this beach is quiet favorite amongst the lovers of nature. There is also a 35 m large sculptural image of a mermaid known as 'Matsya Kanyaka.' This is an ideal place for the sunset watchers. The beach is adjacent to the Thiruvananthapuram international Airport and Veli Tourist Village.
2. *Thangasseri (Kollam):* This beach and its little village has a historical significance to make them popular. This tiny village has the ruins of an old Portuguese fort and churches built in 18th century. There is a lighthouse that welcomes visitors desirous of paying a visit.

3. *Thirumullavaram(Kollam):* With fresh air flowing all around, the Thirumullavaram beach is just perfect to enjoy a walk early in the morning. The swaying coconut palm trees contribute to the tranquil beauty as you watch fishermen setting out to the sea in search of catch. Bathing is quiet a good option in this beach.
4. *Cherai Beach (Ernakulam):* Cherai Beach lies at a distance of 45 km from the Ernakulum city and forms the border of the popular Vypeen Island. It is highly popular amongst tourists because of Dolphins. Dolphins of course radiate an infinite beauty and perhaps even make the hearts of visitors leap out in delight. Swimming is also quiet a good option in the Cherai beach. This lovely beach bordering Vypin Island is ideal for swimming. Dolphins are occasionally seen here. A typical Kerala Village with paddy fields and coconut groves nearby as an added attraction.
5. *Chavakkadu Beach (Thrissur):* This beach is off the usual tourist track. The sea is a brilliant emerald here and along the length of the beach are clusters of coconut palms which provide a natural cover to lie back in the shade.
6. *Nattika Beach (Thrissur):* This coastal village with virgin golden beach and serene ambience is now a must sea destination.Vadanappilli, Chavakkadu, Valappad, Thalikkulkam, Nattika, Perinnnanam, Panangad, Azhikodu are the other attractive beaches in Thrissur.
7. *Padinharekara Beach (Malappuram):* At the end of the Tipu Sultan road near Ponnani, the beach offers a breathtaking view of the confluence of the Bharathapuzha, the Thirur Puzha and the Arabian Sea.
8. *Vallikunnu Beach (Malappuram):* A beach resort set in the middle of the coconut grove is the main attraction here. The Kadalundi Bird sanctuary is just a short distance away.
9. *Tanur Beach (Malappuram):* The small coastal- fishing town of Tanur is one of the earliest settlements of the

Portuguese. It is a belief that St. Francis Xavier visited the place in 1546.

10. *Kappad Beach (Kozhikode):* History comes alive where a small monument commemorates the landing of Vasco da Gama in 1498. With the legends woven around its historic origins and traditions that cast their own spell, the scenic beauty of Kappad is no less enchanting. Set amidst picturesque fishing villages and rock information, the beach is truly lovely.
11. *Kozhikode Beach (Kozhikode):* This beach is a favorite haunt of sunset viewers. Adding to its natural beauty is the old world charm retained in the old light house and the two crumbling piers, each more than a hundred years old.
12. *Payyoli Beach (Kozhikode):* This faces the promonotory, is another stretch of beautiful golden sands and the sea here is quite.
13. *Beypore (Kozhikode):* This one is in the Kozhikode district of Kerala and also an erstwhile significant port city of the state. Right from the very beginning, Beypore has been renowned for its excellent construction of Ur's, the Arabian trading vessel. These ships were in huge demand earlier and even today, shipbuilders, known as Khalasis, have big customer line up from Middle East as well as across Arabian Sea. On your visit to the Beypore beach, you can still find experienced Khalasis at their work (which surprisingly is completely manual). This beach is located at the mouth of the river Chaliar
14. *Ezhimala Beach:* This beach is also located in the Kannur district of Kerala and has a 286 m high hill to add to its majestic look. At the foothill are few noteworthy sites including a carved stone pillars and an ancient burial chamber. The plants that grow on the hill are believed to have medicinal properties. A Naval Academy is being developed here.
15. *Payyambalam Beach (Kannur):* Situated close to the Kannur town, the Payyambalam beach is counted

amongst the best beaches of Kerala because of its serene beauty. An opportunity to relax and sunbathe is plenty. The beach has also a historical significance attached to it in the form of mortal remains of famous personalities like Swadeshabimani Ramakrishna Pillai, A.K. Gopalan, Pamban Madavan and K.G. Marar are buried here. The breezy, subdued sea makes this beach pleasant for viewing sunset.

16. *Dharmadam Beach:* This beach is the pride of an island known by the same name. Spread in an area of five acres, this island is not a public property which means that permission has to be sought before you can actually step on the sands of this beach. The beautiful island with coconut palms and green bushes is located at a distance of 17 km from the Kannur town (in the district of same name) in the northern part of Kerala.
17. *Meenkunnu Beach (Kannur):* This beach is located in Azhikode. This uncrowded beach is very popular among the tourists with its golden sand and surf.
18. *Mapila Bay Beach (Kannur):* Located in the Kannur district, the Moppila Bay shot into limelight during the reigns of Kolathiri. However, the bay is presently recognized as a fishing harbor. For a bit of sightseeing, there are ruins of an old fort (St Angelo's) and a temple. If the weather is favorable a boat cruise to the sea is a memorable experience.
19. *Muzhupilangad Beach (Kannur):* This beach is widely known for its length which is perhaps the largest in entire Kerala. The beach which is located in the Kannur district is pleasantly clean and allows safe waters for swimming. The particular feature of this beach that sets it apart from the other beaches is that it is the only drive in beach in entire Kerala. It is a long and clean beach, and the calm sea makes it ideal for swimming. This is only drive in beach in Kerala. Kizhunna Ezhara beach and Ezhimala beaches are the other major beach centers in Kannur.

20. *Bekal Beach (Kasarcode):* This beach is merely 14 km away from the city of Kasodgarh in the district by the same name in the northernmost part of Kerala. The beach boasts of a 3 century old fort in its background which lends its a historic significance. The panoramic beauty here is breathtaking. Flanked on two sides by long ravishingly beautiful palm fringed beaches, the Bekal fort stands proud on a promontory. The fort's commanding position, with views across the bays to the north and the south are truly breath taking.
21. *Kappil Beach (Kasarcode):* Remote and secluded, this beach is fast becoming a major tourist attraction.
22. *Pallikere Beach (Kasarcode):* This is hardly one km from the Bekal fort. Its relative seclusion, shallow water and great view, it becomes a favorite destination for the tourists.
23. *Chithari beach (Kasarcode):* This is a small tropical island nearby, with an emerald lagoon and a long sandy beach.
24. *Kanwathirtha beach (Kasarcode):* This is on the outskirts of Manjeswaram. Here at regular intervals along the long beach, the sea extends slender arms into the land, each branch resembling a swimming pool.

Marketing of Beach Tourism in Kerala: Ground Realities

Tourism planning and marketing efforts are considered as the chief elements of identifying tourist's preferences and their perception of the destination. The focused marketing efforts of the past few years paved the foundation for the image as a quality destination. Marketing grabs the tourists' attention, arouse their interest, trigger their desire and motivate them to take a decision. Successful marketing strategies create a desire for a product. As an industry, tourism has many components which lead to the travel experience. It includes transportation, accommodation and Locale. For ensuring the consistency and quality of the product the service provides need to work together tour package. (Romila Chawla; 2006)

The beaches in Kerala are experiencing a drop in the tourist arrivals this season. The trend indicates that tourists who spend the day at the beaches head for other destinations by the evening. The weather condition has been not so good in this season and the rains and lack of space at the beaches is making a negative impact on the resort. Complaints like recurrent power interruptions, drug selling, lack of efficient garbage dumping system and drinking water shortage is holding back the resort. And with the growing demand for high profile hotels, it's mainly the small hotels that suffer the loss this season.

The government is planning to develop and promote tourism products with continuous focus on Backwaters, Ayurveda, performing arts, pilgrim centers, cuisines and ecotourism as per the vision 2025, the official tourism policy document for the state of Kerala (Saroop Roy, 2006).It is clear that the Vision 2025 is neglecting the prospects of the development of beach tourism. Rajasenan and Kumar (2002) pointed out that Kerala is a coastal state and beaches are one of its biggest assets. One reason why beaches do not perform up to expectations could be that the state government downplays beach tourism. Kerala wants to be a high end tourism destination and its government is worried that promotion of the beachside will push the state into a low end mass tourist haven. This could be a wrongly placed notion since previous research says that beach tourists visiting Kerala are high spenders; probably they spend more than those who visit in search of heritage and culture. Or, it may be that only high spending beach tourists visit Kerala due to the government's beach de-marketing efforts.

Problems and Prospects

The first and foremost problem is the visibility and awareness about the unexplored beaches of Kerala.The state is concentrating on new products and is not marketing itself as aggressively as it should. Evev if the right products are there,the tourists is going to be swayed by the basic facilities that complete his experience,and the state has to provide the fundamental infrastructure suitable for the beach environment. In general it was found that the beach tourism gave an opportunity rather than a serious threat to bio diversity. Uncontrolled unchecked and irresponsible development and behaiviour by tourism businesses and tourists themselves leads to deterioration of the biodiversity in the destination area.

The development of beach destinations turned out to be a major issue and leads to uncontrolled and unplanned development. T Balakrishnan in his article "Do's and Don'ts in Tourism" stated that while developing beach tourism extreme care should be taken to see that the environment is not adversely affected. Any plan will be cleared only after conducting an environmental impact analysis and the carrying capacity. While tourism can boost local economy and create employment, if it is not planned properly it can also have adverse impacts on the host community. In a state like Kerala where the awareness about the ecology and environmental problems are very high no projects will be taken up before a detailed survey is done.

Beaches have the great potential for growth, but as a wide destination area with lot of components these destinations are facing *a plethora of problems.* Jacob Thomas in his study "adversities of coastal tourism-A quantitative approach" stated that 'resort development' trend was the main culprit .The mushrooming of resorts along the coastal areas had led to the destruction of shorebird habitats, depletion of fisheries, erosion of swimming beaches, poisoning of coral reefs and pollution harbors. The preference of tourists had their adverse effects. The study said the Westerners were always on the look out for under-developed coastal strips. As a result more and more virgin beaches wee falling prey to the rapaciousness of tourism.

Tourism has led to severe water scarcity in most of the leading beach destinations in Kerala. Especially in the peak season, the demand from the hotels and restaurants leads to groundwater depletion, affecting local communities whose purchasing power is far below that of the tourism industry and the tourists. The high consumption of a common good by the tourism industry is an illegal form of water privatization.

The large amounts of waste and sewage generated by tourism have also become a major environmental problem, even affecting tourism as such. The haphazard growth of tourism in Kovalam without proper planning took place to the detriment of local people, many of whom do not benefit from tourism. In response to this problem state government brought a new legislation called Kerala Tourism Act 2005,which is suggesting new tourism zones in any tourist destinations in the state. Which legislations infringing the powers local self-governments. So that it denied the space for local population in tourism planning and implementation (Keralatourismwatch).

The studies on beaches of Kerala revealed that there are so many problems occurring directly and indirectly from the development of beach destinations. The local people pointed out that the lack of proper infrastructure leads to problems like shortage of pure drinking water, frequent power failure, non facility for garbage disposal, in adequate drainage facilities, inadequate market facility and so on. The lack of strretlights on the beaches,poor road networks and absence of sanitary facilities at the beaches are the main problems encountered by the tourists.They also stated that the antisocial elemtnts harassed the women.The the international tourists pointed out that tourists also expres grievence over the lack of proper communication facilities and exploitation by the autorikshaw and taxi drivers.The street vendors and the stray dogs are a persistent problem at the beach.

Conclusion

Kerala tourism is trying to woo tourists from new markets. However the size of the beach and coastal features are important to give full psychological satisfaction to the 'sunlust' visitors. A beach resort needs to be developed as an integrated complex to function as a self contained community. There is a strong need to revive beach tourism in Kerala. Kerala can improve the marketing of its beaches by concentrating integrated packages. Excluding that, as a parent Department the Kerala government has to invest significantly in infra-structure if it has to promote tourism in the region.

An aggressive media policy for the promotion of beach tourism in India and abroad will helps to retain the lost glory of the beaches of Kerala. By organizing FAM Trips to the industry personnel will support our efforts. For lengthening the period of tourist arrivals and stay, the Government has to take efforts to organize fairs and festivals in the beach areas. By placing the locations in the films or the serials makes it possible for the domestic tourists to get the feel of the locations and creates awareness as well.

There is a strong need to formulate a conscious policy to diversify and improve tourism products of Kerala, including beach destinations. strategy for the development of tourism should concenterate the development of adventure sports facilities; designation of special tourism areas; development of specific circuits through external aid. An integrated strategy for the development of tourism has been already developed for synergizing the activities of different infrastructure sectors, the state governments and the private sector for tourism development.

Modern tourists expect to find a range of activities and a variety of experiences. In this respect the beaches of Kerala should have a wealth of assets to give them a distinctive appeal and combination of activities. Beach tourism in Kerala facing increased competition and has a pressing need for major investment, modernization of infrastructure and preservation of the natural assets of sea, beaches, wetlands and so on.Through education of all stakeholders involved in tourism it was felt that greater understanding of the importance of biodiversity could be achieved.

However there are many concerns related to the development of beach tourism in Kerala. There is a strong need to replace mass tourism, because a beach destination attracts always the mass tourists. While adopting the mass tourism in the beach areas the government should take initiatives to replace the mass tourism with sustainable and responsible tourism concepts. This will surely gain the socio economic and environmental fabric of the state.

References

www.keralatourism.org accessed on June 5th, 2009.

Saroop Roy B.R. (2006), "Kerala Tourism: Innovations in God's Own Country; Tourism Kerala; Tourism India Publication p.50.

Shepard, F.P. (1967), 'Submarine Geology', Mc Grew Hill, New York, p.190)

Ravi Bhushan Kumar (1995), Coastal Tourism and Environment, APH Publishing Corporation, New Delhi.

Rajasenan.D. and Kumar,M.K.A. (2002), Demographic, Psychographic and Life-Style Characteristics of Foreign Tourists: An Exploratory Study of Kerala, India. Tourism Recreation Research, 29(3) 51-59.)

Manoj Edward and Babu P George (2008), Destination Attractiveness of Kerala as an International Tourist destination: An Importance-Performance Analysis; paper presented in the Conference on Tourism in India-Challenges Ahead, IIMK.

Impact of Tourism on the Quality and Access to Water Case Studies from Kerala" available at http://www.keralatourismwatch.org/node/18.

T Balakrishnan (August 1993), Do's and Don'ts in Tourism Kerala Calling, Govt. of Kerala.

Romila Chawla (2006),Tourism Marketing and Communications, Arise Publishers, New Delhi.

21

Customer Relationship Management in Hotel Industry

S. Mythili, R. Renuka

Introduction

Today's customer prefer comfortable hotel stay to any other rewards offered. The modern hotel is one that can build a relationship with their customers with a personalized stay – a stay that customers wish to come back again and again. Customers who are once pleased by rewards and prizes care more about the hotel that remembers them. The frequent traveler and the occasional vacationer are more likely to return to a hotel that gets to know them. The use of customer Relationship Management (CRM) application to create a business strategy is an excellent way to increase customer loyalty and customer retention. By personalizing a customer's stay, a hotel can ensure that customers will come back again and again simply by remembering their favourite beverage, pillow or other preferred amenity.

CRM implementation, particularly in hotel industry, is very challenging in hotels. It allow hotels to customize the stay of loyal and valued customers as well as create special loyalty rates for customers who continue to spend quality time and money with the hotel. This is important because customers remember hotels that gave them personalized care. Also a business strategy put into place with CRM ensures that the hotel's technology is up to date and that a hotel can track a customer's satisfaction by creating a close relationship to that customer.

The customers relationship management in general is operationally defined by authors as "a management process of acquiring customers by understanding their requirements, retaining customers by fulfilling their requirements more than their expectations and attracting new customers through customer specific strategic marketing approaches. The process invites total commitment on the part of the entire organization in evolving and implementing relationship strategies that would be rewarding to all concerned".

Hotel is a place where a traveler can receive food and shelter provided he can afford to pay for it. It is also known as the accommodation industry and hospitality industry.

Importance of CRM in Hotel Industry

Today's technology allows a hotel to get to know loyal customers and provide special gifts such as sending flowers or gifts for children simply from remembering how the customer feels about those who are special in their lives. The significance of CRM are:

- Reduction in customer recruitment cost,
- Generation of more and more loyal customers,
- Expansion of customer base,
- Reduction in advertisement and other sales promotion expenses,
- Benefiting customer selectivity approach,
- Increase in the number of profitable customers,
- Easy introduction of new products,
- Easy business expansion possibilities,
- Increase in customer partnering, etc.

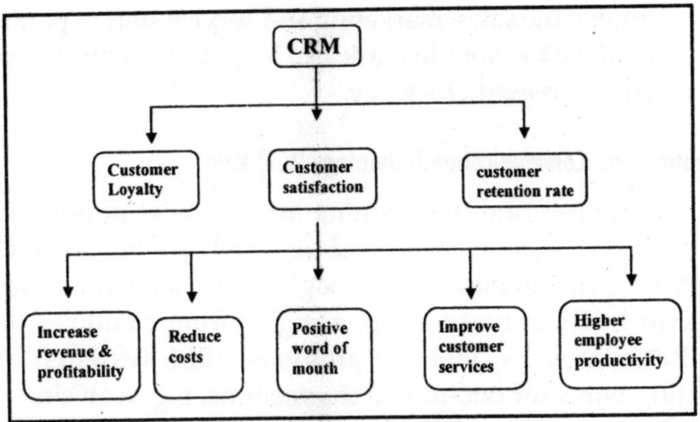

Benefits of CRM

In today's highly competitive business world CRM is becoming the ultimate solution for both customers as well as organizations.

CRM Technologies

CRM Technologies are rapidly evolving and are providing companies a collection of tools to use in order to enhance their customer relationship. According to Stone(2000) the two main forces that influence the need for CRM technologies to support the completion of CRM, are,

- The need for higher quality in CRM in order to meet the needs of the customers, CRM systems are increasingly being used to arrange companies' resources in a proper order.
- The need for greater productivity in CRM. CRM systems are giving the possibility to automate work previously done by hand.

According to Mr. Trepper (2000) there are three crucial requirements that need to be fulfilled by a CRM system. They are:

- Provide a consistent and unified view of each customer who contacts the company.
- Provide the customer with a complete view of the company, irrespective of how the customer contacts the company.

- Enable the sales, marketing and service staff to perform their tasks more like a team, leading to reduced costs and increased efficiency.

Information and Communication Technology (ICT) Role

Data warehouses and data mining are the most popular and highly needed systems for providing CRM capabilities or else for defining, developing and managing "the segment of one". ICT is an instrumental for gathering, storing customer data (e.g. EPOS system, website analysis, IBM systems) and providing ways for one-to-one interactions. e.g. web site, call centre, Kiosks, etc as well as identifying ways for disseminating and assessing information across the organization. CRM uses Information and Communication Technology (ICT) to gather data, which can then be analysed to provide the information required to create a more personal interaction with the customers.

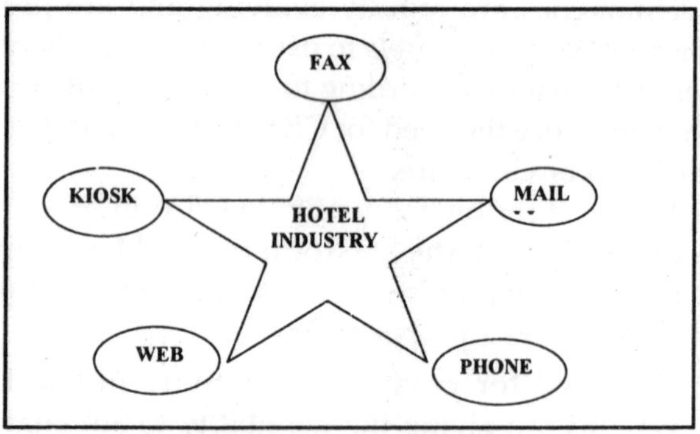

Hotel Industry and eCRM

Knowledge Management (KM)

The success of CRM, heavily depends on the collection and analysis of customer information that is used for developing highly personalized offerings. Romano (2000) and Massey et el (2001) strongly advocated the relation of CRM with KM and specifically customer KM, while the significance of customer knowledge is highlighted in several CRM studies.

CRM'S 4P (Marketing Mix in Hotel Industry)

Marketing mix in hotel industry has Four P's that all of them are tactical elements that required for a successful CRM initiative in any hotel company:

- Profiles
- Preferences
- Precision
- Property

Profiles

Effective profiling is at the heart of having one-to-one communications with hotel's guests. It has little to do with police officers determining whom to pull over or not, and everything to do with capturing relevant information about the guest and their behaviour, both observed and reported. Identifying the data elements to capture and retain represents a major tactical decision in a hotel CRM initiative.

Some of the key elements to consider in defining your profile data include:

- Multiple addresses and telephone numbers
- Payment methods(i.e. credit card numbers)
- Prior visit history,
- Family composition
- Comments
- Correspondence history.

Preferences

Preference data may be either observed or reported. One challenging thing about preferences is that a single guests' preferences vary according to the purpose of a given trip and the destination.

Precision

Precision of data input is a crucial element for any CRM effort in any industry. Sophisticated data hygiene and matching algorithms somewhat address the precision issue but establishing, training and reinforcing data input standards are the effective remedies.

Property (Property Management System)

In the hotel environment the measure of excellence in service almost always comes down to a face-to-face interaction in the hotel with the guest. The PMS is a crucial part of servicing that interaction given the role of the PMS in service delivering an integrated CRM initiative must incorporate two-way data transfer between any third-party system and the PMS. As guest stays are completed, the stay detail and any new master records must get passed from the PMS to CRM platform.

Tourism Package

The Tourism package consists of Accommodation, Recreation, Restaurant, Attraction and Transportation.

Tourism Package

Accommodation	*Recreation*	*Restaurant*	*Attraction*	*Transportation*
Five star, Four star, Three star, Two star, One star, cottages.	Theatre, Pubs, Night life, Music meeting, get together.	Western, Chinese, Indian, others.	Natural scenes, Historic, Artificial, beauties, Socio-cultural, heritages, lake, parks.	Airways, Railways, Roadways, Seaways, subways.

Source: Jha .S.M, Services marketing, Himalaya Publishing House,New delhi. Page No. 295

This table reveals that accommodation is the prime factor for tourism product. In this accommodation hotel capture the major place. For managing the hotel services, it is essential that we are also careful to the hotel accommodation facilities. It is pertinent that hotels are easily accessible to the tourist sites or beaches or shops. The hotel personnel should be trustworthy and competent enough to speak English and other regional languages. They are supposed to be friendly. The management of facilities at hotels need due care. Though the standard of services, amenities and facilities depend upon the grade of hotels still it is essential that hotels offer the promised services to the users. The gap between the services-promised and services-offered should be bridged over. The hotels should be well maintained, the décor should be attractive, possibly a fair mix of eastern and western culture, the atmosphere should be calm and quiet.

Hotel Services

The common law says that hotel is a place where all who conduct, themselves properly and who being able and ready to pay for their entertainment, accommodation and other services including the boarding like a temporary home. It is home away from home where all the modern amenities and facilities are available on a payment basis.

Hotel belongs to service activity. As every one understands hotel is a place where people will stay by paying the prescribed charges. They get personal comforts like comfortable living for any number of days, for which they have to pay on daily basis , and also availing other services like obtaining desired food, calm and independent stay. Besides basic living amenities, one can get entertainment ,sport facilities ,sight - seeing and various other comfortable services on paid basis.

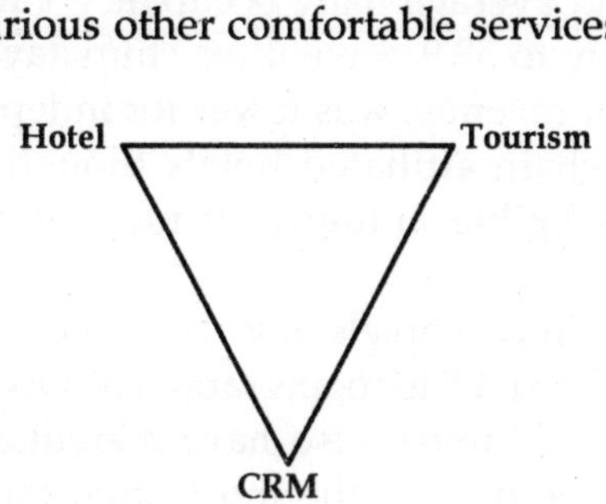

Trends in Indian Hotels

The Indian hotel industry, like any other industry, is facing changes in policy, technology, and customer aspirations, with the opening of the Indian economy in 1991, leading chains have been entering Indian market through joint venture options and franchising.

Some of the trends being witnessed in the Indian hotel industry are the competition in increasing, with the influx of international brands in India, the consumer experience a wide variety of product options and facilities. Consumers are getting better educated and aware of the issues that affect them. There is an increased amount of spending on leisure activities. There is also an increasing blend of business travel with leisure travel.

Too many hotels are being built up with a rapid increase in the metros are a result of which supply would outpace demand. At locations like Mumbai, Delhi, Chennai, and Khajurao, existing capacity outpaces the demand as a result of which there are empty rooms available at most times. Many new projects in the country are being delayed or are stalled due to cash crunch. The main reason for the cash flow problem is that the investor confidence in big hotel projects is very low, mainly because of the fear of increased supply. Where as in smaller towns, there is a dearth of quality hotels in the mid-priced segment. Oberois in India have come up with Trident as a leading brand in the mid-sized segment.

The occupancy levels on an average in Indian hotel industry varies between 51 percent in September to 63.9 percent in December. And average daily occupancy varies from 49.1 percent on Sunday to 59.9 percent on Thursday. Net income, as a percentage of revenue, was lower for independent hotels as compared to chain affiliated hotels though independent hotels spent negligible amount on management fee and franchise fee.

Traditionally, Indian hotels have been room oriented. The Taj group has a 35:65 F&B to rooms ratio. The Oberoi properties in New Delhi and Mumbai also have a similar ratio. Room revenue is considered to be the most important source of a hotel's profitability, representing 56.4 percent of total revenue across all hotels.

Tourism Spots in Tamil Nadu

The state of Tamil Nadu is indeed a tourist's destination. Tamil Nadu offers the terrific combination of tradition with trend. There are the filter coffees, dosas, Bharat Natyam performances, breathtakingly beautiful beaches and the magnificent temples. The exciting past and the beauty of the nature make Tamil Nadu worth more than a visit.

The entire state of Tamil Nadu reveals the beauty of the Indian temple architecture in its various structures. The capital city of Chennai is renowed for its beautiful beach resorts. Then there is the marvelous village of Mamallapuram. At mamallapuram you must check out the terrific temples made in the Pallava rock-cut architecture along the beautiful beach. The kaleidoscopic Kanchipuram reveals its rich heritage and attracts thousands of tourists. The pilgrim centre of Rameshwaram has several spots associated with the Ramayana and terrific temples too. At the southern mos tip of the Indian mainland is Kanyakumari. Kanyakumari is the auspicious meeting point of the Bay of Bengal, the Indian ocean and the Arabian sea. In the middle of the traditional towns like Thanjavur and Tiruchirapalli are the new age destinations of Pondichery and Auroville.

The state of Tamil Nadu boasts of two terrific hill stations of Kodaikanal and Ooty. The marvelous mountains, the fabulous forests and the tea and coffee plantations add to the magic of the serene yet beautiful surroundings. For the animal lovers Tamil Nadu offers the elephants and dholes wild pack-hunting dogd, tigers and leopards at the Mudumalai wildlife Sanctuary amidst the teak dominated deciduous forests. At the Annamalai sanctuary you may spot the lion-tailed macaques and several migratory birds. The state of Tamil Nadu is well connected through air, rail and road. There are enough decent accommodation options in Tamil Nadu and the scene is getting better every passing day. There are a number of star category hotels catering to the needs of tourists coming to explore Tamil Nadu or interesting in exploring the scenic region around.

The Chola regime brought glory to Thanjavur in the period between 10th and 14th centuries. It is situated at 55km east of Trichy and is also the headquarters of the district of the same name. Tanjavur is well known for its traditional handicrafts-art plates, bell metal castings, silk carpets, pith work, bronze icons, and classical Indian musical instruments.

Sri Brihadisvara Temple, Raja Raja Chola I built this temple in the 10th century. The frescoes of the sanctum are comparable to those in the Ajanta Caves. A gigantic statue of Nandi Bull, protects the sanctum.

Kumbakonam known as Temple city because of the presence of 108 temples in this town, is the second bigger town in Thanjavur district, also. It is located about 313 kilometers away from Madras on the south, about 90 kms from Trichy on the east and about 40 kms from Thanjavur on the North East. The town is bounded by two rivers-"River Cauvery" on the north and "River Arasalar" on the south. The city is famous for the "Mahamaham" festival that is celebrated once in 12 years in the Mahamaham tank located in the heart of it. Kumbakonam is flooded with temples of large size. There are as many as sixty temples, in and around Kumbakonam within 40 Kms radius.

In Tamil Nadu there are number of tourist places and temples. Among these Thanjavur district is also an important place for visit. Many people from various parts of our country visit many places in Thanjavur district and they select different kinds of hotel for their stay.

Purpose of Accommodating in Hotel in Thanjavur District

Purpose	*No. of Persons*
Occupation	12
Conference	17
Sight-seeing	13
Relaxation	21
Health	1
Pilgrimage	31
Marriage	16
Others	1

Source: Primary source

The table refers the reasons for lodging in the hotel industry like occupation, conference, sight-seeing, Relaxation, Health, Pilgrimage, Marriage and others. It infers that reasons pilgrimage shares major percentage when compared with other purpose of staying in hotel. The reason is Thanjavur district is the one of the oldest and famous pilgrimage centre.

IT Variables and Use of Internet in Hotel Industry

There are lot of facilities that could be implemented and used in hotels with the help of IT for customer satisfaction such as providing website, 24 hour on line reservation, TV welcome messages, TV menu ordering, credit card facilities and room services like wireless, internet, music and video on demand. IT facilities that could be offered for customer satisfaction using credit card facility, film and music on demand in rooms having web sites are the most important factors for guest.

Internet provides tremendous marketing opportunity. Internet should be used as a sales and marketing tool. In addition, it has also commended as a means to make reservation to promote, and to build awareness. Hotels could also extend their loyalty programme online by having special features for their potential and existing customers such as general information, online enrolment, restricted guest area, create customer profile, special web offer, and request rewards online. Service is a core source of differentiation for each hotel, internet as a powerful tool, enables hotels providing considerable novel services to customers.

Conclusion

Now a days the hotel industry faces increased globalization, competition, higher customer turnover, growing customer acquisition costs and rising customer expectations. The hotel industry's performance and competitiveness is significantly dependent on their ability to satisfy customers efficiently and effectively. To enhance guest satisfaction and profitability, hotels must focus on implementing Customer Relationship Management (CRM) strategies that aim to seek, gather and store the right information, validate and share it throughout the entire organization and then use it throughout all organizational levels for creating personalized, relationship and unique guest's experiences.

Thus customer satisfaction will result in customer loyalty and retention. Dyche stated that 5 percent increase in customer retention results in a 25 to 95 percent increase in profits.

A successful implementation of CRM with more satisfied and loyal customer have a lot of benefits for hotels such as increase in the rate of retention, increase revenue and profitability, reduce internal costs, decrease marketing costs, improving customer service, positive word of mouth, market share growth, improve marketing methods, streamlined business process, better understanding of customer requirements, higher employee productivity and protect marketing investment with maximize returns. All these benefits of a hotel can be a source for long term and sustainable competitive advantage.

References

Books

Jha. S. M, "Services Marketing", Himalaya Publishing House, New Delhi.

Jha. S. M, "Hotel Marketing", Himalaya Publishing House, New Delhi.

Manish Ratti, " Hotel Tourism and Hospitality Management", Rajat Publications, New Delhi. A Step-by- Step Approach, Vikas Publishing House Pvt Ltd,New Delhi.

Peeru Mohamed. H. and A. Sagadevan," Customer Rerlationship Managemement".

A Step-by-Step Approach, Vikas Publishing House Pvt Ltd., New Delhi.

Ravi sankar,"Services Marketing the Indian Perspective", Excell Books Publishers, New Delhi.

Website

www.tourism.gov.in.

22

Customer Relationship Management in Hotel Industry

P. Nithya Preetha, N. Markkandeyan

This article will provide a brief overview about customer relationship management with the concept of hospitality industry, the importance of hospitality marketing to ensure customer satisfaction and business growth. It was suggested that players in hospitality industry should realize that hospitality product is different, that is in fact, something intangible that they are selling and as both product and reasons for buying it are different also different so it demands a different marketing strategy, something like hospitality marketing that requires customer centered hospitality need identification, specific segmentation & positioning and 'the hospitality marketing mix'.

CRM stands for *Customer Relationship Management.* It is a process or methodology used to learn more about customers' needs and behaviors in order to develop stronger relationships with them. There are many technological components to CRM, but thinking about CRM in primarily technological terms is a mistake. The more useful way to think about CRM is as a process that will help bring together lots of pieces of information about customers, sales, marketing effectiveness, responsiveness and market trends.

Customer relationship management helps businesses use technology and human resources to gain insight into the behavior of customers and the value of those customers. Customer relationship management is more than the practice of collecting guest-centric data. It's the art of using historical, personal, and experiential information to personalize a guest's stay while generating incremental revenue opportunities.

With the latest offerings in CRM, hoteliers can:

- Develop comprehensive guest profiles from reservation information and demonstrate to guests that the property is in touch with their needs.
- Drive guest-centric data down to the transaction level, allowing employees and guest-facing technology to deliver value to the guest.
- Generate a realistic profile on the spending and stay patterns of guests, allowing the property to create guest-centric marketing for increased loyalty and spending.

Customer relationship management is normally relying on the following items:

1. Marketing
2. Service and
3. Sales

It can be easily understood with the help of the Fig: 1 given below.

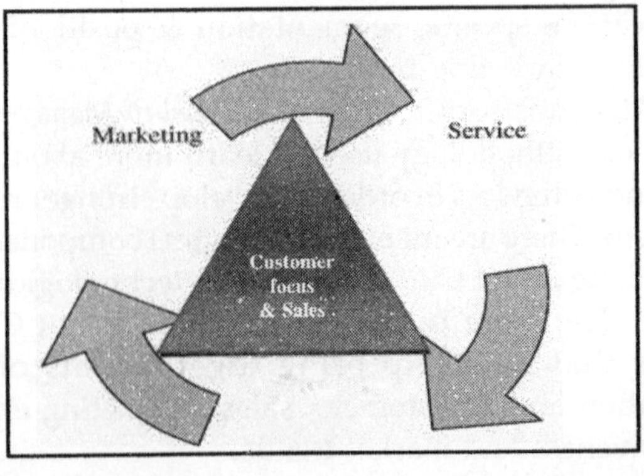

Marketing

Marketing may be performed through any combination of channels, using information stored in a customer data warehouse to personalize transactions and select appropriate products to be offered to potential customers. One specific loyalty program member may have a history of regularly staying in a particular hotel between Monday and Thursday, over a prolonged period. Using advanced analysis techniques, this traveller may be segmented as having a profile typical of someone working on a temporary business assignment, where repetitive behavior is demonstrated over a finite period. As with many business hotels, the hotel in question is promoting weekend breaks to address the problem of low weekend demand. The campaign management system receives information saying that this traveller is a likely candidate for a weekend break with their spouse. The contact management system is used to discover which communications medium the traveller most often uses to make bookings. This guest usually books through the hotel Web site. Since the traveller is a member of the hotel chain loyalty program and has entered his Internet e-mail address as part of the program registration, the campaign management system sends the traveller details of the offer in the form of a direct e-mail appended to the booking confirmation of the traveller's next business stay. If the traveller had a history of booking directly with the hotel, then the campaign management system may have selected the hotel outbound call center as the chosen communication media, or may even have sent a text message to his registered mobile telephone. Additional information in the passenger's profile may result in the offer being communicated in the customer's natural language or even, in co-operation with a partner airline, may include convenient air travel information for the customer's spouse.

Service

It is a department which serves food and beverage to the guest in a very attractive and pleasing manner, which creates good impression on the guest. There is several kind of food and beverage outlet like restaurants, Bars, Coffee shops, take away banquets etc. It is *second most revenue* producing department of the hotel by selling different types of food and beverage to the guest. The primary function of the service department is to provide food and drink to a hotel's guests; this was a fairly simple task. Today, however, providing food and drink is much complicated. A large hotel might well have a coffee shop, a gourmet restaurant, a poolside snack bar, room service, two banquet halls, and ten function rooms where food and beverages are served. It might also have a lounge, a nightclub, and a lobby bar. On a busy day (or night) it's quite likely that functions will be booked in many outlets at the same time. In addition, some outlets may have multiple events scheduled for a single day. As you can see, there is great diversity in the types of activities performed by a service department, requiring a significant variety of skills on the part of its workers.

Because of the diversity of services provided, the service department is typically split into subunits. The executive chef, a person of considerable importance and authority in any full-service hotel, runs the food production, or kitchen, department. A variety of culinary specialists who are responsible for different aspects of food preparation report to the executive chef.

The actual serving of food in a large hotel's restaurants is usually the responsibility of a separate department, headed by the assistant food and beverage director. The food service department is composed of the individual restaurant and outlet managers, maitre d's, waiters, waitresses, and bus help.

Because of their special duties and concerns, many large hotels have a separate subunit that is responsible only for room services. Because of the high value and profit margins associated with the sale of alcoholic beverages, some hotels have a separate department that assumes responsibilities for all outlets where alcoholic beverages are sold. The person responsible for this department is the beverage manager.

Most full-service hotels also do a considerable convention and catering business. The typical convention uses small function rooms for meetings and larger rooms for general session, trade shows, exhibits, and banquets. As a hotel or lodging business increase the use and its personnel are introduced to the client, a meeting planner, or an association executive by the marketing and sales department. The convention services department then handles all of the client's meeting and catering requirements. Individually catered events include parties, wedding receptions, business meetings and other functions held by groups. To provide for the unique needs of these types of customers, hotels often organize separate catering and convention departments.

Depending on the size of the hotel, the job of cleaning the food and beverage outlets themselves as well as of washing pots and pans, dishes, glasses. And utensils are often delegated to a subunit known as the stewarding department.

It is only through continuous co-operation and co-ordination that a hotel's food service function can be carried out effectively. A guest who is dinning in a hotel restaurant requires the joint efforts of the kitchen, food service, beverages, and stewarding departments. A convention banquet cannot be held without the efforts of the convention and catering department along with the food production, beverage, and stewarding departments. The sequence of events and co-operation required among the food and beverage staff is even more important than in the rooms department, thus increasing the importance of communication between managers and employees alike. Another challenge faced by management is the diversity of the employees in the food and beverage department; the dishwasher in the stewarding department is at a dramatically different level than the Sous chef in the kitchen.

Sales

Co-ordination is not as important an issue in the sales department, which is generally much smaller than the service department. The primary responsibility of the sales managers who make up the sales department is sales, or the selling of the hotel facilities and services to individuals and groups. Sales manager sell rooms, food and beverages to potential clients through advertising, attendance at association and conference meetings, and direct contacts. The sales department is also removed from most of the day-to-day operational problems faced by other departments. The division of work among the sales managers is based on the type of customers a hotel is attempting to attract. Individual sales managers often specialize in corporate accounts, conventions, or tour and travel markets. Sales managers' accounts are sometimes subdivided along geographical lines into regional or national accounts. The sales staff of the largest full-service hotels usually does not exceed a dozen or so. These sales managers work more or less independently in their particular market segments.

Conclusion

Customer focus is the main motto of this industry. In hospitality industry, customer satisfaction is considered as a more significant one than others. In short, we can say that the hospitality industry is a customer-centered industry/business. So their focuses will be laid only on their customers alone. Right from check -in till check-out, the hotelier will be held responsible for the customer's satisfaction in all the aspects as per their customers wish, because the customer is the only person who is considerable to run the whole industry. The functions of other departments like production, service, front office, house keeping, maintenance, etc are also pedestal on these customers with their satisfaction. In order to maintain the will in this competitive hospitality industry each and every one has to work hard with endurance to satisfy the customer need. Customer may be of any nature, but the hotelier has to know how to handle them with care. Hence the discussion may conclude that, the hospitality industry provided ever needed services rendered to their customers.

Reference

www.wikipedia.com

www.salesforce.com

en.wikipedia.org
searchcrm.techtarget.com
www.crminfoline.com
www.twocrows.com
and more

23

CRM in Commercial Banks

J. Arunachalam

Banking Industry

Over the last five years that Market Intelligence has conducted annual surveys of local banks, the most important point that has continued to emerge strongly from managers is the need for dynamism to keep pace with the constantly changing needs of their clientele. As customers become more and more enlightened, they are demanding innovative and convenient services from their financial providers. In fact in this year's customer survey, customers came out as very conscious of how their preferred banks utilize information and communication technology to enhance efficiency, convenience, and to gain competitive edge. IT consumes a considerable R&D fund for any bank (and indeed any other company) that aspires to be a leader in service delivery. One company that has endeared itself among banks by providing IT related solutions in Africa is Fintech. We take a look at the company, its partners, products and services.

Having recently celebrated its tenth anniversary, Fintech, a wholly owned subsidiary of Loita Holdings Corporation Africa touts itself as a leader in enterprise technology services and solutions. The company, registered in Mauritius, provides a wide range of products in accounting, banking and financial systems, specifically developed software solutions, cheque clearing system, ATM switching solutions, security solutions, storage solutions, document management solutions, networking solutions, enterprise MICR reader systems, training, outsourcing, consulting as well as IT project management. Apart from Kenya, Fintech is present in Uganda, Tanzania, Malawi, Angola, Zimbabwe and Tunisia with a strong staff of over 150 professionals who are trained to deliver world class IT solutions.

However it is almost impossible for any single company to offer quality service in as many areas without partnering with other experts in relevant fields. Fintech is backed by a broad network of best-of-breed international solution providers and serves its customers with professionalism and support in keeping with international standards. These partners include i-flex solutions, Mosaic Software, Unisys, Microsoft, Oracle, HP, Microsoft Business Solutions, Computer Associates, Hypercom, Checkpoint and Hitec Labs. In addition Fintech has a dedicated software development company, Data Integration Technologies (DIT) which has some of the leading technology designers and programmers in Kenya. Further, the company incorporates a training firm, Loita Institute for Finance and Technology (LIFT) which leverages off the group's Pan African presence, technical and banking expertise to provide courses that address the IT and banking training requirements of institutions and individuals in the market. And lastly, there is Fincom, which focuses on enterprise hardware solutions, networking, ATM's and maintenance services.

The company, which occupies the whole 16th floor of AmBank House and is always a buzz with activity has end-to-end capabilities for managing technology lifecycle from application development, system integration to training. From defining the IT strategies, Fintech can design, implement and manage an organisation's technology aspect and handle changes if and when they arise. Additionally the company manages multifaceted business and technology projects using proven techniques and automated tools for organisations.

Some of the banking software used by local financial institutions provided by Fintech is currently in use by other leading banks in over 100 countries around the world. Fintech's banking technology partner - i-flex solutions, is a leading global provider of solutions to the financial services industry worldwide. i-flex is the architect of Flexcube, an end-to-end product suite for consumer corporate, investment and internet banking, asset management and investors servicing. It is a universal banking solution which is a reliable, industry-strong, multi-currency, multi-lingual, one-stop solution that offers integrated delivery of all the banking products across the branch network, telephone, ATM, POS and internet. Flexcube is a comprehensive, integrated yet modular core banking solution that caters for all the needs of a modern financial institution. Since its launch in 1997, more than 140 financial institutions across 65 countries have implemented Flexcube. It has been ranked the number one selling universal banking solution in the world by International Banking Systems.

Framework that lets financial institutions create and deploy financial applications over the web and other customer contact points such as ATM, PDA.WAP and telephone. It provides the financial institutions with a ready suite of web applications in areas of retail banking commercial banking mutual funds, securities trading and bill payment. This is a financial middleware that extends the organisations other businesses like credit cards and insurance into its customers' lives quickly and rapidly.

India's largest product software company and offers a comprehensive range of products and customised services that enable financial institutions to cut costs, respond rapidly to market needs, enhance customer service levels and mitigate risks. Its other financial service solutions include Prime Sourcing, which is a customised application software development and deployment methodology. PrimeSourcing allows financial institutions to cut costs and reduce risk because it is supported by SEI-CMM Level 5 processes and Centre of Excellence that remain focused on domain and technology areas such as Business Intelligence, CRM, Insurance and

Payment Systems, Java and e-services. Then there is Reveleus which is the industry's only metadata-driven information management infrastructure, coupled with a suite of integrated analytical applications and improves the quality and consistency of information, thereby helping organisations reduce risk and improve efficiencies in information gathering, analysis and distribution.

Financial Industry

MICR Cheques clearing systems - dubbed "ChequePoint", this system automates the cheque clearing operations within the bank's branches and with other banks. The system uses MICR technology to read the cheques MICR code line which is unique to every cheque. ChequePoint has been the preferred MICR system because of its unique features which include, cheques imaging (front/back), Amount entry using cheque images, cheque statement distribution, post dated cheques handling, Stopped cheques detection, missed items reconciliation, comprehensive reporting & graphing, commendable security & audit features etc.

Leasing Management Systems-dubbed "LeasePAC" the system automates asset financing businesses which include, leasing, hire purchase, Business and personal loans, Insurance Premium Financing, Stocking Plan, Factoring & Discounting, Treasury Management, Deposits etc. The system comes with comprehensive reporting, security and Audit capabilities.

E-banking products-The system dubbed "E-bridge" enables customers to access their banking solution through various delivery channels like ATMS, POS, Telephone, Internet and Dialup. E-bridge is interfaced with the core banking system to offer online services. E-bridge is currently running in 15 banks in 6 different countries in Africa, managing over 100 ATMs and POS terminals.

Other product offerings include:

- Pension Funds Management System-dubbed "FinPen".
- Signature capture module-dubbed 'microImage'
- Workflow Solutions-dubbed "Fintranets"

Having been the first Microsoft support Centre in Kenya, DIT has standardised its development on Microsoft platform. This includes the use of Visual Basic as its development language, SQL as database engine, and Windows as the operating system.

Fintech also provides EFT businesses with a wide range of solutions, including linking ATM's to banks and processors, collecting and managing in-store data and transactions through retail point-of-service (POS) payments, and switching millions of transactions to EFT networks or hosts. Fintech is the technology provider for Kenswitch and Zimswitch in projects that are helping set the standard for e-business in Africa in the 21st century.

As a Microsoft Gold Certified Partner, Fintech has passed the highest level of requirements from Microsoft. The Gold designation means Fintech has demonstrated the most robust, efficient and scalable implementations of Microsoft technologies where the focus is typically on one or more solution specialties. Fintech's technical and professional services include design and implementation, consulting, project management, audit, outsourced IT administration, maintenance and support services.

One of the most ingenious services on offer is IT personnel outsourcing. If for example an IT expert in an organisation abruptly quits or is infirmed, Fintech can forward an equally trained and experienced person to step in either temporarily or permanently. This ensures uninterrupted and consistent technology flow within an organisation. Their consultants can leverage their strong management capabilities and past experiences to enhance the value of the organisation's IT.

The company mitigates information risk by evaluating, planning and implementing an organisation's security program, process and technologies. Their consultants use their knowledge and real life techniques to evaluate an organisation's vulnerabilities and risks then help to resolve and monitor them. In addition to integrating network technology solutions, the company delivers customised focused software solutions on standard third-party platforms to meet client needs. They plan, manage, assess, design, develop, re-engineer, implement and support software solutions to address client requirements.

Fintech is responsible for maintaining and supporting over US$20million in software and systems implementations on behalf of its clients. Its stated mission is 'To provide our customers with the most effective solutions to empower them to better serve their customers.' Its sister company Loita Capital partners International Limited, is an investment banking firm focused on Africa. Loita provides services in the arrangement and funding of debt transactions, advisory services and capital-raising for equity transactions, bank management, correspondent banking, asset management and other corporate-oriented financial services.

Customer Service Management

Rapidly changing customer demographics, sophisticated business needs and margin pressures in an industry characterized by increased regulation, globalization and continuous M&A activity are forcing banks to improve their operations and rethink their customer acquisition and retention strategies. Selling increasingly commoditized products and outward bound, document-based transaction processing at customer touch points are not enough to compete effectively. Customers want convenient, secure access and they want their bank to know who they are. To attract and retain profitable customers you must deepen your customer relationships and enrich the customer experience. This means offering a complete range of integrated banking services and channels, from branch networks and call centres to ATMs, internet and mobile banking. It also means providing the right products, services and channels. You must be able to view disparate customer data, analyze the information, identify opportunities and launch customer programs that are targeted to suit your customer's banking needs.

Banking Center of Excellence Showcases

The Banking Center of Excellence showcases CSC's business expertise and technology prowess in the retail banking industry. The Center provides banking solutions for clients worldwide in the areas of core banking, card and electronic payment systems, customer relationship management, remittance processing, loan processing and servicing, and check image archiving. Some of the world's largest financial institutions rely on these function-rich, scalable solutions to support mission-critical processing.

The Center and IBM have joined forces to deliver world-class solutions that combine CSC's hands-on systems integration proficiency and deep industry knowledge with the Web-based design and open-standards-based technology of IBM. CSC and IBM have teamed together to leverage IBM software and hardware to develop prepackaged, repeatable enterprise applications and next-generation solutions.

Organizations can leverage the Center to:

- Achieve dramatic improvements in process efficiency by participating in technology frameworks or business transformation discussions that create innovative options for technology and business users.
- Evaluate and pilot the configuration of new bank products, methodologies and concepts using CSC's banking systems.
- Access performance benchmarks and scalability studies that have been completed for CSC's banking solutions.
- Complete a core banking system functional analysis that identifies functions that a bank can further exploit to realize additional business value.
- Access hands-on learning environments to further understand system parameters for business-case scenario development.
- Review a full range of SWIFT (Society for Worldwide Interbank Financial Telecommunication) service options that are available in the Germany Center.
- Attain total immersion and solid system knowledge transfer by attending the system training that is part of the Center.

- Analyze the latest compliance and regulatory updates to develop risk management strategies and practices.
- Complete a (European) cross-border gap analysis for retail banking functionality (regulatory requirements, banking product terms and conditions, process definition) and develop a central development cross-border roll-out operational model.
- Perform a core banking process and best practices analysis that identifies a retail banking best practices architecture (from a business point of view) and a service repository (from a Service-Oriented Architecture perspective).
- Reduce the total cost of ownership (TCO) for IT by examining a variety of technology options and frameworks generated through TCO "yellow pad" briefings.

Resources

Is staffed by over 350 banking and cards industry and application experts, project managers, solution programmers and solution architects from a global resource pool. This pool provides a range of capabilities customized for retail banking: business assessments, business process engineering, systems design, solution implementation, systems integration, technical architecture services, training and customer support.

Dominant Banking Industry Trends

Customers Redefine the Rules of the Game

Over the next ten years, the retail banking industry will be forced to adapt to rapidly changing customer expectations. Customer diversity and individualism will pervade buying behavior, and how customers perceive value will change as a result of pronounced shifts in demographics and value systems. "Norms" will become increasingly rare. Population growth will increase the relative numbers of both the oldest and youngest customer segments, posing significant new challenges and opportunities for banks. While older customers tend to require more high-touch service but are generally more loyal, youthful customers are fickle, technology savvy, and highly inclined to research and negotiate the best deals. And across all age groups, long-standing life stage patterns are becoming more unpredictable. People are marrying later, divorcing more, having second families, and starting second and third careers. These changes are leading to unprecedented diversity in the financial needs of households. Customers' decision patterns will become more complex. Value-oriented buying, based on the price-quality dynamic, is becoming increasingly influenced by personal views and the desire to express those views outwardly. Customers will demand low prices for basic goods but pay premiums for products and services that matter more to them personally.

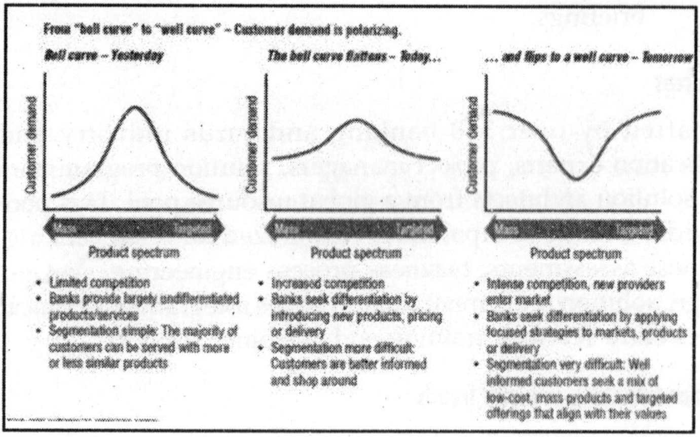

Overall, banking customers are becoming more handson and more mistrustful – trends that are even stronger in younger generations. Banks are experiencing defection rates reaching as high as 30 percent as customers are less inclined to think that banks act in their best interest. Less than one-third of the customers of top 10 U.S. banks (32 percent), for example, consider their banks to be advocates.5 More importantly, about as many (31 percent) believe that their bank does what is best for its bottom line at the expense of customers.6 And as time progresses, technology and competition will continue to make it easier to research, compare, and form and break relationships -driving switching costs toward zero.

So, what are the implications of these trends? By 2015, better-informed, more discerning customers will redefine the rules of the game by demanding greater advocacy and control in their banking relationships. To be sure, banks will need to develop (or attain) the capabilities necessary to sense and respond rapidly to their customers' increasingly eclectic demands and unpredictable patterns of banking behavior. To delight their customers, banks will need to provide greater perceived value relative to their competition. Having the ability to offer greater choice and personalization of products and services in the future will be critical–and yet not enough. Becoming a true customer advocate will require banks to use information about customers to anticipate and proactively suggest banking solutions that meet their life and lifestyle needs.

What's more, in 2015, bank customers will demand relationships with greater transparency–there will be no tolerance for "fine print" with vague terms and conditions. Banks will have to simplify their fee structures and implement trusted processes that help customers avoid unnecessary fees.

Our research across the banking and retail industries, including discussions with senior executives worldwide, reveals that extraordinary service and a superlative customer experience are the most sought-after capabilities, yet also the most difficult to scale and replicate consistently. In the future, retail banks will have immense opportunity to use service and experience to decommoditize their offerings and to encourage and reward customer.

There are a number of cues that banks can take from retailers to support their move in this direction:

- Thorough understanding of the needs and buying patterns of segments they aspire to serve and delight
- Extraordinary service standards and follow through
- Strong emphasis on people empowerment

- Extensive client associate training
- Reward structures designed to elicit desired behaviors with clear, measurable goals.

Universal Banks and Ultra-focused Niche Players Thrive

By 2015, the results of two prominent competitive forces will be clearly visible: a "middle squeeze" of traditional banks, and the emergence of far greater numbers of industry specialists and non-bank banks–each with distinct competitive growth strategies.

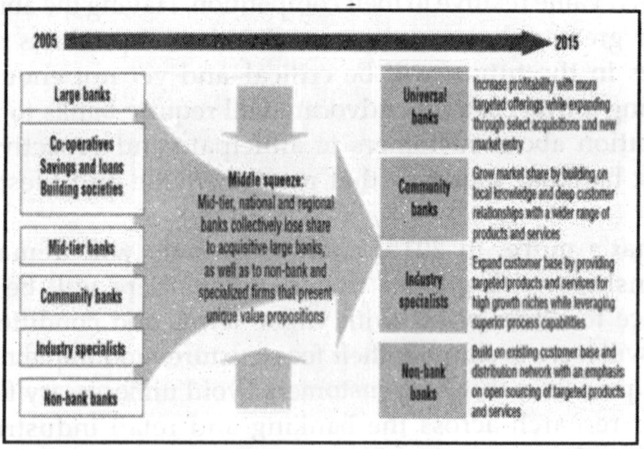

The industry will witness consolidation at its middle as it continues to be affected by large banks spreading their reach, and the emergence of specialized banking players that will set new cost and service level standards. Acquisitions led by large banks, however, will continue to be less attractive until the acquirer and potential target valuation gap narrows. Currently, acquirers (as represented by large banks) are valued at approximately ten times 2006 earnings, while potential targets (as represented by regional banks) are valued at 13 times 2006 earnings.10 More likely, regional banks will look to consolidate among themselves or will seek investors from outside their home countries to grow into more powerful players in the market.

Non-traditional participants in the banking ecosystem, including specialized banks, specialist service providers, and non-bank banks, will have a significant impact in altering the competitive dynamics of the industry as well. Specialized banks, for example, will continue to enhance their market differentiation and will be well-positioned to offer greater choice and personalization to customers. These banks are expected to compete aggressively with traditional banks to control select, more-profitable market segments. A good number will also become attractive acquisition candidates for larger banks looking to target specific markets, customers or products.

Conclusion

2015 will present tremendous challenges for the retail banking industry. Customers will become increasingly individualistic and, at the same time, more controlling in their relationships with banks. Ubiquitous information will empower customers to compare offerings across the market and transact increasingly on their own terms. For banks, traditional segmentation approaches and go-tomarket techniques will become obsolete.

How retail banks compete in the marketplace will also change dramatically. Universal institutions will compete directly with community banks offering unique value propositions to targeted groups of customers. A flood of industry specialists and non-bank banks will both compel and enable traditional banks to become specialized enterprises themselves.

On the flip side, 2015 will present tremendous opportunities for retail banks, particularly with respect to harnessing product, service and process innovation to serve customers better, to differentiate themselves in an increasingly crowded marketplace, and to de-commoditize current products and services. Moreover, advances in technology will enable unprecedented levels of global connectivity, IT functionality and the ability to realize the enormous potential of data.

References

Brenmer Robert "Business Banking, Banking Technology' News.

Chawla A.S & Others – Indian Banking Towards 21st Century, Deep & Deep Pub., New Delhi.

Parameswaran. R – Indian Banking Theory, S. Chand & Co. New Delhi.

Varshney PW & Sundaram– Banking and Financial System, Sultan Chandra Sons, New Delhi.

24

Marketing Strategies of Tourism Product in Kanniyakumari

R. Rathiha, G. Sweetlin Subi, S. Priya

Introduction

Tourism is a smokeless industry and is one of the fast growing business world over. The tourist flow to various countries serves as an indicator through which we can foresee a process of cultural assimilation and economic development in destination countries. Every country has something to offer to a tourist, it may be in the form of natural products like scenic spots or man-made wonders like Disneyland in U.S.A. Many of the developing countries are blessed with such a vast amount of cultural heritage, material artifacts and life styles embedded with fairs and festivals that tourism industry can serve as a great source of revenue generation. Despite the nature's gift in abundance in countries and particularly in South Asia, the tourist traffic has remained dismally low and the region receives a minute percentile of the global traffic.

Tourism promotion, like other forms of marketing, largely depends on the customer traffic. If there is a growing customer traffic trend then more and more money shall flow to an economy in the form of gross revenue earnings and also as foreign direct investments for tourism destination marketing.

The product marketing does not involve much complex phenomenon because the number of uncontrollable factors in more than the number of mix variables.

Tourism first of all, is a service. So production and consumption take place at the same time. The problems of marketing in tourism are somewhat different from the problems of traditional product marketing. To be successful, an industry must sell its product in the market place. Since tourism product is immobile and its potential customers need to build and compare destination images before they travel, some form of intermediary is required. This is the function of the travel agent, who must successfully match a tourist image and tourist product. The industry is also highly dependent on the goodwill and co-operation of host communities. Hence it is the citizen who needs to see how his community is packaged and sold as a tourist product on the world market.

"Marketing is a management philosophy which, in light of tourist demand, makes it possible through research, forecasting and selection to place tourism products on the market most in line with the organization's purpose for the greatest benefit."

Burbart and Medlick opine, "Tourism marketing activities are systematic and co-ordinated efforts extended by National Tourist Organization / or tourist enterprises at international, National and local levels to optimize the satisfaction of tourist groups and individuals in view of sustained tourism growth".

About Kanniyakumari

Kanniyakumari occupies a unique place among the tourist centers in India. It is a place of hoary antiquity and derives its name from Kanniyakumari the Virgin Goddess. It is the land's end of the Indian peninsula, where the Arabian sea, the Indian ocean and the Bay of Bengal confluence. This is one of the important pilgrim centers of India of fine beach landscape with sands of myriad colour. From the beautiful beach, one can simultaneously witness the glorius sight of the moon, rising up and the sun setting in the west, on a full moon day. It is the meeting place of Tamil and Malayalam and even Tamil is spoken differently like Malayalam with nationalized accent.

Kanniyakumari Bagavathy Amman temple like Swami Vivekananda rock memorial Ganthi memorial, Thiruvalluvar statue, Bay Watch, Government museum, Church, Sothavilai beach, Mathoor flulme, Suchindram, Thirparappu waterfalls, Muttom etc. were the places of interest in Kanniyakumari.

Statement of the Problem

Kanniyakumari is a beautiful place with a huge variety of tourist centers. Yet, these tourist centers remains unidentified by vast number of tourists. Tourism will bring more tourists to Kanniyakumar District and help in creating more employment opportunities to the local poor. This has intended the researcher to analyse tourism marketing in Kanniyakumari.

Objectives of the Study

- To exhibit the preference of tourists regarding the multi-dimensional tourist products like accommodation, transportation, recreation, restaurant, shopping etc.,
- To analyse the level of satisfaction of tourists regarding tourist products.

Preferential Attributes for Tourism Product

A survey was conducted among tourists visiting Kanniyakumari. 12 foreign tourists and 88 Indians tourist were considered for intensive study and the study revealed the following:

- 8 percentage of the foreign tourists prefer 5 star hotels and 34 percentage prefer 4 star hotels which are lacking in Kanniyakumari. However 38 percentage of Indian tourists prefer cottages, havelis and other accommodation other than star hotels.
- 66 percentage of foreign tourists prefer Indian food. However 49 percentage of Indian tourists prefer Tamilian food and 46 percentage prefer Indian food.
- Most of the foreign tourists prefer airways but most of the Indian tourist prefer road transport when compared to other means of transport.

- Tourists visiting Kanniyakumari, both foreign as well as Indian tourists prefers to buy handicrafts. Their second preference is artistic products.

  (Refer Annexure I, II, III and IV)

Satisfaction regarding tourism product

The survey reveals that 64 percentage of visitors feel that their stay is excellent at Kanniyakumari, 27 percentage feels good and only, 2 percentage feel fair. No one feels unsatisfactory, where as the other 7 percentage feel satisfactory. In a nut shell, majority of the visitors are satisfied by their visit to Kanniyakumari. Level of satisfaction is high in the case of tourists upto 55 years of age and low in case of 55 and above age group. With regard to sex, the level of satisfaction is more in case of female and low in case of male. Level of satisfaction is low in case of Christians while in case of Hindus the level of satisfaction is high and the satisfaction level for Muslims is on an average level. Level of Satisfaction is low in case of highly educated visitors when compared to low educated visitors. Level of satisfaction is high is case of low income group than in high income group. All the foreign visitors and local visitors are enjoying the visit. 67 percentage of the foreigners feel their visit as excellent and 25 percentage as good whereas 64 percentage of local tourists feel as excellent and 27 percentage as good. Level a satisfaction in high in case of tourists who stay for a long period in Kanniyakumari than in case of tourists who say for a short period of 1-5 days. Level of satisfaction is high in case of visitors who visit Kanniyakumari more than 3 times.

Chi-square test has been applied to find out whether there is any significant relationship between demographic factors and level of satisfaction and the results were exhibited in Table 1.

There is significant relationship between education, income and level of satisfaction. However other factors like age, sex, religion, native place, length of stay, frequency of visit etc have no significant association with the level of satisfaction

Table 1
Demographic Factors and Level of Satisfaction

Factor	*Calculated Value*	*Table Value*	*Significance*
Age	0.227	3.84	Insignificant
Sex	0.065	3.84	Insignificant
Religion	1.961	3.84	Insignificant
Education	4.12	3.84	Significant
Income	4.52	3.84	Significant
Native Place	0.41	3.84	Insignificant
Length of Stay	1.382	3.84	Insignificant
Visit	1.76	3.84	Insignificant

Source: Primary data

Recommendations

- Based on the above findings, following suggestion were given for the better utilization of tourism product in Kanniyakumari.
- For any foreigner, a visit to India must have a profound cultural impact, and in its broader sense, tourism in India involves a large content of cultural contact. The various aspects of cultural tourism in Kanniyakumrai district, which can be revived in the light of prevailing condition are listed below.
    - Archaeological and historical monuments scattered throughout Kanniyakumari District should be developed as tourist spots.
    - Traditional music and dance programmes should be arranged in tourist sports. Foreign visitors would be delighted to have the opportunity of witnessing the performance of professional dancers and musicians.
- India has wide varieties of traditional arts and crafts. As per the survey most of the tourists visiting Kanniyakumari like to purchase handicrafts and handloom work. Centers of artistic value can be started in Kanniyakumari which will have a good impact on tourism.
- Survey indicates the preference of five star hotels by tourists. Five star hotels can be constructed in Kanniyakumari and proper roads should be constructed to facilitate smooth traffic.

- Domestic and international air capacity will be an added facility to tourism. Hence an airport can be constructed in Kanniyakumari which will bring more foreign tourists to Kanniyakumari.
- Market planned can focus an holiday tourism like beach holidays, mountain holidays, etc, which will bring more tourists to Kanniyakumari District. Holiday villages can be established at warm sea sides and in the regions which offer certain facilities for the tourists. The village complex should be a center of accommodation providing extensive sports and recreation facilities, riding, swimming, tennis, volley ball, foot ball, mini golf, badminton, table tennis and yoga. The accommodation can be sold for a week or a fortnight at an all inclusive pritel.

Conclusion

Marketing viewed from the customer's end is relatively a new phenomenon in India. The liberalization of economy during the last five years has led to a new resurgence of spirit of enterprise fuel led by completion tourism is no exception to the spirit that prevails. Both the department of tourism which is Indian National Tourism Administration (NTA) and the travel agency must try to adjust to the new environments.

References

Tapan K. Panda, Sitikantha Mishra, *"Tourism Industry in India"* Excell Books.

Chandralekha Chandra *"Tourism Marketing in India"*.

Jha. S.M. *"Service Marketing"*.

Ratan Deep Singh *"Tourism Marketing"* Kanishka Publishers & Distributors, New Delhi.

Bhatia. A.K. (1994), *"International Tourism Fundamental and Practices"* ©1991, Reprint.

Subburaj V.V.K., *"Tourist Guide to Tamil Nadu"*.

Meena V., *"Kanyakumari A Tourist Guide"*.

Reports of Tourist Officers, Kanyakumari.

Annexure 1
Preferential Attributes for Accommodation

Accommodation	*Tourists*			
	Foreign Tourists		*Indian Tourists*	
	No. of Respondents	*Percentage*	*No. of Respondents*	*Percentage*
5 Star Hotel	1	8	1	1
4 Star Hotel	4	34	4	5
3 Star Hotel	3	25	10	11
2 Star Hotel	-	-	1	1
1 Star Hotel	1	8	3	3
Cottages, Havelis	3	25	33	38
Others	-	-	36	41
Total	12	100	88	100

Source: Primary Data

Annexure II
Restaurant Preferred by Tourists

Restaurant	*Tourists*			
	Foreign Tourists		*Indian Tourists*	
	No. of Respondents	*Percentage*	*No. of Respondents*	*Percentage*
Western	2	17	-	-
Chinese	2	17	3	3
Indian	8	66	40	46
Tamilian	-	-	43	49
Others	-	-	2	2
Total	12	100	88	100

Source: Primary Data

Annexure III
Preferential Attributes for Transport

Transportation	*Tourists*			
	Foreign Tourists		*Indian Tourists*	
	No. of Respondents	*Percentage*	*No. of Respondents*	*Percentage*
Airways	9	75	-	-
Railways	2	17	17	19
Road Ways	1	8	71	81
Sea Ways	-	-	-	-
Total	12	100	88	100

Source: Primary Data

Annexure IV
Preferential Attributes for Shopping in Kanyakumari

	Tourists			
	Foreign Tourists		*Indian Tourists*	
Shopping	*No. of Respondents*	*Percentage*	*No. of Respondents*	*Percentage*
Artistic	3	25	7	7
Handicrafts	6	50	36	41
Handloom	-	-	11	13
Books	2	17	14	16
Garments	1	8	11	13
Jewelery	-	-	9	10
Total	12	100	88	100

Source: Primary Data